Medium Law

Why should anyone care about the medium of communication today, especially when talking about media law?

In today's digital society, many emphasise on convergence and seek new regulatory approaches. In *Medium Law*, however, the 'medium theory' insights of Harold Innis, Marshall McLuhan and the Toronto School of Communication are drawn upon as part of an argument that differences between media, and technological definitions, continue to play a crucial role in the regulation of the media. Indeed, Mac Síthigh argues that the idea of converged, cross-platform, medium-neutral media regulation is unattainable in practice and potentially undesirable in substance. This is demonstrated through the exploration of the regulation of a variety of platforms such as films, games, video-on-demand and premium rate telephone services. Regulatory areas discussed include content regulation, copyright, tax relief for producers and developers, new online services, conflicts between regulatory systems and freedom of expression.

This timely and topical volume will appeal to postgraduate students and post-doctoral researchers interested in fields such as Law, Policy, Regulation, Media Studies, Communications History, and Cultural Studies.

Daithí Mac Síthigh is Professor of Law and Innovation at Queen's University Belfast.

Routledge Studies in Law, Society and Popular Culture

www.routledge.com/Routledge-Studies-in-Law-Society-and-Popular-Culture/book-series/RSLSPC

Series Editors: Steve Greenfield and Guy Osborn
School of Law, University of Westminster, UK

1 **Cricket and the Law**
The Man in White is Always Right
David Fraser

2 **Gigs**
Jazz and the Cabaret Laws in New York City, Second Edition
Paul Chevigny

3 **Readings in Law and Popular Culture**
Edited by Guy Osborn and Steve Greenfield

4 **Television and the Legal System**
Barbara Villez

5 **Voicing Dissent**
American Artists and the War on Iraq
Violaine Roussel and Bleuwenn Lechaux

6 **Medium Law**
Daithí Mac Síthigh

Medium Law

Daithí Mac Síthigh

Routledge
Taylor & Francis Group
LONDON AND NEW YORK

First published 2018
by Routledge

2 Park Square, Milton Park, Abingdon, Oxfordshire OX14 4RN
52 Vanderbilt Avenue, New York, NY 10017

Routledge is an imprint of the Taylor & Francis Group, an informa business

First issued in paperback 2019

British Library Cataloguing in Publication Data
A catalogue record for this book is available from the British Library

Library of Congress Cataloging in Publication Data
A catalog record for this book has been requested

ISBN: 978-1-138-67771-5 (hbk)
ISBN: 978-0-367-87636-4 (pbk)

Typeset in Times New Roman
by Wearset Ltd, Boldon, Tyne and Wear

For Bláthnaid

The convergence of media law and Internet regulation has caused some to question the need for medium-specific laws: a claim firmly rebutted in this comprehensive review of medium-specific law basing itself on the insight of the 'Toronto School' scholars Innis and McLuhan. Mac Síthigh's excellent monograph provides meticulous case studies in the vagaries of medium law, essential reading for all those interested in the construction of medium-specific regulatory regimes, their evolution and their continued relevance.

Chris Marsden, *Professor, Sussex Law School, University of Sussex, UK*

Medium Law provides a rich and detailed overview of the tensions that exist in some of the less-charted areas of UK media law – from the regulation of online radio and video games, to live relay of opera in the cinema, music apps, and video-on-demand. Mac Síthigh challenges us to reconsider the role of the medium, alongside the message, in framing our media regulation of the future.

Rachael Craufurd-Smith, *Reader in EC Law Director of Learning and Teaching, University of Edinburgh, UK*

This timely and highly ambitious book confronts head-on the debate on the development of technology-neutral, future-proof legislation across media platforms. By providing a careful and in-depth analysis of the laws concerning radio, film, TV, games, on-demand services and other entertainment platforms, this insightful book explains why the medium will continue to play a pivotal role in media regulation. Highly recommended.

Peter K. Yu, *Professor of Law and Director, Center for Law and Intellectual Property, Texas A&M University School of Law, USA*

Contents

Table of cases

United Kingdom: Supreme Court, House of Lords, Privy Council

England and Wales

Scotland

Australia

Ireland

New Zealand

United States

Court of Justice of the European Union

European Court of Human Rights

Table of statutes

Acts of the UK Parliament

Acts of the Scottish Parliament

Acts of the Northern Ireland Parliament (1922–1972) and Northern Ireland Assembly (1999–)

UK secondary legislation, including 'direct rule' legislation in respect of Northern Ireland (1972–1999)

European Union legislation

Series editors' foreword

We are delighted to see the publication of this latest addition to the series *Studies in Law, Society and Popular Culture. Medium Law* is an important and timely text and its aims are bold. In examining, in its broadest sense, the area of media law, Mac Síthig privileges the notion of the medium itself and, after McLuhan, goes beyond the idea of the medium being (solely) the message. He begins by challenging the notion that the medium of communication has become redundant and goes on to argue that, in fact, the medium is increasingly important. This, he argues, necessitates a more nuanced approach to regulation. As he himself notes, '... will propose that the idea of converged, cross-platform, medium-neutral media regulation is unattainable in practice and potentially undesirable in substance' (page 2, Chapter 1).

To illustrate his argument, an eclectic mix of areas are drawn upon and some innovative examples explored. This is the beauty of the book. The examples Mac Síthig chooses are well thought through and apposite, and beautifully delivered. Some of the chapters utilise, in part, previous work that some readers may be aware of, particularly perhaps important earlier interventions relating to computer games and film, but here they are skilfully woven into this broader theoretical frame. These perhaps more traditional or recognisable areas of media law are supplemented by the examination of fields such as licensing law and further utilises forays into areas as diverse as planning and ecclesiastical law, allowing a truly unique and innovative take on media law.

This ground-breaking text is the sixth book published in the series, and follows previously published texts on jazz and the cabaret laws; television and the legal system; and the relationship between cricket and the law amongst others. *Medium Law* is a worthy addition to this canon of work, we would be delighted to receive more proposals for texts to add to this list and encourage prospective authors to contact us.

Guy Osborn
Steve Greenfield
Series Editors, Routledge Studies in Law Society and Popular Culture
Email: G.Osborn@westminster.ac.uk

Acknowledgements

I first sketched out what became this book through two invited lectures in Scotland; many thanks to Lilian Edwards (Strathclyde) and Jane Cornwell and Judith Rauhofer (Edinburgh) for the invitations. I have also had the opportunity to present draft chapters to a number of other audiences over the following years, including the Law and Emerging Technologies group at the University of Leeds, the Law, Innovation, and Society research group at Newcastle University, the Media and Communications Law section of the Society of Legal Scholars, and the British and Irish Law, Education and Technology Association (BILETA).

My thanks also go to former colleagues at Newcastle University, the University of Edinburgh and the University of East Anglia. Special thanks to those who read a draft of the manuscript or commented on specific chapters: Keith M. Johnston, Irini Katsirea, Karen Mc Cullagh, Colin Murray, Ole Pedersen, Muireann Quigley, Mathias Siems, Ian Ward, Lorna Woods, and Paul Wragg. I also appreciated a number of very useful conversations with Emily Laidlaw, T. T. Arvind, and Tom Phillips, with whom I worked on other research projects while working on this book. I also drew upon the advice of previous employers and mentors, including that dispensed well before work started on this project: David Mead, Alastair Mullis, Eoin O'Dell, and Liora Salter. Additional thanks to Chris Marsden for encouragement and for coining the phrase medium law (even though I may have reinterpreted it for my own purposes …).

Constant support at home came from my wife NíChaoimh Dewdney and from our family and friends.

Work was carried out in a number of excellent libraries, including the 'Lit & Phil' in Newcastle, the university libraries at Durham and Edinburgh, and the Institute for Advanced Legal Studies. The Law Library and Interlibrary Loan teams at Newcastle University were most helpful.

I have attempted to state the law as of 1 January 2017.

Daithí Mac Síthigh
Newcastle upon Tyne, Lá 'le Seanán, 2017

1 Introduction

The age of the message

Why should anyone care about the medium of communication today, especially when talking about media law? Jeremy Hunt MP, while Secretary of State for Culture, Media and Sport in the UK, argued that 'sensible cross-platform regulation' was a prerequisite if the British media were to develop 'world-beating cross-platform offerings'.[1] Ed Richards, as chair of the communications regulator Ofcom, foresaw a future where media would be the subject of a 'single regulatory system ... underpinned by a common set of core principles'; it would 'simplify where possible for the digital age' and not grow 'piecemeal in light of events'.[2] In 2013, the House of Lords Communications Committee waxed lyrical about the many ways in which users could access content in light of technological and market change, and called for 'placing much audiovisual content on an equal regulatory footing'.[3] One could be forgiven for thinking that all sensible lawmakers would ignore the medium if at all possible, or at least look forward to the day when broad, clear laws on content regulation can be promulgated.

These views are not without their supporters beyond the ranks of politicians and regulators, either. In the 1980s, Pool pointed out that 'convergence' between different means of communication, brought about through technological innovation, challenged the historic separation of different media,[4] while Kittler set out in the following decade (albeit with considerably less optimism than Pool) how digital technologies 'erase the very concept of the medium'.[5] An extensive inquiry by the Australian Law Reform Commission in the present decade identified a number of different forms of convergence (e.g. economic,

1 Jeremy Hunt, 'Boldness be my friend' (Speech at the Royal Television Society Cambridge Convention, 14 September 2011) www.gov.uk/government/speeches/royal-television-society–2

2 Ed Richards, 'Speech to the Oxford Media Convention' (25 January 2012) www.theguardian.com/oxfordmediaconvention/ed-richards-speech

3 House of Lords Select Committee on Communications, *Media convergence* (HL 154, 2012–2013) 5.

4 Ithiel de Sola Pool, *Technologies of freedom* (Harvard University Press 1983).

5 Friedrich Kittler, *Gramophone, film, typewriter* (Geoffrey Winthrop-Young and Michael Wutz trs, Stanford University Press 1999) 2.

technological) and how this challenged the 'silos' recognised within media regulation.[6] As a typical account of media history put it, the present day position is that 'all the accepted wisdom about … copyright, censorship … is now being called into question'.[7]

In this book, I will set out the case for continuing to acknowledge within regulation, and in some cases use as the basis for special regulation, the medium. This is not to say that every silo ought to be defended on equal terms. There are plenty of examples where the lines drawn for legal purposes make no sense, and may have never made sense in the first place. We will encounter Morris dancers and lap dancers, space invaders and streaming video, and surprisingly detailed consideration (by regulators) of everything from ringtone subscriptions to titles and credits in audiovisual works. But I will propose that the idea of converged, cross-platform, medium-neutral media regulation is unattainable in practice and potentially undesirable in substance.

Revisiting the medium

In Chapter 2, I set out the conceptual basis for studying the medium within law. Within communication and media studies, a sustained engagement with the medium is found in the work of Canadians Harold Innis and Marshall McLuhan. Innis and McLuhan studied the history of communications, making arguments about the relationship between a medium and its social or economic impact. They distinguished between media, often situating the emergence of a new medium against the affordances of an older one (i.e. what it can be used for or what we think it can be used for). Their work, and the work of others, sits within the labels of the 'Toronto School' or 'medium theory'; echoes are found in other work, including the 'apparatus' tradition within film studies. I summarise the main contentions of Innis and McLuhan, and respond to the criticism that the study of the medium is unhelpful because of the tendency to attribute excessive agency to technology, i.e. technological determinism. I then develop an argument in favour of using the Toronto School's perspective as a tool for analysis of law, particularly media law. I note that searching for the role of the medium in media law allows for the examination of whether differences in the treatment of the 'same' content can be justified, as well as whether applying the same rule across more than one medium could lead to differing results depending on the characteristics of a particular medium. This means that although much of this book is an attempt to identify and explain what the law is, there is a strong normative dimension in that asking questions in this way is based on an assumption (which some would contest) that there is value in categorising media regulation in this fashion.

6 Australian Law Reform Commission, *Classification – content regulation and convergent media* (ALRC Report 118, 2012) Chapter 3.

7 Roger Parry, *The ascent of media: from Gilgamesh to Google via Gutenberg* (Nicholas Brealey 2011) 365.

The other contention made in Chapter 2 is that the medium of communication is the basis for regulation, or for the application of one set of rules over another, well beyond the area of media law. I support this argument through discussion of two examples in specific fields of law, and a broader argument regarding human rights law. The first example is ecclesiastical law, and more precisely a set of cases and statutory provisions relating to 'ritual' in the Church of England during the nineteenth century. These controversies demonstrate that the choice of medium is closely related to the desired communication or effect, but that regulating by reference to the medium presents opportunities for innovative legal arguments and, in some cases, avoiding the intended impact of regulatory intervention. The second example is how planning law treats the flying of flags. Flags are readily identified as a means of communication, but once more, there are flag-specific rules and also situations where a flag is deliberately used in preference to another medium. Finally, I highlight how human rights law (specifically, freedom of expression and of assembly) interacts with the medium used for communication; I find examples of this phenomenon in the legal control of advertising, processions, and the like.

Film and games: two labels, many mediums

Chapters 3 and 4 contain a detailed treatment of two broad themes: 'film' and 'games'. Film is without doubt a contested label, especially in relation to its status as a medium. Legally, there are significant differences between the arguably narrower categories of 'cinema' and 'video', although there are also areas of overlap with, for instance, broadcasting law. Games (by which I mean video, computer or digital games) might have a certain deal of attraction as a category, but even this younger sector has seen definitional and regulatory challenges, such as in relation to casual games and smartphone/tablet apps. In both cases, the goal is to identify and assess the regulation of the medium or media in question, with particular emphasis on how boundaries are set and how specific rules apply to a medium – whether that is above and beyond that applicable to other media, or copied from or influenced by the rules already in place elsewhere.

Within these chapters, I attend to both internal and external aspects of the legal definition of a medium. The internal dimension is the consistency (or otherwise) of the way that the terms are used in law. The external dimension is the way in which audiences and the industry relate to the definitions and the specific technologies or platforms covered by a definition, in the light of technological, social and economic change.

Note that both chapters include a discussion of tax relief and (primarily regarding games rather than film) copyright law. These provide an important contrast with the more familiar discussion of content regulation. For instance, the offering of favourable conditions under tax law to particular aspects of the creative industries requires Parliament to identify both the rationale for doing so and the conditions of eligibility. Unsurprisingly, these conditions involve identification of a relevant medium (not necessarily in the same fashion as in content regulation), and in turn form part of the analysis of what rules apply within a given medium and how particular they are to that medium. Similarly, copyright depends in part on assumptions made about a medium (e.g. whether to treat something as 'software' or 'art' and therefore applying the relevant set of rules) and can form part of the overall regulatory environment for and constitution of a medium, especially in light of technological change.

Medium law at the media margins

Each of the following three chapters are then dedicated to the analysis of medium specificity within three fields: radio and audio, video-on-demand (VOD), and premium rate (telephone/SMS) services (PRS). As Marsden has highlighted through his work on net neutrality[8] and on Internet co-regulation[9] (while also using the label 'medium law'), there is a need to identify aspects of content regulation even where not obvious at first glance (e.g. in his work, telecommunications law). The three sectors discussed in Chapters 5, 6 and 7 have been chosen because they all fall, to some extent, outside the major preoccupations of media law. VOD is an emerging area and may take on more significance in future work, while PRS has been around for a while longer, but is re-emerging as an influential regulatory model in light of technological and market changes. The detailed investigation of press regulation through the Leveson Inquiry saw renewed discussion of the plethora of regulatory models used within media, although some remain better known than others. Textbooks and syllabi may deal with areas like radio to some extent, but often with much less detail than those issues of interest to television and the press. Of course, the regulation of television is still discussed throughout the book, often through comparing it with film, radio and VOD.

The same marginalisation may also be observed within media studies. As Benson argued, even the emergence of the interdisciplinary study of video and new media saw pre-recorded video treated as the 'bastard child of cinema and television' deserving of little critical attention.[10] Dymek proposes that an industry such as video games can only be properly understood as a subcultural industry working within a subcultural industry logic; the transition between such and becoming a 'mass-cultural medium' therefore requires attention.[11] This also justifies the separate treatment of premium rate services; it is more tenuous in the case of radio, although as the chapter deals with a broad range of audio services (including podcasts, streaming, and the like), some similar tensions and questions can be observed.

8 Christopher Marsden, *Net neutrality: towards a co-regulatory solution* (Bloomsbury Academic 2010) 216–19.

9 Christopher Marsden, *Internet co-regulation: European law, regulatory governance and legitimacy in cyberspace* (Cambridge University Press 2011) Chapter 5.

10 Caetlin Benson-Allott, *Killer tapes and shattered screens: video spectatorship from VHS to file sharing* (University of California Press 2013) 23.

11 Mikolaj Dymek, 'Video games: a subcultural industry' in Peter Zackariasson and Timothy Wilson (eds), *The video game industry: formation, present state, and future* (Routledge 2012).

I contend that even in these arguably marginal areas, the significance of medium law can be tested. Indeed, it may be more relevant because of the growing pains or revisionist challenges that they are currently facing (e.g. the future of positive obligations within radio). The chapters therefore have the dual purpose of *identifying the coherence* of the regulation of the field through how the medium is defined by various means, and of *interrogating the significance* of the medium within the operation of the regulatory system.

Let me entertain you

The final substantive chapter could fall within what is sometimes labelled as 'media and entertainment law', although again the focus of scholarly attention and of teaching tends to be elsewhere (e.g. regulation of the music industry more broadly, aspects of intellectual property). This chapter instead considers the regulation of entertainment through the Licensing Act 2003 and other provisions. The 2003 Act is a notable high water mark of Parliamentary attempts to consolidate and to approach regulation in a demonstrably more 'converged' fashion. It is therefore significant that, not just in the Act itself but in subsequent amendments, the result has been the creation of a very complex set of medium-based categories and subcategories. The story of entertainment licensing serves as an illustration of the conflict between convergence and complexity, and the enduring appeal of the medium – even if the distinctions between one medium and another are sometimes beyond parody.

Approaches and methods

Unsurprisingly, the influences on this book are drawn from media studies and from law. Chapter 2 is based on a reading of Innis, McLuhan, and others who study the media (including through other disciplines; Innis was after all an economist and a historian, first and foremost). But even in later chapters, engagement with media studies is valuable. The question of defining a medium is a long-standing preoccupation of media scholars, especially in relation to a medium as it comes into significance, such as television; Ellis summarises this as an attempt to 'define what is new and special about their medium' beyond existing media e.g. theatre or radio.[12] Much of this relates to a search for legitimacy or identity, which may be easier to demonstrate if medium specificity is identified.[13] In particular, evidence from media studies can inform an assessment of the characteristics of a medium (as required by the medium theory perspective), which can then be used in problematising the way in which the law identifies and regulates that medium.

12 John Ellis, 'Defining the medium: TV form and aesthetics' in Glen Creeber (ed.), *Tele-visions: an introduction to studying television* (BFI 2006) 12.

13 William Uricchio, 'Film, cinema, television … media?' (2014) 12(3) *New Review of Film and Television Studies* 266, 273; John Belton, 'If film is dead, what is cinema?' (2014) 55 *Screen* 460, 466.

Beyond its primary concern with the regulation of media and entertainment, this book might also be characterised as one about categorisation. Categories, including those derived from statute or from the actions of regulators, have political and ethical consequences.[14] An area of law like judicial review is infused with attempts to work out whether the actions of a regulatory body are consistent with the categories established by a statute. What is the difference between a washhouse and a laundry?[15] Are structures used for Hindu cremations 'buildings' under the law on cremation?[16] Is bridge a sport?[17] Is a lanyard containing a list of gig dates and football fixtures a newspaper?[18]

Research in the 'cyberlaw' field already recognises the need to identify and critique regulation through the design and affordances of different technologies, as an alternative to or in conjunction with formal legal rules and other forms of control.[19] But I also seek to respond to a challenging question outlined by Julie Cohen in 2012, who contends that legal scholarship on information and communication still tends to marginalise how 'social practices of information use are mediated by context', including cultures, artefacts, and networks.[20] So even though it might be surprising to see some of the examples that follow (in this chapter and throughout the book), the intention is to utilise the spirit of the call for appreciating the centrality of the medium, as explained in Chapter 2, in a range of legally significant communicative contexts, as considered in the following chapters.

14 Geoffrey C. Bowker and Susan Leigh Star, *Sorting things out: classification and its consequences* (MIT Press 1999).

15 *AG* v. *Fulham Corporation* [1921] 1 Ch 440.

16 *R (Ghai)* v. *Newcastle City Council* [2010] EWCA Civ 59, [2011] QB 591.

17 *R (English Bridge Union)* v. *English Sports Council* [2015] EWHC 2875 (Admin).

18 *Davis* v. *Westminster City Council* [2012] EHWC 2303 (Admin).

19 Lawrence Lessig, *Code and other laws of cyberspace* (Basic Books 1999) Chapter 7; Andrew Murray, *The regulation of cyberspace* (Routledge 2007)

20 Julie Cohen, *Configuring the networked self: law, code, and the play of everyday practice* (Yale University Press 2012) 5.

2 The medium and the media

Introduction

In the first half of this chapter, I outline the main attributes of research in the 'Toronto School', including a discussion of its two major figures, Harold Innis and Marshall McLuhan. Both Innis and McLuhan wrote on media and communication; Innis did so in the 1940s and 1950s, while McLuhan's best-known works were published in the 1960s. Recent work has seen a number of attempts to assemble the work of Innis, McLuhan, and others into a 'school' of thought or of complementary analysis – the Toronto School of Communication(s) (or for some, the Toronto School of Communication Theory). Initially, two key contentions associated with Innis in particular are discussed: the significance of space and time, and the concept of the monopoly of communications. Then, I address two contentious aspects of the School, with more of an emphasis on later work – susceptibility to technological determinism, and the emergence of 'medium theory'. Finally, I set out my reading of the relationship between medium theory and media law. The second half of the chapter then applies these perspectives to a number of areas of law, and links them to an established debate in human rights law.

The Toronto School

Space, time, and monopolies

The origins of the Toronto School can be traced to the economist Harold Innis (1894–1952), whose career can be divided into two rough phases: earlier books on 'staples' (the study of Canadian economic and regional development in relation to the likes of fishing, hunting, and trade),[1] and the study of the history of communications.[2] In work on the latter topic, Innis sets out a partial vision for

1 For instance, Harold Innis, *The fur trade in Canada* (Yale University Press 1930).

2 There is a continuing debate on the extent of the link between these two phases. See for instance Marshall McLuhan, 'The later Innis' (1953) 60 *Queen's Quarterly* 385 ('he shifted his attention from the trade-routes of the external world to the trade-routes of the mind'); John Bonnett, *Emergence and empire: Innis, complexity, and the trajectory of history* (McGill-Queen's

how communications and media ought to be researched. A key contribution is the way in which Innis highlights the space-binding and time-binding aspects of different form of communications. The former is associated with influence over an increasingly broad territory (such as daily newspapers), while the latter provides continuity across generations (such as the medieval Church). In three collections (*The bias of communication*,[3] *Empire and communications*,[4] and *Changing concepts of time*[5]), Innis applies his concepts regarding time and space to changes in communication throughout (primarily Western) history. He also argues that new forms can develop in opposition to existing forms (e.g. print culture challenging the limited dissemination of information on parchment),[6] but in turn become established and thus serve as the orthodoxy against which even newer forms may emerge.

This idea of identifying the characteristics of a medium is picked up by Marshall McLuhan (1911–1980) in his work on media published in the 1960s, especially *Understanding media.*[7] As is widely known beyond media studies, McLuhan summarised much of his work in the now-familiar statement that 'the medium is the message'[8] – focusing his attention on the attributes of a medium and its relationship with social change and (what we would now call) globalisation. He contended that the world could be studied in an epochal fashion; oral, typographic, and electronic, with the electronic epoch being the twentieth century in particular.

McLuhan presented his work as following on from that of Innis.[9] McLuhan's axes (or as Robert Babe puts it, dialectics) are different, in that he focuses on the 'audile-tactile' as opposed to the visual,[10] or the 'high' and 'low' definition of

University Press 2013) 5 (arguing that the whole work 'can and should be viewed as a sustained exploration of change, and more specifically the variant of change that governs human history'); Robert Babe, 'Innis' great transformation: staples thesis/medium theory' (2015) 40 *Canadian Journal of Communication* 489, 491; William Buxton, 'The rise of McLuhanism, the loss of Innis-sense: rethinking the origins of the Toronto School of Communication' (2015) 37 *Canadian Journal of Communication* 577, 578.

3 Harold Innis, *The bias of communication* (University of Toronto Press 1951).

4 Harold Innis, *Empire and communications* (Clarendon Press 1950). (The version cited in this book is that published by Dundurn Press in 2007.)

5 Harold Innis, *Changing concepts of time* (University of Toronto Press 1952).

6 Innis, *Empire and communications* (n 4) 138, 150.

7 Marshall McLuhan, *Understanding media: the extensions of man* (McGraw-Hill 1964). (The version cited in this book is that published as the 30th anniversary edition by MIT Press in 1994).

8 Ibid. ch 1.

9 E.g. Donna Flayhan, 'Early medium theory, or, roots of technological determinism in North American communications theory' in Lance Strate and Edward Wachtel (eds), *The legacy of McLuhan* (Hampton 2005) 241–3; Marshall McLuhan, *The Gutenberg galaxy* (University of Toronto Press 1962) 216; Marshall McLuhan, 'Introduction' in Innis, *The bias of communication* (n 3) (1964 edition).

10 Robert Babe, 'McLuhan and Canadian communication thought' in John George Moss and Linda M. Morra (eds), *At the speed of light there is only illumination: a reappraisal of Marshall McLuhan* (University of Ottawa Press 2004) 41–2.

different forms. McLuhan expressed this as a distinction between 'hot' and 'cool' media, based on the extent to which the user has to supply additional information (e.g. movies and radio are, in his account, hotter, while telephones and televisions are cooler).[11] The space/time and hot/cool contrasts have in common a back-and-forth or equilibrium state.[12]

Innis wrote about communications history across a number of centuries, and his work was published in the 1950s (with some discussion of early twentieth century phenomena, such as radio). What does it therefore offer to a project like the present one? Later writers highlight the gravity of the 'changing spatial-temporal configurations of empire and communications'[13] in the present day, and so argue for the use of aspects of Innis's scholarship beyond his specific case studies. Examples are found regarding mobile media (whether smartphones constitute a paradigm shift),[14] YouTube (on creeping co-option by the commercial media),[15] the global televising of live news and events,[16] the political economy of video games,[17] and the Internet more generally (an initial but soon abandoned rediscovery of orality and community).[18] Similarly, though more obviously, McLuhan's work is often revisited as an aid to understanding the growth in popularity of the Internet and its implications,[19] and other media such as video games.[20] Finally, the well-observed phenomenon where criticism of a new medium (e.g. ebooks and apps) uses similar tropes to criticism of much earlier developments (e.g. books)[21] serves as an important warning that contemporary media criticism may not be as novel as it first seems.

A second concept found in the work of Innis, and picked up by others, is that of the monopoly of knowledge. Potentially an early articulation of what subsequently

11 McLuhan, *Understanding media: the extensions of man* (n 7) 22.

12 However, Levinson argues that the space/time and hot/cool contrasts have in common a back-and-forth or equilibrium state: Paul Levinson, *Digital McLuhan: a guide to the information millenium* (Routledge 1999) 110.

13 Ian Parker, 'Innis and the geography of communications and empire' (1993) 37 *Canadian Geographer* 353, 354.

14 Jason Farman, 'Historicizing mobile media: locating the transformations of embodied space' in Noah Arceneaux and Anandau Kavoori (eds), *The mobile media reader* (Peter Lang 2012).

15 Michael Strangelove, *Watching YouTube: extraordinary videos by ordinary people* (University of Toronto Press 2010) 133.

16 Sara Compton and Edward Connor, 'The integrated news spectacle, Live 8, and the annihilation of time' (2007) 32 *Canadian Journal of Communication* 29.

17 Stephen Kline, Nick Dyer-Witheford and Greig De Peuter, *Digital play: the interaction of technology, culture and marketing* (McGill-Queen's University Press 2003) 31–3.

18 Megan Mullen, 'Space bias/time bias: Harold Innis, empire and communications' (2008) 50 *Technology and Culture* 175, 181–2.

19 Levinson (n 12), especially Chapter 9; Susan Barnes, 'The global village versus tribal man: the paradox of the medium and the message' in Lance Strate and Edward Wachtel (eds), *The legacy of McLuhan* (Hampton 2005).

20 Timothy Wilson and Peter Zackariasson, 'Through the looking glass sharply' in Peter Zackariasson and Timothy Wilson (eds), *The video game industry: formation, present state, and future* (Routledge 2012) 252–3.

21 Alison Gopnik, *The gardener and the carpenter: what the new science of child development tells us about the relationship between parents and children* (Random House 2016) 220–1.

emerged in various disciplines as the notion of hegemony[22] or the 'propaganda model' in media studies,[23] Innis's concern was with what he considered as the success and failure of civilizations.[24] He provides examples of how access to a medium of communication is leveraged by elites in order to control the dissemination of knowledge and thus aspects of political and economic power, such as a fourteenth-century restriction on dictation at the University of Paris.[25] Carey draws out a theme in Innis's work, of scepticism about broad legal protections for freedom,[26] in the face of the enormity of control over a medium;[27] I have in other works argued that a careful reading of Innis's comments on media regulation supports a 'right to communicate' rather than a focus on freedom of expression or the rights of the press, as is the case in many constitutions and human rights instruments.[28] While the monopoly framework is not the direct focus of this present work, it informs the value of using medium theory in that, in some cases, a more precise identification of the legal treatment of a particular medium can be an aid to a critique of whether this phenomenon is emerging and/or how it ought to be responded to through regulation.

Beyond determinism

An account of media regulation that is unduly influenced by technological determinism would not be useful. There is little for the legal scholar to say if broad assumptions about the consequences of technological change are left unchallenged. There is a strong streak of anti-determinism in legal writing on technology, ranging from Reed's renewed emphasis on jurisprudence and the qualities of good lawmaking and the rule of law[29] to the libertarian critique of those who would adopt an overly pessimistic account of technological change or call for greater regulation of Internet markets.[30] Similarly, Graeber calls into question the

22 Robert Babe, *Cultural studies and political economy: toward a new integration* (Lexington 2009) 66; Paul Heyer, *Harold Innis* (Rowman & Littlefield 2003) 77.

23 Robert Babe, 'Innis and the news' (2006) 13(3) *Javnost – The Public* 43, 48.

24 For a more detailed discussion of how Innis conceived of civilizations, and linked his communications work to this concept, see Robert Cox, 'Civilizations: encounters and transformations' (1995) 47 *Studies in Political Economy* 7.

25 Innis, *Empire and communications* (n 4) 161.

26 Innis, *Changing concepts of time* (n 5) 11, 78; Innis, *The bias of communication* (n 3) 32; Innis, 'The concept of monopoly and civilization' (1951, reprinted in Daniel Drache, *Staples, markets, and cultural change* (McGill-Queen's University Press 1995)); William Buxton, 'Harold Innis' "French Inflection": origins, themes, and implications of his 1951 address at le Collège de France' (2004) 29 *Canadian Journal of Communication* 171.

27 James Carey, *Communication as culture: essays on media and society* (Unwin Hyman 1989).

28 Daithí Mac Síthigh, 'From freedom of speech to the right to communicate' in Monroe Price, Stefaan Verhulst and Libby Morgan (eds), *Routledge handbook of media law* (Routledge 2013).

29 Chris Reed, *Making laws for cyberspace* (Oxford University Press 2012).

30 E.g. Christopher Yoo, 'Technological determinism and its discontents' (2014) 127 *Harvard Law Review* 914.

tendency in popular discourses on technology to overstate the causal role of particular technologies, which masks the contribution of bureaucratic systems, legal assurances and social practices.[31]

So why turn to the Toronto School? Scepticism is understandable, as technological determinism has been the subject of a great deal of criticism within media studies in recent decades; McLuhan is often pointed to as a chief offender,[32] though Innis does not escape criticism either.[33] The case for the prosecution is considerably weaker in the case of Innis, and indeed other scholars who attend to the significance of the medium. Carey described Innis as a 'soft' determinist ('unlike McLuhan'),[34] while Babe dismissed the allegation entirely through emphasizing Innis's engagement with how technology is used.[35] Di Norcia does the same, to a lesser extent, by highlighting the struggle for control over technology by various forces,[36] while Buxton focuses on Innis's interest in institutions, whether individual or social.[37] Speaking about the Toronto School rather than Innis specifically, Deibert characterises contemporary work by such scholars as addressing how 'the changing modes of communication have effects on the trajectory of social evolution and the values and beliefs of society'.[38] Kroker's extended discussion of Canadian scholarship on technology emphasises Innis as a 'technological realist'[39] while Carey, many years after his initial comment, added that Innis's approach to communications was echoed in the emerging concern with globalization and its interaction with technology and communications,[40] pointing to its socio-political rather than technological value. Bonnett's 2013 work argues that Innis was exposed to work on emergent change, self-organising systems and what we would now call the science of complexity.[41]

31 David Graeber, *The utopia of rules: on technology, stupidity, and the secret joys of bureaucracy* (Melville House 2015) 34–5.
32 Most famously, Raymond Williams, *Television: technology and cultural form* (Fontana 1974) 126 ('The work of McLuhan was a particular culmination of an aesthetic theory which became, negatively, a social theory'), 128 ('if the effect of the medium is the same, whoever controls or uses it, and whatever apparent content he may try to insert, then we can forget ordinary political and cultural argument and let the technology run itself').
33 Bonnett (n 2) 187 (summarizing Czitrom and others and offering mild criticism of the reasoning normally offered to dismiss the allegations; he ultimately concludes, however (at 290–1), that it is a 'charge without foundation' because of the attention paid to cyclical factors by Innis, which arises out of his wider role as an economist).
34 James Carey, 'Harold Adams Innis and Marshall McLuhan' (1967) 27 *Antioch Review* 5, 7.
35 Babe, *Cultural studies and political economy: toward a new integration* (n 22) 36.
36 Vincent di Norcia, 'Of stone, books and freedom' (1986) 12(3) *Visible Language* 344, 348.
37 Buxton, 'The rise of McLuhanism, the loss of Innis-sense: rethinking the origins of the Toronto School of Communication' (n 2) 584.
38 Ronald Deibert, *Parchment, printing, and hypermedia: communication in world order transformation* (Columbia University Press 1997) xi.
39 Arthur Kroker, *Technology and the Canadian mind: Innis, McLuhan, Grant* (New World Perspectives 1984).
40 Introduction to Innis, *Changing concepts of time* (n 5) xi.
41 Bonnett (n 2) 10 (in general), 16 and 40 (influence of Veblen and challenging the risk of determinism through combining the study of economic, social, religious (etc.) practices).

There is, admittedly, a tension between McLuhan's account of technology and that of clearly non-determinist media scholars, such as Raymond Williams.[42] However, Acland argues that Innis's interest in 'multiple forces of determination', including history, means that his work can be reconciled with Williams' culture-centred critique of technology;[43] Uricchio notes the tension between the work of the 'inspiring' McLuhan and 'convincing' Williams, but acknowledges that they share an interest in media, beyond the 'text-centric' concerns of, for instance, aspects of film studies.[44] Moreover, an engagement with history (more characteristic of Innis than of McLuhan) allows the scholar to 'avoid the trap of the technological sublime – the hope for technological salvation'.[45] Kline *et al.* even argue that their work on the video games industries uses Williams as a foundation, alongside a careful reading of Innis and McLuhan, allowing them (unlike McLuhan, in their account) to attend to inequalities of power or specific meanings in the 'message' regarding, for instance, gender.[46]

Medium theory

McLuhan himself told Innis that 'an entire school of studies' could be organised around aspects of *Empire and communications*.[47] What I refer to in this book as the Toronto School, though, will take some more precise exposition. A starting point is an acknowledgement that early twentieth century work in communication studies assumed a linear, transmission model that was based on the communication of messages from sender to receiver; in the US, this was succeeded by a practice, within media research, of focusing on the effects of the media on audiences and society. Toronto School scholarship, on the contrary, considers more carefully the implications of technological change and the relationship between

42 Williams (n 32). On the relationship between the two bodies of work, see Babe, *Cultural studies and political economy: toward a new integration* (n 22) 78–81; Nick Stevenson, 'Marshall McLuhan and media and cultural studies' in Paul Grosswiler (ed.), *Transforming McLuhan: cultural, critical, and postmodern perspectives* (Peter Lang 2010) 26 (though, Stevenson goes on to argue (at 28) that, despite problems with McLuhan's approach, Carey and Meyrowitz have demonstrated how media has an impact on social life above and beyond the specific content transmitted through a medium).

43 Charles Acland, 'Harold Innis, cultural policy and residual media' (2006) 12 *International Journal of Cultural Policy* 171, 178.

44 William Uricchio, 'The greatest art form of the twentieth century' (2014) 13 *Journal of Visual Culture* 104, 105.

45 Flayhan (n 9) 240.

46 Kline, Dyer-Witheford and De Peuter (n 17) 30–6. On studying the history of information and communications in order to understand power, see the extensive treatment of the subject in Jeremy Black, *The power of knowledge: how information and technology made the modern world* (Yale University Press 2015) (summarised at 7 in the contention that 'information was cause and outcome, a form of knowledge, and also a social product shaped by demands, institutions and practices').

47 Marshall McLuhan, 'Letter to Harold Adams Innis (1951)' in Eric McLuhan and Frank Zingrone (eds), *Essential McLuhan* (House of Anansi 1995) 72.

media and society.[48] As such, it was not surprising that critics of the transmission model in the US, such as James Carey and Daniel Czitrom, both explicitly drew upon on the work of Innis.[49] Meyrowitz is among the first to discuss 'medium theory', as one of the two strands of thinking brought together in his 1985 book *No sense of place.*[50] He derives this from a reading of Innis and McLuhan, but adds others (including Ong, Eisenstein and Havelock), concluding that medium theorists (in which he includes himself, to some extent) argue that 'the form in which people communicate has an impact beyond the choice of specific messages'.[51]

The editors of a recent collection summarise the Toronto School as based around three themes: communications as a *process* rather than a structure, an interest in effects *and* consequences, and a 'sharp focus on the technology of communication'.[52] As noted in the introduction to this chapter, the Toronto School emerges from more recent work as a retrospective grouping of the work of Innis, McLuhan, and others. De Kerckhove, writing in 1989, places some emphasis on the significance of the University of Toronto, but goes on to emphasise the intellectual commonality of scholarship addressing the structure of a medium and its distinguishing features, identifying a number of later scholars working with the same assumptions.[53] Lauder has recently argued that the specifically *Toronto* dimension, in terms of influences upon Innis, benefits from further study.[54] Yet there are those who would place Innis as the backdrop to rather than the founder of a School.[55] Meyrowitz's more recent writing emphasises the continued relevance of medium theory, but adding that it should be thought of as McLuhanesque rather than specifically McLuhan's theory.[56]

Toronto School scholarship is important, however, not only for the specific object of attention in a given piece, but also for the approach that is taken to

48 For an example of the framing of Toronto School work in opposition to the transmission tradition, see Babe, 'McLuhan and Canadian communication thought' (n 10) 57–8.

49 Carey's approach is of media as ritual. See further Carey, *Communication as culture: essays on media and society* (n 27) 15–18; Daniel Czitrom, *Media and the American mind: from Morse to McLuhan* (University of North Carolina Press 1982) Chapter 6.

50 Joshua Meyrowitz, *No sense of place: the impact of electronic media on social behavior* (Oxford University Press 1985) 12–15.

51 Ibid. 19.

52 Menahem Blondheim and Rita Watson, 'Innis, McLuhan, and the Toronto School' in Menahem Blondheim and Rita Watson (eds), *The Toronto School of Communication Theory: interpretations, extensions, applications* (Hebrew University Magnes Press 2007) 9.

53 Derrick de Kerckhove, 'McLuhan and the "Toronto School of Communication"' (1989) 14 *Canadian Journal of Communication* 76.

54 Adam Lauder, 'Bertram Brooker and the Toronto School of Communication' (2012) 27 *Topia: Canadian Journal of Cultural Studies* 67.

55 Buxton, 'The rise of McLuhanism, the loss of Innis-sense: rethinking the origins of the Toronto School of Communication' (n 2) 590.

56 Joshua Meyrowitz, 'From tribal to global: a brief history of civilization from a McLuhanesque perspective' in Lance Strate and Edward Wachtel (eds), *The legacy of McLuhan* (Hampton 2005).

questions of media and communication – and how the study of communication and technology informs a range of inquiries in the humanities and social sciences. Babe's argument here is that there is still merit in work that cuts across the decades-long 'split' between two traditions in media studies – one focused on cultural studies (primarily textual analysis and in the humanities) and one utilizing the tools and methods of political economy (predominantly social scientific in orientation, though with a preoccupation with structures rather than audiences).[57] He characterises this potential reunification as 'critical political economy', which he glosses as non-Marxian, institutionalist and based around medium theory.[58] A different but complementary reading is that of Mullen, who puts forward Innis in particular as a middle point between the behaviourist leanings of US scholars[59] and the 'sometimes impenetrable' postmodernists and cultural theorists long found in European universities.[60] Creeber, working in television studies, points to medium theory and Meyrowitz in particular as providing an innovative starting point for research on media aesthetics, because it is neither art criticism (pure judgment of meaning) nor dominated by the Frankfurt School's critical take on mass culture.[61]

Meyrowitz's definition of medium theory extracts from Toronto School work the idea that you cannot reduce a medium to the content of its messages, emphasizing the deliberate adoption of the singular *medium* (as each medium has its own characteristics).[62] From a different starting point (including psychoanalysis), 'apparatus' theory within film studies, popular in the 1970s in particular, similarly places an emphasis on the impact (including through specific technologies) of watching film in (for instance) a cinema environment.[63] As a recent work on video emphasises, the 'meaning-making process of watching a movie necessarily includes the mechanics of viewing' *and* the content and the person watching;[64] even in literary analysis, there is scope for a renewed engagement with 'media-specific analysis', provoked by technological change but significant across the history of the book.[65]

57 Babe, *Cultural studies and political economy: toward a new integration* (n 22) 4–5.
58 Ibid. 20.
59 The ability of Innis and McLuhan to work from outside of this tradition (by virtue of being employed at Canadian universities) is often observed; see for instance Czitrom (n 49) 147; Elihu Katz, 'The Toronto School and communication research' in Menahem Blondheim and Rita Watson (eds), *The Toronto School of Communication Theory: interpretations, extensions, applications* (Hebrew University Magnes Press 2007) 3.
60 Mullen (n 18) 177.
61 Glen Creeber, *Small screen aesthetics: from TV to the Internet* (Palgrave Macmillan 2013) 5–7.
62 Meyrowitz, *No sense of place: the impact of electronic media on social behavior* (n 50) 16.
63 Toby Miller, 'Apparatus theory' in Robert Stam and Toby Miller (eds), *Film and theory* (Blackwell 2000).
64 Caetlin Benson-Allott, *Killer tapes and shattered screens: video spectatorship from VHS to file sharing* (University of California Press 2013) 15.
65 N. Katherine Hayles, 'Print is flat, code is deep: the importance of media-specific analysis' (2004) 25 *Poetics Today* 67 (noting at fn 1 how 'in many ways this is a return to the agenda set by Marshall McLuhan'). See also the argument that consideration of the role of communications in history has focused too much on the print 'leap' rather than a wider set of technological developments: Black (n 46) 27.

Medium theory and media law

It can therefore be concluded that the Toronto School, and its concept of medium theory, promotes the study of the attributes of different mediums and of how technological change is related to social and political change. I conclude this section by contending that although Innis and many of those who come after him did not often engage with legal questions (especially regarding media law), their *approach* to the medium contains valuable lessons for the study of the law and of media law in particular. (In this I draw upon how Meyrowitz describes scholarship in medium theory as being more appropriately unified by a perspective rather than a theory.)[66]

A Toronto School approach allows one to widen the subject matter[67] and methods[68] of research, which in turns supports the consideration of context, multiple causes, and a sensitivity to balance. A possible downside, however, is the risk of determinism, as set out above. Assuming this can be overcome, then, we must also think of Innis's approach as conceptual and provocative,[69] or a starting point rather than a grand theory. (If this is not understood, the risk is that Innis's arguably baffling work – described as such even by those who study his work in detail[70] – is confined to its own facts.)

It may also be necessary to look beyond those elements of Innis's work that are explicitly identified as legal. Rather than focus on Innis's take on the First Amendment or the development of civil codes, consider instead something like his discussion of different scripts in language.[71] Innis sets out his argument here as part of his analysis of the consequences of changes in the medium. I have argued elsewhere that there is a thread running from churches competing to evangelise particular populations, through printed newspapers right through to current difficulties in regulating Internet domain names.[72] A Toronto School approach recognises that this is not simply something of technical interest, but something that a scholar of history or culture or even law and regulation ought to pay attention to. The affordances of a medium in terms of individuals and

66 Meyrowitz, *No sense of place: the impact of electronic media on social behavior* (n 50) 22.

67 Robert Babe, *Canadian communication thought: ten foundational writers* (University of Toronto Press 2000) 51.

68 See for instance Vincent di Norcia, 'Communications, time and power: an Innisian view' (1990) 23 *Canadian Journal of Political Science/Revue canadienne de science politique* 335.

69 An example is how David Godfrey characterises Innis as presenting a series of facts as the basis for further consideration 'like a modern novelist', in his foreword to the 1986 edition of *Empire and communications* (n 4) at xiii.

70 E.g. Heyer (n 22) 43 (on 'Minerva's Owl' in *Bias*, 'a baffling read of insightful observations followed by statements that seem to make no logical connection to what preceded them'), 60 ('by all accounts his oral delivery was just as baffling to audiences as his writing'); Bonnett (n 2) 3 ('Harold Innis is an awful read').

71 Innis, *Empire and communications* (n 4) 144.

72 Daithí Mac Síthigh, 'More than words: the introduction of internationalised domain names and the reform of generic top-level domains at ICANN' (2010) 18 *International Journal of Law and Information Technology* 274.

societies – and, I contend, the interaction between these points and the matrix of regulation – is part of the history of a period or of a society. It may even contribute to a more nuanced anticipation of future developments.

The Toronto School is a minority tradition within media studies,[73] and even new approaches in media studies that seem medium-driven, such as 'platform studies', tend to be characterised by a focus on the digital rather than on a broader discussion of the significance of the medium.[74] Moreover, media studies is not the first place that legal scholars turn when trying to understand the complexity of regulation.[75] However, the potential rewards are not without significance. Using medium theory in law offers an opportunity to explain some of the unresolved issues in the field, such as good lawmaking in relation to technological change,[76] the success or failure of particular regulatory approaches at different points in time, especially in the context of innovation,[77] and the appropriate balance between broad principles and detailed regulation in fast-moving sectors.[78] This does not mean defending all aspects of medium-specific regulation, but it does mean that the broad promises that the law might some day soon pay no heed to the medium at all will be called into question.

Differential regulation

In this section, I build upon the argument that greater attention ought to be paid to the medium in law by identifying that dimension in two different areas of law: ecclesiastical law and planning law. Both share some links with the broad media and communications focus of this book. They are highlighted in these early pages so as to demonstrate the broader significance of the concepts set out in this chapter, and their applicability to the study of law and regulation, beyond the more obvious audiovisual focus of the chapters immediately following.

73 Robert Babe, 'Innis and the emergence of Canadian communication/media studies' (2008) 1(1) *Global Media Journal – Canadian Edition* 9, 11 (arguing that it is typically only Canadian media scholars who cite Innis or identify Toronto School concepts, even where there is significant similarity or overlap); Flayhan (n 9) 237 (arguing that Innis and McLuhan differ from 'all other North American communication scholarship', and were more marginal within Canada than other commentators acknowledge).

74 Benson-Allott (n 64) 23.

75 Cohen argues that the failure to engage with work in science and technology studies has undermined the contribution of the dominant code-is-law approach to cyberlaw: Julie Cohen, *Configuring the networked self: law, code, and the play of everyday practice* (Yale University Press 2012) 27. I agree, although as is clear from this section, I see the potential of the Toronto School (which was not considered by Cohen) as a similarly useful set of influences.

76 Reed (n 29).

77 Tim Wu, *The master switch: the rise and fall of information empires* (Atlantic 2011).

78 Ian Brown and Christopher T. Marsden, *Regulating code: good governance and better regulation in the information age* (MIT Press 2013).

Ecclesiastical law

A protracted dispute regarding 'ritualism' in the nineteenth-century Church of England is thought of[79] as the last time that national political life was, for a time, dominated by questions of canon law in the established church – although it is hardly the subject of much present-day research. Of course, the Church of England remains established, but (through a combination of legal changes and the non-exercise of other powers) church matters are not typically debated in the Commons or Lords to any great extent. Where there is wider public interest in a given matter (such as the ordination of female bishops), it is the proceedings of the Church of England's own lawmaking and deliberative structures that are the subject of media coverage and public debate.

The ritualism controversy can be seen, in part, as a theologically-led debate regarding law and communicative acts. The spiritual dimension means that it would be unrealistic to engage in blunt comparison with the secular activities discussed in the later chapters of this book. Nonetheless, the celebrated cases, before various courts, highlight a number of pertinent issues regarding defining and regulating different forms of communication, as well as the different values or meanings attributed to various formats. As recorded in the standard introductory work on canon law, it may seem unusual to many that matters of ceremony, furnishing and decoration give rise to so many cases, but over time they have 'aroused the strongest feelings'[80] and often serve as a proxy for key points of departure within religious communities, despite striking present-day readers as 'unbelievably trivial'.[81] The ritualist 'tradition of resistance to the law'[82] (motivated by a view that the law was out of step with the true law of the church) was undoubtedly a factor, too.

In the mid to late nineteenth century, Church, Parliament and courts found themselves grappling with important questions of doctrine, primarily concerning the work of Anglo-Catholic clergy – those who were within the Church of England, but some of whom promoted ritual and 'Romish' (i.e. Roman Catholic) approaches or ideas. The 'Catholic revival' was the source of significant conflict in the Church of England in this century, not least in respect of liturgy and ritual.[83] The key tensions are those that come after the earlier rise in influence and profile of the 'Oxford Movement' or the 'Tractarians'.[84] Ritualism is aptly

79 James Bentley, *Ritualism and politics in Victorian Britain: the attempt to legislate for belief* (Oxford University Press 1978) 1; Peter Marsh, *The Victorian church in decline: Archbishop Tait and the Church of England, 1868–1882* (Routledge 1969) 158.

80 Timothy Briden, *Moore's introduction to English canon law* (4th edn, Bloomsbury 2013) 133.

81 Nigel Yates, *The Oxford Movement and Anglican ritualism* (Historical Association 1983) 32.

82 Bentley (n 79) 81.

83 DG Paz, *Popular anti-Catholicism in mid-Victorian England* (Stanford University Press 1992) 131.

84 Named after the *Tracts for the times* published by a number of prominent theologians. See generally e.g. S. A. Skinner, *Tractarians and the 'Condition of England': the social and political thought of the Oxford Movement* (Oxford University Press 2014).

described as the 'aesthetic expression' and 'tangible poetry' of the Oxford Movement,[85] though also associated with the subsequent decades (the period of interest here because of the cluster of relevant cases heard by the English courts). Moreover, the emphasis on architecture and furnishing, in light of historical evidence from the medieval period, by groupings such as the Cambridge Camden Society[86] provided support for what became a set of liturgical claims and (in the eyes of some) innovations.

The English Church Union, favourably disposed towards ritual, identified 'six points' of key importance: the wearing of Eucharistic vestments, facing east at the Eucharist, using altar lights (i.e. candles), mixing water and wine in the chalice, using wafer bread and the use of incense.[87] A broader set of controversial practices is recorded in the *Purchas* judgments[88] of 1870, setting out the legality and illegality of 35 diverse activities. More generally, Bentley summarises ritualist practices as 'every motion or gesture' and every item of clothing becoming meaningful,[89] while Purchas himself argued in a widely circulated mid-century book, *Directorium Anglicanum*, that 'ritual and ceremonial are the hieroglyphics of the Catholic religion, a language understanded of the faithful, a kind of parable in action'.[90] A related contention, though one long understood in religious communication,[91] is that 'the poor learnt more by the eye than by the intellect',[92] and the 'town labourer … came in noticeably larger numbers where he found ornament and colour and movement'.[93]

In the midst of the various legal challenges to ritualist practices, Parliament intervened by way of the Public Worship Regulation Act 1874 (PWRA). The Act put in place a new and considerably more detailed procedure for dealing with disputes of this nature, and strengthened sanctions against those found to be acting in violation of canon law. It set up a new special court, exercising the distinctive sanction of inhibition (treating the incumbent as if he were dead) but also being able to order imprisonment, as it did on a number of occasions. The Act had been popular because of a perception that it would 'halt the drift to Rome'[94] through the adoption of Roman Catholic practices within the Church of

85 Marsh (n 79) 112.
86 Yates (n 81) 15–16.
87 In a resolution of 1875, consolidating practices in dispute up to that date. See further Michael Chandler, *The life and work of John Mason Neale, 1818–1866* (Gracewing 1995) 115; Bernard Palmer, *Reverend rebels: five Victorian clerics and their fight against authority* (Darton, Longman & Todd 1993) 6.
88 *Elphinstone* v. *Purchas* (1869–1872) LR 3 A & E 66; *Hebbert* v. *Purchas* (1869–1871) LR 3 PC 605.
89 Bentley (n 79) 3.
90 John Purchas, *Directorium Anglicanum* (1858), reproduced in Elisabeth Jay, *Faith and doubt in Victorian Britain* (Macmillan 1986) 43.
91 Black (n 46) 88 (highlighting the importance of signs and images in daily life; 'the doings of the day were suffused with Christian action and thought').
92 Owen Chadwick, *The Victorian church* (2nd edn, A & C Black 1972) 308.
93 Ibid. 311.
94 Michael Yelton, *Anglican Papalism: a history: 1900–1960* (Canterbury Press 2005) 65.

England (an attack on what Disraeli, Prime Minister at the time of the Act's adoption, called 'the Mass in masquerade'[95]), and saw the strong influence of the avowedly anti-ritualist Queen Victoria.[96]

The nature of the approach to communication taken by ritualist clergy can be easily observed. Take, for instance, Alexander Mackonochie – the 'Martyr of Ritualism' according to his biographer and to many of his supporters. Aptly, he is described in the Dictionary of National Biography as 'heroically stubborn and not averse to a little legal hair-splitting', with the entry asking the reader to consider, in this regard, 'his distinction between kneeling, genuflecting, and bowing'; another source notes that he had a 'degree of sheer bloody-mindedness'.[97] Mackonochie himself described his object as '[seeing] how far I could obey the law of the Church without disobeying the law of the state'.[98] Mackonochie's legal troubles came before and after the PWRA, and concerned his work as the priest in charge of the new church of St. Alban's, Holborn.[99] The anti-ritualist Church Association, acting through a willing resident of the parish, challenged his practices under the Church Discipline Act 1840,[100] returning to compel enforcement, to seek committal for contempt, and then under the new provisions of the PWRA. These practices included, amongst others, processions with banners, crucifix and candles, making the sign of the cross and wearing vestments.

Some clergy approached the legal difficulties of ritualist practices within a less than obviously ritualist church through exploring the affordances of what we would now think of as a multimedia performance. For instance, the Reverend E. O. Humphrey Whitby, of St. Mary's, Bourne St, used the text of the Book of Common Prayer, but 'disguised' the words through accompanying ceremonial actions and gestures, and the occasional rearrangement of the text itself.[101]

Fr. Arthur Tooth, of St. James', Hatcham (Surrey) was the first to be imprisoned (for nearly a month) under the PWRA. Again, his stubbornness is recorded in colourful terms, with one historian noting that he was 'endowed less with a great power of will than an enormous power of won't'.[102] As with Mackonochie, the Church Association supported complaints against him. Tooth did not appear in his

95 Palmer (n 87) 11; Bentley (n 79) 69.

96 Marsh (n 79) 159–60.

97 Palmer (n 87) 66.

98 Ibid. 95.

99 St. Alban's was 'built entirely according to ritualist principles' (Bentley (n 79) 17) and was supported by a patron, with no pew-rents (Palmer (n 87) 82).

100 Providing for cases concerning clergy (non-criminal matters such as those concerning doctrine) to be heard by the responsible bishop sitting with a judge and clergy as a commission, or to be referred (as in this case) to the Provincial Court.

101 Yelton (n 94) 9. Not a new response either; in the sixteenth century, those who resisted the new Book of Common Prayer reacted by singing in English while making it 'sound as much like the Latin as possible': Andrew Gant, *O sing unto the Lord: a history of English church music* (Profile 2015) 84.

102 Palmer (n 87) 121.

defence, and disobeyed various initial sanctions (e.g. three months inhibition). He was imprisoned (under the Ecclesiastical Courts Act 1813, which provided for imprisonment instead of excommunication as the penalty for contempt of an ecclesiastical court), but was ultimately released on the application of the complainants.

Various examples of issues disputed in the cases demonstrate the complexity of regulating communicative acts, even in the specifically ecclesiastical context. The first is the ringing of bells. For those concerned with these controversies, the question was less about whether a bell was rung, and more about when (e.g. at the elevation of the host, a deliberate decision of ritualist clergy). Another is how to ascertain the legal status of a procession. As noted above, ritualist clergy were enthusiastic processors, often with visual displays, music, incense and the like – a genuinely multi-sensory experience, and far from unusual within religious history, whether Christian or otherwise. But the law could not simply forbid all processions, without recognizing that (for instance) a celebrant would need to get to and from the altar. Ritualists therefore recognised and sometimes exploited this ambiguity, in arguing (while before a court) that they were engaged in necessary transit, while being satisfied that they were engaging in spiritually and liturgically appropriate practices. Similar distinctions were made in respect of candles – permitted when necessary for purposes of light, but forbidden when used in other situations (i.e. as part of ritual).[103] Due to the nature of the judicial process, a process of testing the limits of the law was often observed; Mackonochie, for one, responded (as noted above) to a finding of 'excessive kneeling' by instead genuflecting, and then bowing, before finally running out of options.[104]

The credibility of the Act was greatly affected by the imprisonment of priests (and by provocative actions such as the forced sale of property to pay legal costs), and its impact had essentially fallen to nothing by the end of the nineteenth century. Liturgical disputes, of course, continued into the twentieth century. It does however demonstrate, even in a purely secular sense, a recognisable struggle between the regulator and the regulated, including a protracted search for a definitive interpretation of the law, in the light of practices that convey different meanings to different people. Present-day disputes about the position of, for instance, religious dress in a liberal and primarily secular society, or the association between faith and political extremism, are also not as unprecedented as sometimes presented.

Planning law

My second example relates to flags and banners, including how they are treated by planning law (primarily in England). I highlight how the medium of the flag or banner is the subject of special regulation, but that not all are treated in the same way (e.g. special treatment for particular symbols).

103 *Westerton* v. *Liddell* (1857) Moore's Special Report; see Marsh (n 79) 124 (adding that this particular point 'caught Disraeli's sense of humour').

104 Ibid. 125.

Flags are without doubt a means for communication, and objections may be provoked by the content of a flag and the motivation underlying its display; in particular, as discussed in the final section of this chapter, human rights provisions dealing with speech may be applicable. This can be complicated by debate over the meaning of a given flag, as in a dispute in New York on whether a 'Gadsden' flag (a coiled rattlesnake and the term 'Don't tread on me')[105] was the flag of the 'Tea Party' movement or an apolitical one with historic significance.[106] Regulation can also extend to the use of flags in other ways, such as in the US Supreme Court's famous application of the First Amendment to laws governing the burning of the US flag.[107]

The passions aroused by the display of flags, or by restricting such displays, are easy to understand. In South Carolina, a long-running debate on the flying of the Confederate flag at the state legislature culminated in legislation and the removal of both flag and flagpole, with the flag being transferred to a museum.[108] In Northern Ireland, the latest attempt to strengthen and extend the post-Belfast Agreement institutions includes a new commission on flags and emblems.[109] Indeed, specific legal provisions in relation to the display of flags were in force in Northern Ireland for many years; a 1954 Act (repealed in 1987) provided for the control of the display of an emblem in a way that may occasion a breach of the peace – although it was specified that 'the expression "emblem" includes a flag of any kind other than the Union flag'.[110]

105 Michael Corcoran, *For which it stands: an anecdotal biography of the American flag* (Simon & Schuster 2007) 26.

106 Peter Applebome, 'Veterans group, flying a flag with a message, ruffles a city' *New York Times* (New York, 7 August 2013) A13.

107 *Texas* v. *Johnson* (1989) 491 US 397 (overturning a conviction for violation of a State law on respected objects); *US* v. *Eichman* (1990) 496 US 310 (invalidity of subsequent federal legislation specifically dealing with flag desecration).

108 Richard Fausset and Alan Blinder, 'South Carolina settles its decades-old dispute over a Confederate flag' *New York Times* (New York, 10 July 2015) A16; Richard Fausset, 'Era ends as South Carolina lowers Confederate flag' *New York Times* (New York, 11 July 2015) A9.

109 Northern Ireland Office, 'Stormont House Agreement' (2014) [15]. This was prompted in part by a series of protests in late 2012 and early 2013 regarding the flying of the Union flag by Belfast City Council; see for instance Lesley-Anne McKeown, 'Protesters attempt to storm Belfast city hall after flag vote' *Irish Independent* (Dublin, 4 December 2012). The new Commission was appointed, after a number of delays, in June 2016: Northern Ireland Executive, 'Foster and McGuinness announce membership of the Commission on flags, identity, culture and tradition' (20 June 2016) www.northernireland.gov.uk/news/foster-and-mcguinness-announce-membership-commission-flags-identity-culture-and-tradition

110 Flags and Emblems (Display) Act (Northern Ireland) 1954; Public Order (Northern Ireland) Order 1987, SI 1987/463, s 27. The use of this provision was the basis for a notable set of actions in 1964, when the display of the Irish tricolour in the window of the office of a republican candidate led to confiscation, criticism by a soon-to-become-famous Ian Paisley (subsequently an MP, leader of the Democratic Unionist Party, and ultimately First Minister of Northern Ireland from 2007–2008), and protests and disorder; see Brian Hanley and Scott Millar, *The lost revolution: the story of the Official IRA and the Workers' Party* (Penguin 2010) 35–6; Ewan Morris, *Our own devices: national symbols and political conflict in twentieth-century Ireland* (Irish Academic Press 2005) 202–5.

More generally, a flag can be an 'advertisement' and therefore subject to control (on amenity and public safety grounds) in England and Wales under the Town and Country Planning Act 1990, and similar provisions in other parts of the UK. The statute does not specifically refer to flags, but it frames advertisements in broad terms, referring to form (any word, letter, model, sign, placard, board, notice, awning, blind, device or representation, whether illuminated or not) and to function (in the nature of, and employed wholly or partly for the purposes of, advertisement, announcement or direction).[111] Moreover, a Scottish court interpreting a similar definition found it easy to find that flags fell within the definition.[112] However, in many situations no application for permission will be required, either because the flag is 'excepted' from the requirement to obtain consent, or enjoys deemed consent.[113]

The exceptions are found in Class H of the supporting statutory instrument, and (through provisions adopted in 2007) include national flags, the flags of the EU, UN and Commonwealth, English county flags, and the flag of a saint within that saint's county. In 2012, flags of the armed forces, flags of cities, parishes and the like, and certain other specified flags (e.g. the flags of St. Patrick and St. David) were added to Class H.[114] The exceptions only apply where the flag is unmarked, although a black ribbon can be added without causing the exemption to be lost. The 2012 changes did address, to some extent, a press critique of the original exception that it gave the flag of the European Union the 'same legal status' as the Union flag;[115] the EU flag is still protected, but now sits alongside a much broader range of flags and not just those of nation states. Similarly, instances of the restriction of the flying of flags related to the armed forces were reported (albeit erroneously in some cases, such as that it was a 'Council ban' rather than the application of national legislation); one disappointed resident sought to highlight the absurdity of the rules by flying the flag of Saudi Arabia instead.[116]

Deemed consent, found in class 7 of the same source, applies more narrowly; for instance, it is not available within areas of outstanding natural beauty. Flags that meet certain criteria as to form (height, positioning, etc.) are deemed to have consent, if the content of the flag falls within a range of stipulations (e.g. the name and logo of an event). Again, the class has been extended through

111 Town and Country Planning Act 1990, s 336 (although 'awning' and 'blind' were added a year later: Planning and Compensation Act 1991, s 24). The same definition is found in Planning Act (Northern Ireland) 2011, s 250.

112 *Taylor* v. *Secretary of State for Scotland* 1997 SC 179, considering Town and Country Planning (Control of Advertisements) (Scotland) Regulations 1984, para 2(1).

113 Town and Country Planning (Control of Advertisements) (England) Regulations 2007, SI 2007/783, sch 3.

114 Town and Country Planning (Control of Advertisements) (England) (Amendment) Regulations 2012, SI 2012/2372, para 2(2).

115 James Chapman, 'EU flag is given national status' *Daily Mail* (London, 16 March 2007) 36.

116 Aidan McGurran, 'Barmy flag ban: council tells Dave to take down troop tribute' *Daily Mirror* (London, 17 September 2008) 23.

subsequent legislation, and now includes the flags of sports teams.[117] This will make it more difficult for the local press to highlight the unfairness of sports fans being told to take down their unlawful advertisements in the form of flags demonstrating where their loyalties lie.[118] The changes also facilitate the use of flags associated with specified awards (e.g. Ecoschools), and (described through a list of colours rather than name) the Pride flag ('six horizontal equal stripes of red, orange, yellow, green, blue, and violet').[119]

In *Westminster City Council* v. *Haw*,[120] the late protester who stood outside the Houses of Parliament for many years was alleged to be obstructing the highway without lawful authority or excuse. Although the case turned on other points, it was found that Haw's placards were not advertisements, as (working through the three sub-categories in the statute) they did not constitute advertisements (as they did not promote a product or service), announcements (as he was not announcing anything), or directions (as he did not direct anyone anywhere or to do anything). The decision lacks detail and appears to narrow the scope of the planning legislation. In contrast, a later High Court, in *Butler* v. *Derby City Council*,[121] found that a campaigner's large banner (a little under two square metres), on a single issue rather than in an election campaign, did require planning permission; it thought it would be a 'pointless semantic exercise' to assess the three categories and thought that the definition of advertisement in the statute was 'deliberately broad'.

The *Butler* case meant that the courts were confronted with the relationship between flags and freedom of expression. It dismissed the Article 10 arguments of the applicant for two reasons: the local authority could not refuse consent because of the content, and the restriction was justifiable because it protected the rights of others (against visual intrusion) and was governed by a consent mechanism rather than a general ban. The problem with this analysis is that the result of the regulation of the medium is a de facto restriction on the message. This becomes more contentious when it is noted that other advertisements (e.g. relating to a travelling circus and to the letting or selling of property) benefit from deemed consent, under class 3F and 3A respectively. In short: planning law, through controlling a vast array of aesthetic matters, cannot avoid influencing communicative actions, even if such analysis takes place in a context far removed from classic media law or freedom of expression analysis.[122]

117 Town and Country Planning (Control of Advertisements) (England) (Amendment) Regulations 2012, SI 2012/2372, para 2(3)(c).

118 See for example Chris Bishop, 'Canaries fan from King's Lynn threatened with £2,500 fine for flying a Norwich City flag in his back garden' *Norwich Evening News* (Norwich, 5 November 2011).

119 Town and Country Planning (Control of Advertisements) (England) (Amendment) Regulations 2012, SI 2012/2372, para 2(3)(c).

120 [2002] EWHC 2073 (QB).

121 [2005] EWHC 2835 (Admin).

122 For a provocative analysis of the similarities between theatrical censorship and planning law, and a discussion of repressive measures regarding architecture around Europe, see John Delafons, 'Planning and censorship' [1993] *Journal of Planning and Environment Law* 527.

Flags and banners are not the only means of communication to attract specific provisions in planning law. Some provisions relate to content (e.g. political advertisements during election periods, signs for bed and breakfasts), but others to positioning (e.g. displayed on a vehicle that is normally moving) or medium (captive balloons, but only for ten days in a year). The boundaries of medium-specific exceptions are tested from time to time.[123] The person wishing to 'speak' through non-verbal means will therefore be affected by the choice of medium, because making this choice will then determine, in part, whether permission will be required. The medium-specific provisions themselves speak to a sense of what ought to be regulated and what ought to be left alone, and in doing so tries to make an assumption about the communicative power, potential, and significance of that particular medium. Even the more controversial provisions and interventions, such as the history of flags in Northern Ireland discussed above, arise in part because of the choice of a flag (rather than another medium) as the means by which a particular image is displayed or political cause endorsed.

Indeed, lawmakers have a certain appreciation of this point. When the 2012 changes discussed above (extending exceptions and deemed consent) came into force, the proposing Secretary of State allowed himself to reflect on why flags were important. He argued that, alongside the broader goal of removing 'municipal red tape', flags represented 'our sense of self, of the communities we belong to, our interests and beliefs and our pride in being British', and welcomed 'gradual cultural change' regarding the flying of flags.[124] While the specific arguments might be open to criticism, the comments disclose both a belated recognition of the flag as a medium with its own significance and the need to think hard about the purposes of medium-specific regulation.

Human rights law and the medium of communication

Constitutional and similar provisions in respect of freedom of expression have required courts to pay attention to medium-specific restrictions on the exercise of a right for many years. In US law, there are clearly established precedents for the regulation of the 'time, manner and place' of speech, in a way that is accepted by the federal courts to be compatible with the broad prohibition on the regulation of speech contained in the First Amendment, so long as it is 'content

123 A limited exception exists, for instance, for estate agent signs, conditional on the removal of the sign 14 days after a tenancy is granted: Town and Country Planning (Control of Advertisements) Regulations 1992, sch 3, as considered in *Barbara Rees Ltd* v. *Cardiff City Council* [2006] EWHC 1617 (Admin).

124 Department for Communities and Local Government, 'Spirit of the summer realised with relaxation of flag flying rules' (20 September 2012) www.gov.uk/government/news/spirit-of-the-summer-realised-with-relaxation-of-flag-flying-rules

neutral'.[125] Furthermore, the Supreme Court identifies the significance of the medium. For instance, it acknowledged in *Metromedia* v. *City of San Diego*, a case on the regulation of billboards, that each method of communication is 'a law unto itself' and so the law must respond to differences between media, in terms of their 'natures, values, abuses and dangers'.[126] European human rights law sees both a recognition that principles developed in respect of the press are applicable in respect of television and radio, and a further contention that

> the potential impact of the medium concerned is an important factor and it is commonly acknowledged that the audiovisual media have often a much more immediate and powerful effect than the print media ... conveying through images meanings which the print media are not able to impart.[127]

Innis and McLuhan would easily recognise this contention, which is also echoed in the argument by Fish that time-manner-place restrictions have the effect of meaning that different groups have different 'speech opportunities'.[128]

These tensions have been particularly prominent in cases on media regulation; in *Burstyn* v. *Wilson*, in upholding a challenge to statutory regulation of cinema, the court noted how a medium 'present(s) its own particular problems',[129] while the tolerance for a greater deal of content regulation on radio is explained by reference to the need to deal with 'each medium of expression' differently under the First Amendment.[130] Nonetheless there is a search for the application of general rules; *Burstyn* is a turning point regarding the role of the arts within the First Amendment,[131] and more recently is cited in a 2011 decision on video games (discussed further in Chapter 4, below) as authority for the proposition that the emergence of a 'new and different medium for communication' is still approached in light of free speech principles.[132] Even where the Supreme Court is clearly applying strict scrutiny to a content-based restriction, it identifies

125 See for instance Eric Barendt, *Freedom of speech* (2nd edn, Oxford University Press 2005) 80; Timothy Zick, *Speech out of doors: preserving First Amendment liberties in public places* (Cambridge University Press 2009) 56–8; David Feldman, 'Content neutrality' in Ian Loveland (ed.), *Importing the First Amendment: freedom of speech and expression in Britain, Europe and the USA* (Hart 1998); *Ward* v. *Rock against Racism* (1989) 491 US 781, 798 ('a regulation of the time, place, or manner of protected speech must be narrowly tailored to serve the government's legitimate, content-neutral interests, but that it need not be the least restrictive or least intrusive means of doing so').

126 *Metromedia* v. *City of San Diego* (1981) 453 US 490, 501.

127 *Jersild* v. *Denmark* (1995) 19 EHRR 1 [31].

128 Stanley Fish, *There's no such thing as free speech ... and it's a good thing too* (Oxford University Press 1994) 15.

129 *Burstyn* v. *Wilson* (1952) 343 US 495, 503.

130 *FCC* v. *Pacifica* (1978) 438 US 726, 748.

131 Edward de Grazia, *Girls lean back everywhere: the law of obscenity and the assault on genius* (Random House 1992) 293.

132 *Brown* v. *Entertainment Merchants' Association* (2011) 564 US 786.

the need to identify, in respect of the medium in question rather than in general, whether less restrictive measures are available.[133]

Advertising is another area where medium-specific regulation can often be found. Moreover, in considering the acceptability of laws on advertising, courts find themselves confronted with evidence on the features of the regulated medium, as well as whether suitable alternatives are available through other media. So, in a challenge to the prohibition of political advertising on television and radio in the UK, the House of Lords drew comfort from the availability of other means of advertising,[134] such as in print and online; the European Court of Human Rights was similarly reassured that the prohibition was not a total one.[135] The court also considered the impact of different media, albeit without referring to any specific evidence; Baroness Hale highlighted how the TV advertisement which was not aired would prove 'much more powerful than a static image on a bill-board or printed page'.[136]

Beyond the regulation of the electronic media, other cases on the application of the First Amendment have seen a range of types of communication discussed, including but not limited to the flying of a red flag (as a 'sign, symbol or emblem of opposition to organised government'),[137] the wearing of a jacket on which an offensive word was printed,[138] and dancing while undressed or wearing a limited amount of clothing.[139]

The continued relevance of the medium within human rights law can also be identified through a brief discussion of the control of public protest.[140] A public procession (beautifully defined as 'a procession in a public place') is the subject of specific control, through a requirement to notify the police in England and Wales,[141] to notify both local authorities and the police in Scotland,[142] and by

133 Compare *Sable Communications* v. *FCC* (1989) 492 US 115 (inability to control access by children to pornographic telephone services justified a ban) and *US* v. *Playboy* (2000) 529 US 803 (time restriction on sexually explicit cable programmes not constitutionally acceptable, as although a broader ban was necessary in respect of broadcast television, the technological characteristics of cable made it feasible for service providers and users to control unwanted access).

134 *Animal Defenders International* v. *Secretary of State for Culture, Media and Sport* [2008] UKHL 15 [32]. The prohibition is contained in Communications Act 2003, s 319(2).

135 *Animal Defenders International* v. *United Kingdom* (2013) 57 EHRR 21 [117].

136 [2008] UKHL 15 [50]. The same theme is discussed in ECtHR decisions, e.g. *Murphy* v. *Ireland* (2004) 38 EHRR 13 [69] (prohibition of religious advertising on radio).

137 *Stromberg* v. *California* (1931) 283 US 359 (the Supreme Court finding that the provision was contrary to the Constitution, although note Butler J's argument in dissent, that the 'mere display of a flag as an emblem of a purpose' had not been established as falling within constitutionally protected speech (at 376).

138 *Cohen* v. *California* (1971) 403 US 15.

139 *Barnes* v. *Glen Theatre* (1991) 501 US 560; *Erie* v. *Pap's AM* (2000) 527 US 277.

140 A much more extensive treatment of this subject is found in David Mead, *The new law of peaceful protest* (Hart 2010); Michael Hamilton, 'Processions, protests and other meetings' in Brice Dickson (ed.), *Human Rights in Northern Ireland* (Hart 2015).

141 Public Order Act 1986, s 11(1).

142 Civic Government (Scotland) Act 1982, s 62.

way of more detailed provisions in Northern Ireland, including a Parades Commission with the power to set conditions and a requirement for more advanced notice (four weeks rather than six days).[143] Such processions must also be distinguished from static demonstrations. In England and Wales and in Scotland, such demonstrations would be classified as public assemblies. Assemblies do not require notification,[144] and cannot be banned outright (unless involving trespass[145]), but can be the subject of conditions imposed by the police (in advance or on the spot).[146] In Northern Ireland, 'open air public meetings' can be the subject of police directions or even banned by ministerial order,[147] while 'protest meetings' (broadly, open air public meetings held to oppose a procession) fall within the initial jurisdiction of the Parades Commission (including a notification requirement), and can be regulated or prohibited.[148] Yet even within the field of parades and the like, further issues related to the fine line between medium and message arise. If a marching band plays a well-known tune without words, and that tune is known by some through its use in a sectarian song, is that a problem? If the tune is played outside a church of a different religious community, does that make a difference?[149]

Moreover, both the drafting of the definitions on processions and the distinction between processing and demonstrating highlights a theme to which I will return again and again in this book. That is how legislatures seek to target particular forms of communication and make provision for exceptions, in order to avoid absurdity or unintended consequences; in turn, this requires the rest of us to scrutinise who or what is being favoured or disfavoured by the law's categories, and how a well-briefed individual might seek to place themselves in one category or another. In respect of processions in England and Wales, the exception is one that dispenses with the requirement to notify the police where a procession is a funeral procession organised by a funeral director, or is a procession 'commonly or customarily held' in the area.[150] This concept has been tested in

143 Public Processions (Northern Ireland) Act 1998.

144 Other than in in the vicinity of the Houses of Parliament.

145 Public Order Act, s 14A, inserted by Criminal Justice and Public Order Act 1994, s 70.

146 Public Order Act, s 14.

147 Public Order (Northern Ireland) Order 1987, SI 1987/463, s 5(1).

148 Public Processions (Northern Ireland) Act, s 7.

149 Ultimately the subject of a number of convictions for breach of the peace: Alan Erwin, 'Loyalist Famine Song bandsmen convicted "outrageous" sectarian behaviour outside Catholic church' *Belfast Telegraph* (Belfast, 30 April 2015) www.belfasttelegraph.co.uk/news/northern-ireland/loyalist-famine-song-bandsmen-convicted-outrageous-sectarian-behaviour-outside-catholic-church-31183254.html. The tune in question is that of the Beach Boys ('Sloop John B'), and the association drawn by the court was with the text of the 'Famine Song'. The same text has been considered in the Scottish courts: *Walls* [2009] HCJAC 59, and under subsequent legislation on offensive behaviour at football. See discussion in Simon McKerrell, 'Hearing sectarianism: understanding Scottish sectarianism as song' (2012) 9(4) *Critical Discourse Studies* 1.

150 Public Order Act 1986, s 11(2).

the courts, in cases regarding 'Critical Mass' cycle rides.[151] The exception was never part of the law in Northern Ireland (perhaps understandable given that the most contentious of processions are likely to include customary processions). In Scotland, most exemptions (including for customary processions) were removed from the statute in 2006, although a power to create or recreate such exemptions is exercisable by way of secondary legislation.[152] The funeral exception survived.

This sketch of the appreciation of the medium within human rights law affirms the objectives set out in the first part of the chapter, and demonstrates the broad range of legal evidence that can be assessed as part of a study like the present one. It does highlight, as indeed also emerges from the explorations of ecclesiastical and planning law, that the search for the role of the medium is not always the priority of litigants or indeed of scholars. The chapters that follow are influenced by these initial findings at the level of principle, although the specific question of the human rights consequences of medium-specific regulation will be considered throughout and returned to in the final chapter.

151 *Kay* v. *Metropolitan Police Commissioner* [2008] UKHL 69; see also *Powlesland* v. *DPP* [2013] EWHC 3846 (Admin).

152 Civic Government (Scotland) Act 1982, s 62(11B), inserted by Police, Public Order and Criminal Justice (Scotland) Act 2006.

3 Film, cinema and video

Introduction

The three legal areas considered in this chapter, as in the following chapter on games, are content regulation, tax relief and copyright.[1] Under the first heading, the key questions are whether a work requires classification, under the requirements for exhibition of a film now found in the Licensing Act 2003 and/or for classification of video works under the Video Recordings Act 1984 (VRA). This includes the treatment of various novel or unforeseen situations, such as the screening of live and as-live performances in cinemas, and the use of exemptions in the VRA. We see therefore not just a top-level medium-based distinction (between cinema and video), but also a series of sub-divisions – some also distinguishing on the basis of technology, and some creating other distinctions which are not based on a medium but only apply within a medium (e.g. the exemptions for certain videos on the grounds of their subject matter). The second area concerns the availability of a tax credit for the production of some – but not all – films; it is not that there are no distinctions between media, but that the line is drawn in a different place. Copyright is treated in less detail, but the emphasis is on how the availability or otherwise of protection relates to the type of work, and how this has affected the development of the relevant industries. The final part of the chapter is a reflection on film as a medium, and how the legislation on cinema and on video interacts with notions of the value and purpose of film.

Content regulation

Exhibition and the Licensing Act 2003

Responsibility for regulating admission to cinemas, where films are exhibited, is and has since 1909 been vested in local authorities. Indeed, as all students of public law know or will once have known, the infamous definition of unreasonableness in

1 An earlier discussion of some of these issues, with a different focus, appears in Daithí Mac Síthigh, 'Principles for a second century of film legislation' (2014) 34 *Legal Studies* 609.

English administrative law arises out of a claim brought by a cinema exhibitor against a local authority, in *Wednesbury*.[2]

Prior to 1909, the debate on the regulation of cinemas centred on whether such exhibitions fell within the Disorderly Houses Act 1751, which required the licensing of 'public dancing, music or other public entertainment of the like kind'. Indeed, as what became the 1909 Act was under consideration, some judges were prepared to find at least some cinemas did, because of the use of piano performance or recorded sound.[3]

The Cinematograph Act 1909 provided the power for local authorities to regulate cinemas on fire safety grounds (i.e. the exhibition of inflammable films),[4] but authorities exercised these new powers to regulate Sunday opening within weeks of the Act coming into force.[5] Before long, the courts had confirmed that local authorities could impose more general conditions, so long as those conditions are not unreasonable.[6] The BBFC was established as an industry body in 1912 (as the British Board of Film Censors),[7] as such conditions quickly began to include the restriction of the admission of children and broader questions of censorship. It enabled local authorities to rely on its decisions, rather than each and every authority engaging in the separate scrutiny of each film released for exhibition. An early hiccup was the finding that local authorities could not simply delegate their powers to the BBFC, although if an authority generally agreed to follow BBFC recommendations while reserving the right to make its own decision, this would be acceptable,[8] as subsequently confirmed in *Mills*.[9]

2 *Associated Provincial Picture Houses* v. *Wednesbury* [1948] 1 KB 223; moreover, many of the authorities cited in *Wednesbury* also pertained to cinemas, including those cases on the 1909 Act discussed in this chapter.

3 *R* v. *Hallinan* (1909) 73 JPN 458. See further David Williams, 'The "Cinematograph Act" of 1909: an introduction to the impetus behind the legislation and some early effects' (1997) 9 *Film History* 341.

4 Stuart Hanson, *From silent screen to multi-screen: a history of cinema exhibtion in Britain since 1896* (Manchester University Press 2007) 17–19 and 36.

5 Thomas Hunnings, *Film censors and the law* (George Allen & Unwin 1967) 46; Williams (n 3) 49; David Williams, 'Never on Sunday: the early operation of the Cinematograph Act of 1909 in regard to Sunday opening' (2002) 14 *Film History* 186.

6 *London CC* v. *Bermondsey Bioscope* [1911] 1 KB 445. See further Simon Brown, 'Censorship under siege: the BBFC in the silent era' in Edward Lamberti (ed.), *Behind the scenes at the BBFC: film classification from the silver screen to the digital age* (British Film Institute 2012) 5–6.

7 Tom Mathews, *Censored: the story of film censorship in Britain* (Chatto & Windus 1994) 21–5.

8 *Ellis* v. *Dubowski* [1921] 3 KB 621; the Home Office supported the wide use of BBFC recommendations through model conditions and a 1923 circular explaining how an *Ellis*-compatible condition could be adopted by local authorities: Brown (n 6) 12. Indeed, the BBFC has had acquiescence and tacit support from Government throughout the twentieth century: Jeffrey Richards and James Robertson, 'British film censorship' in Robert Murphy (ed.), *The British cinema book* (3rd edn, Palgrave Macmillan 2009) 68–9; James Robertson, *The hidden cinema: British film censorship in action, 1913–1975* (Routledge 1993).

9 *Mills* v. *London County Council* [1925] 1 KB 213. For a similar discussion in Scottish law, see *Classic Cinema* v. *Motherwell District Council* 1977 SLT (Sh Ct) 69.

Further changes came about in 1952 (extending regulation to the exhibition of all films, not just inflammable films)[10] and 1982 (confirming that e.g. an exhibition of a video on a screen was subject to the regulatory system, despite conventional projection technologies not being used).[11] The system of local authority licensing was confirmed in the consolidating Cinemas Act 1985 and is now found in the Licensing Act 2003. When a licence for a premise in which films will be exhibited (defined as 'any exhibition of moving pictures') is issued, section 20 of the 2003 Act requires a mandatory condition to be included in the licence restricting the admission of children in accordance with the recommendation of the 'film classification body' (i.e. the BBFC)[12] or the local authority. A premises licence can include other activities, such as the serving of alcohol, the performance of music, and so forth (see further discussion in Chapter 8). The position is different in Northern Ireland, where holding a licence under the Cinemas (Northern Ireland) Order 1991 provides a broad exemption from the need to hold a licence for other forms of entertainment.[13]

The emphasis upon the regulation of *exhibition* was confirmed by the House of Lords in a 1988 decision concerning games played in amusement arcades.[14] Trade body BACTA successfully persuaded the court that Parliament had successively amended the specific references to specific *technologies* of exhibition, but had not intended to dispense with the *concept* of exhibition. An exhibition, according to the court, means showing a film to an audience. As such, the moving pictures on the machine played by a player were not, for the purposes of this statute, exhibited.

The livecast conundrum

A cinema today, however, is a place where a range of things can be seen. 'Livecasts'[15] or 'alternative content' is an emerging category, which encompasses performances, such as relays of concerts and plays from venues like the Royal Opera House or the National Theatre. The Metropolitan Opera in New York is given particular credit as the first mover,[16] although it was quickly followed by

10 Cinematograph Act 1952; see further Hunnings (n 5) 118.

11 Cinematograph (Amendment) Act 1982. The legislation therefore no longer referred to the production of pictures 'on a screen by means which include projection of light', and simply excluded two types of exhibition (the showing of television and cable programmes).

12 By way of a cross reference to the body designated under the Video Recordings Act 1984 (discussed below).

13 Cinemas (Northern Ireland) Order 1991, SI 1991/1462; Local Government (Miscellaneous Provisions) (Northern Ireland) Order 1985, SI 1985/1208, sch 1, clause 1(7)(a). But a recent review of licensing in Northern Ireland recommended that this exemption be removed: Entertainment Licensing Review Group (Northern Ireland), 'Entertainment licensing review' (2015) www.communities-ni.gov.uk/sites/default/files/consultations/doe/council-consultation-entertainment-licensing-review-2015.pdf 19

14 *British Amusement Catering Trades Association* v. *Westminster City Council* [1989] AC 147.

15 Martin Barker, *Live to your local cinema: the remarkable rise of livecasting* (Palgrave Macmillan 2013).

16 Elizabeth Guider and Ian Mohr, 'Pop goes the opera' *Variety* (New York, 2 April 2007) 5.

others, albeit with an initial focus on opera and similar genres.[17] For theatres, these livecasts have made an appreciable contribution to the viability of performances and reached new audiences.[18] Sport and e-sports (competitive computer gaming) have also been the subject of livecasts for some years now.[19] More recently, transmissions to cinemas from art galleries and museums have been added to the mix, often branded as a 'private view' of a new exhibition.[20]

A contributing technological factor is the installation of digital facilities (suitable projectors and screens) in cinemas, as this facilitates the showing of livecasts. The number of digitally-equipped screens rose (across Europe) from 5,000 screens in 2009, to 10,000 in 2010, and 35,000 by 2014 – about nine in ten screens. Over the course of a decade, with support from the UK Film Council, the UK moved from having few digital screens (4%) to the current position of 100% digital.[21] This shift was particularly important for smaller 'arthouse' cinemas with a small number of screens, many of whom benefited from Film Council financial support. Although the overall share of cinema revenues attributable to alternative content is small (in the region of 1%, though above 10% for some arthouse groups), it is identified as a growth area and one with the potential to attract new patrons, even at times of the day when seats are harder to fill.[22]

Screenings of this nature also provoke an interesting debate; on one hand, the screenings may attract new audiences to opera and classical music,[23] but they also challenge the historic role of the cinema through favouring a 'broadcast' or 'amusement' model,[24] could displace the time and screens available for films

17 Sean Perkins, 'Film in the UK, 2001–10: a statistical overview' (2012) 9 *Journal of British Cinema and Television* 310, 324.

18 Matt Trueman, 'The surprise success of NT Live' *Guardian* (London, 10 June 2013) www.theguardian.com/stage/2013/jun/09/nt-live-success

19 Geoffrey MacNab, 'The big switch' *Sight and Sound* (London, September 2009) 46; Ian Mundell, 'Digital starts to make good on promises of riches' *Variety* (New York, 15 June 2009) 1.

20 Jonathan Jones, 'Look and learn: live art screenings, a new global phenomenon' *Guardian* (London, 19 June 2013) www.theguardian.com/artanddesign/jonathanjonesblog/2013/jun/18/live-art-screenings-cinema-pompeii

21 British Film Institute, *Statistical yearbook 2016* (BFI 2016); earlier statistics adapted from Diana Lodderhose, 'Live feeds fatten exhibs' *Variety* (New York, 8 August 2011) 5; 'Digital cinema over the tipping point' *Screen Digest* (London, April 2011) 109; Media Salles, *European cinema yearbook* (24th edn, 2015). See also Film Policy Review Panel, 'It's still about the audience: two years on from the Film Policy Review' (2014) www.gov.uk/government/uploads/system/uploads/attachment_data/file/274265/1316-A_Film_Policy_Doc_ACCESSIBLE.pdf 4. On digital projection in technological and economic terms, see Charlotte Crofts, 'Cinema distribution in the age of digital projection' (2011) 30 *Post Script* 82.

22 Robert Cookson, 'Alternative content draws in the masses' *Financial Times* (London, 15 June 2013) 18; Chuck Tryon, *On-demand culture: digital delivery and the future of movies* (Rutgers University Press 2013) 88.

23 Vanessa Thorpe, 'Cinemas open screens to opera and ballet' *The Observer* (London, 4 March 2012) 22. See also praise in Film Policy Review Panel, 'A future for British film' (2012) www.gov.uk/government/uploads/system/uploads/attachment_data/file/78460/DCMS_film_policy_review_report-2012_update.pdf 29

24 Chuck Tryon, *Reinventing cinema: movies in the age of media convergence* (Rutgers University Press 2009) 74.

(especially of niche interest)[25] – and raise questions about the future of theatre and performance and the choices made by producers in preparing and filming a performance.[26] However, this emergent market is not an entirely new one. During the 1940s, film studios worked to promote 'theatre television' (television broadcasts shown in cinemas) and subscription television, so as to 'bring the direct-sale economics of film exhibition to the broadcasting business'.[27] Theatre television was not a success,[28] although it did raise issues regarding the role of regulation in supporting or opposing initiatives of this nature – issues left unresolved and therefore presenting the challenge which will be considered in this part of this chapter.

This new business model, or cultural form, is not easily managed within the current UK legal framework for cinema exhibition. Indeed, it highlights a possible weakness in this framework, through challenging the relevance of the definitions used in the Licensing Act. In legal terms there are three types of alternative content: live, 'as live' (or 'delayed'), and recorded. The short answer is that live screenings fall outside of both the Licensing Act and the regulation of broadcasting, while as-live screenings fall in between. Recorded screenings are arguably easier to understand as they are simply treated as exhibitions of moving pictures as long understood under the Act.

The reasons for offering an exemption to live relays are unclear (beyond what was intended in 1982 as breaking the link between regulation and specific technologies of protection, as discussed above), and it is difficult to identify a deliberate decision to do so. The original exclusion (of what was never included in the first place) in 1982 used the language of television and cable programmes already found in the legislation of the time. Now, the simultaneous reception and playing of part of a 'programme service' falls outside of the definition of 'regulated entertainment' in the Licensing Act 2003, along with a remarkable range of other exemptions (some of which are considered in Chapter 8 of this book).[29] For a cinema, this means that although a premises licence may be required for other reasons (e.g. for the sale of alcohol), there is no requirement to restrict admission on BBFC grounds, where all that is shown is a programme service, received and played simultaneously.

But what is a programme service? There are two separate definitions in UK law. One is narrow, being the services regulated and licensed by Ofcom under

25 Leo Barraclogh, 'Arthouses hedge bets' *Variety* (New York, 29 November 2010) 15.

26 Liz Schafer, 'Alice in Cameraland' *Times Higher Education* (London, 18 January 2015) www.timeshighereducation.com/features/culture/the-royal-ballet-alices-adventures-in-wonderland/2017857.article

27 Michele Hilmes, *Hollywood and broadcasting: from radio to cable* (University of Illinois Press 1990) 117.

28 Douglas Gomery, 'Theatre television: the missing link of technological change in the US motion picture industry' (1985) *Velvet Light Trap* 21, 54; Peter Kramer, 'The lure of the big picture: film, television and Hollywood' in John Hill and Martin McLoore (eds), *Big picture, small screen: the relations between film and television* (University of London Press 1994) 32–5.

29 Licensing Act 2003, sch 1, pt 2. Programme services are exempted in para 8.

sections 362(1) and 405(1) of the Communications Act 2003, such as a radio service or a digital television service). The other is broad, and found in s 201 Broadcasting Act 1990 (as amended by s 360 Communications Act 2003). It including everything in the narrower definition,[30] as well as other services, such as sounds or images sent through a communications system and intended 'for reception at a place in the United Kingdom for the purpose of being presented there to members of the public or to any group of persons'.[31] This would probably include live relays in a cinema – although such transmissions would not be caught by the narrower definition. There are a number of other statutes where the broad definition is used, such as regarding incitement to hatred.[32]

The result is an unusual situation where certain material – including live transmissions for showing in a cinema – is neither subject to the Licensing Act nor the Communications Act. Indeed, the Communications Act[33] amended the Cinemas Act 1985 to provide that the latter Act did not regulate Communications Act programme services (i.e. the narrow definition), but when the Licensing Act 2003 replaced the Cinemas Act shortly afterwards it, without explanation, exempted programme services under the Broadcasting Act (i.e. the broad definition). As the explanatory notes to the Communications Act show an awareness of the two definitions,[34] it is difficult to say whether the Licensing Act's effective reversal was a deliberate reversal, a correction of an error, or an accidental one (i.e. without having noticed the change).

It could be argued that the Licensing Act and Communications Act are rightly excluded from application, because the event being shown in a cinema is subject to regulation through other means. However, what remains of theatre legislation in the Theatres Act 1968 (part of which has been incorporated into the Licensing Act) makes this difficult. As part of the liberalisation of the theatre, licensing authorities are strictly limited in the exercise of their licensing powers. In particular, and as discussed in Chapter 8, authorities may only impose conditions in regard to public safety, and are explicitly prohibited from regulating the content of plays; 'no condition may be attached to the licence as to the nature of the plays which may be performed, or the manner of performing plays.'[35] Some limited constraints remain through a statutory prohibition on obscene performances.[36] Restrictions as to the age of attendees, then, are generally a matter for a

30 Through Communications Act 2003, s 201(1)(aa).

31 Communications Act 2003, s 201(1)(c)(ii).

32 Public Order Act 1986, s 22.

33 Communications Act 2003, sch 17, para 74.

34 Explanatory notes to the Communications Act 2003, para 930.

35 Theatres Act 1968, s 1(2); Licensing Act 2003, s 22(1). The limits of this provision are discussed by Nicholas de Jongh, *Politics, prudery and perversions: censorship of the English stage, 1901–1968* (Methuen 2000) 250–2. However, as Barendt points out (Eric Barendt, *Freedom of speech* (2nd edn, Oxford University Press 2005) 129), both plays and films were often treated as similarly dangerous and therefore in need of regulation.

36 Theatres Act 1968, ss 2–4. These provisions do not apply to a play being filmed for inclusion in a broadcast or programme service or as a record or cinematograph film, but only if no-one other than those involved in the filming are present. This is not normally the case for livecasts.

given theatre than for local authorities, and theatre licensing relates to the premises rather than the content (and therefore has no bearing on a livecast). The position is a little different for exhibitions in galleries, which are not subject to the Licensing Act in England and Wales at all (though may be subject to public entertainment licensing in Scotland), but are caught by legislation such as that on obscenity.

A non-live showing of an event remains an exhibition subject to the Licensing Act. This will include an unedited version with a short delay – e.g. where a play is performed at 1 pm but shown 'as live' in a cinema at 6 pm. The BBFC therefore created a new system for as-live materials, so that cinemas could 'fully pursue this new business model and remain within the law'.[37] This response was a creative one, and acknowledged the logistical problems in classifying a live event in what could be a short period between its appearance on the National Theatre's stage and its delayed showing on a cinema screen. However, it does call into question the regulatory approach for other films shown in a cinema. According to the BBFC, 'the public will accept a slightly lighter-touch regulatory regime' for events reshown within seven days of the live event'.[38] The light touch approach is that the distributor supplies information to the BBFC, which in turn makes a recommendation without viewing the work. This system is also less expensive than usual – a flat fee initially of £100 (rather than the £100 + £7/minute for normal theatrical classification), which has subsequently risen to £102.52.

In the first couple of years (after the October 2010 launch of the scheme), only a handful of submissions were made – on average one or two per month. By the end of 2016, however, over 200 showings had been classified through this route. The BBFC declares that its new scheme is 'based on existing legislation', i.e. its power to make recommendations under s 20 Licensing Act 2003. The Board applies a default classification of 12A, and notes that it will incorporate restrictions on access to the live event into classification of the as-live exhibition, ensuring that the cinema showing is no less restrictive than the original performance[39] (although of course the latter is likely to be at the discretion of the venue rather than in pursuit of a legal obligation). So far, 14 submissions have been classified at 15, and four further submissions at 18. While this is legally sound, the ease with which it was done suggests that major changes could be made to the current system of classifying films more generally without fear of contradicting the Licensing Act.

Recorded events, on the contrary, are easily categorised as exhibitions of moving pictures and are treated (and can be classified) in the same manner as the

37 British Board of Film Classification, 'As Live' (2010) www.bbfc.co.uk/industry-services/theatrical-ratings/as-live

38 Ibid.

39 British Board of Film Classification, 'Guidance for distributors: submitting a work for As Live classification' (2010) www.bbfc.co.uk/sites/default/files/attachments/As%20Live%20-%20Guidance%20for%20Distributors.pdf

films that have long been exhibited in cinemas. Nevertheless, the potential for inconsistency is still present. Some recorded events, such as concerts, could be exempted from the application of the Video Recordings Act, in terms of sale or supply of the recording. The VRA provides for certain exemptions (discussed further below) on the grounds of the low risk associated with the content, but there is no parallel provision in the text of the Licensing Act, which is (in this regard, at least) neutral as to the content.

Indeed, the *creation* of an effective exemption for classes of exhibition seems to be at cross purposes with the various attempts to *reduce* the scope for exemptions under the Video Recordings Act. The disavowal of content regulation in this specific regard could call into question why films (whatever the content) are subject to a greater degree of regulation than the National Theatre's *Frankenstein*,[40] or even encourage circumvention of BBFC requirements through doing in front of a camera connected to a live relay what could not be done on celluloid or disc. The scheme also, unsurprisingly, can lead to differing results. A number of performances were also classified at 12A under the as live scheme, and then at 15 on subsequent full classification;[41] conversely, on one recent occasion, an as live rating of 15 was replaced by a film rating of 12A at later showings.[42]

Further changes to exhibition

Film exhibition was partially deregulated through two recent legislative changes. One change was included in what became the Deregulation Act 2015, and put non-profit film screenings in community premises (e.g. church and village halls) outside of the Licensing Act, as long as BBFC or local authority age ratings are enforced, and where the audience does not exceed 500 and the screening takes place between 8 am and 11 pm.[43] The measure was framed, in an earlier DCMS consultation, as being about providing support for access to films in rural areas and to niche films in urban areas.[44] Indeed, it is striking that although some aspects of the cinema sector are doing well, there are areas of limited coverage; in Scotland, one-quarter of local authority areas contain no full-time cinemas.[45] The British Film Institute (BFI) has provided support for 'neighbourhood

40 Classified at 15 (the first to be given this classification), decision published at www.bbfc.co.uk with reference AFF277625. On the theatrical production, see Catherine Bennett, 'Teenagers won't be shocked by a naked man on the stage' *The Observer* (London, 27 February 2011) www.theguardian.com/commentisfree/2011/feb/27/catherine-bennett-frankenstein-children

41 E.g. *The Hard Problem* (National Theatre, 2015): references ALF324893 (as live) and BFF324893 (film).

42 *King Lear* (RSC, 2016): references ALF344734 (as live) and AFF344734 (film).

43 Deregulation Act 2015, s 76, inserting new para 6A into Licensing Act 2003, sch 1.

44 Department for Culture, Media and Sport, 'Community film exhibition: a consultation' (2013) www.gov.uk/government/uploads/system/uploads/attachment_data/file/210729/Community_film_consultation.pdf 3

45 BOP Consulting, 'Review of the film sector in Scotland' (2014) www.creativescotland.com/__data/assets/pdf_file/0018/25245/Review_of_the_Film_Sector_in_Scotland_-_Jan_2014.pdf 11

cinema' through extensive advice and guidance[46] and an equipment fund, where community venues could ask the BFI to purchase equipment such as projectors, DVD players, and seating. (Note however that preference was given to venues which gave a majority of screen time to 'specialised' and independent British film; the former concept, which was also used in previous funding schemes for the installation of digital screens in cinemas, is a non-statutory definition which includes documentaries, subtitled films in foreign languages, programmes comprised of short films, and the like.)

The second change relates to 'incidental' film, i.e. where moving pictures are exhibited as part of a non-regulated activity. Examples provided by the Department for Culture, Media and Sport (DCMS) included charity race nights and home movies during street parties.[47] The cumulative effect of regulatory change is seen, though, in how the clause would exempt films shown as part of a play, as the play would not be regulated under an earlier round of changes to the Licensing Act 2003.[48] The DCMS took care to point out how the new exception would not apply to showing music DVDs on large screens in pubs, because of the risk of unsuitable videos being shown to children; what goes unsaid is, as already noted above in the context of the treatment of livecasts, is that there is already an exemption for showing a television broadcast. This might be presumed to carry lower risk because of the Ofcom regulation of broadcasting and, in particular, its 'watershed' which provides for some measure of de facto age classification of television. However, it is perfectly possible for a licensed premises to admit children during a post-watershed period, and show through a TV channel what could not be seen on the same screen by means of a DVD player (unless it had a licence to exhibit films).

Regulating video

The Video Recordings Act 1984 governs (through the criminal law) the sale and supply of video recordings. The Act establishes various offences and a requirement for classification of video works, and provides for the designation of an authority; the BBFC has always been so designated. It is an example of legislation attempting to apply the regulatory model for a prior medium (cinema) to an emerging one (as video was in the early 1980s). However, as is so often the case, simply copying out the existing provisions would not work. The nature of video (as a technology used for distribution and ultimately offered for purchase by individuals in the form of videotapes) was a factor. Just as important, perhaps, was the desire of the Government of the day to provide, despite favouring free

46 www.bfi.org.uk/neighbourhoodcinema/

47 Department for Culture, Media and Sport, 'Legislative Reform (Entertainment Licensing) Order 2014: explanatory document' (2014) www.gov.uk/government/uploads/system/uploads/attachment_data/file/328492/Entertainment_Licensing_Legislative_Reform_Order_Explanatory_Document.pdf [10.4].

markets in other sectors, for a high level of regulation of violent and sexually explicit material.[49] As such, the VRA emerged as a distinctive, video-specific regime rather than a simple transposition of the system of licensing and the BBFC that was already in use for cinema.

The VRA is silent on the *criteria* for classification, as opposed to the existence of these criteria. This means that, for example, the boundary between two age categories is determined by the BBFC.[50] However, the Act does provide some guidance, for example through the requirement that 'special regard' be had by the classification authority to harm.[51] This requirement was added in 1994[52] and relates to works dealing with themes such as criminal behaviour, human sexual activity and violence. Furthermore, the High Court has been asked to clarify the meaning of the statutory reference to harm on two occasions.[53] The BBFC's most recent classification guidelines, moreover, utilise the concept of harm as a particular justification for regulation, arguably more explicitly than in previous iterations.[54]

Incorporated into the working criteria of the BBFC are a number of further questions of criminal law, which the BBFC will consider when making its decisions. The relevant provisions include the Obscene Publications Acts and the Protection of Children Act 1978; these are acts of general application which affect films as well as other media. Although the purpose of regulation is normally understood as controlling what the audience can see, it is the distributor who is subject to legal control (through the criminal offence of sale or supply of an unclassified video recording), but awareness of the BBFC's approach is crucial to the production process too.

In one specific (and anomalous) case, that of cruelty to animals, statute law is even used to influence the *method* of production, through what are in legal terms restrictions on distribution and exhibition. One 1937 statute criminalises *exhibiting* a film (produced anywhere in the world) where a scene in its *production* was 'organised or directed in such a way as to involve the cruel infliction of pain or terror on any animal',[55] while a more recent provision creates the offence of

48 See Chapter 8.

49 A conflict between the Government's initial favouring of a free market model and pressure from the tabloid press: Kate Egan, *Trash or treasure?: Censorship and the changing meanings of the video nasties* (Manchester University Press 2007) 80–3; Julian Upton, 'Electric blues: the rise and fall of Britain's first pre-recorded videocassette distributors' (2016) 13 *Journal of British Cinema and Television* 19.

50 British Board of Film Classification, 'Classification guidelines 2014' (2014) www.bbfc.co.uk/sites/default/files/attachments/BBFC%20Classification%20Guidelines%202014_5.pdf. Note too how the BBFC labels, with some small changes made, predate the VRA: Julian Upton, 'Innocence unprotected? Permissiveness and the AA certificate 1970–82' (2017) 14 *Journal of British Cinema and Television* 64, 73.

51 Video Recordings Act 1984, s 4A, inserted by Criminal Justice & Public Order Act 1994.

52 Colin Manchester, 'Criminal Justice and Public Order Act 1994' [1995] *Criminal Law Review* 123; Paul McDonald, *Video and DVD industries* (British Film Institute 2007) 90.

53 *R (BBFC)* v. *Video Appeals Committee* [2008] EWHC 203 (Admin); *R* v. *Video Appeals Committee ex parte BBFC* [2000] EMLR 850.

54 Emma Pett, 'A new media landscape? The BBFC, extreme cinema as cult, and technological change' (2014) 13 *New Review of Film and Television Studies* 83, 84–5.

55 Cinematograph Films (Animals) Act 1937.

supplying, publishing, showing or possessing for supply a video recording of an animal fight (although in this case only referring to fights that have taken place in the UK).[56]

Exemptions from the VRA

The Video Recordings Act has also been revisited in recent years (as well as being re-enacted without change for reasons of compliance with EU law),[57] with questions on what it does and does not control being at the core of the debate. A number of amendments were made to the VRA in the Digital Economy Act 2010. The one that attracted most attention was the creation of a parallel system (and separate classification authority) for video games, which is discussed in detail in the following chapter. However, the 2010 Act also contained a new provision (added at a late stage in debate, and responding also to a Private Members Bill)[58] authorising the future amendment of the VRA (through secondary legislation) to vary the criteria for exemption from classification requirements.[59]

Aside from video games, the two categories exempted from the classification requirement (and therefore capable of being lawfully sold or supplied without classification) under the 1984 Act were works 'designed to inform, educate or instruct' or 'concerned with sport, religion or music'. The exemption was lost (i.e. classification is required) if the work met specific criteria set out in the Act (such as depicting to a significant extent 'human sexual activity or acts of force or restraint associated with such activity'). In the 1994 changes to the Act, the scope for exemption narrowed a little, through new provisions providing for the loss of exemption in respect of works (again depicting to a significant extent) techniques likely to be useful in committing a criminal offence or criminal activity in a way that is likely to encourage the commission of offences. These exemptions do *not* apply to cinema, and are not drawn from existing legal concepts – they are specific to the VRA.

This system came under criticism during the technical re-enactment of the VRA and while the Digital Economy Bill was being considered, and was presented by its critics as a 'loophole' allowing children to access material that was

56 Animal Welfare Act 2006, s 8(3).

57 Resulting from a failure to notify the VRA to the European Commission under the Technical Standards Directive (then 83/189/EEC; now Directive 2015/1535 of 9 September 2015 laying down a procedure for the provision of information in the field of technical regulations and of rules on information society services [2015] OJ L241/1). The result was the (properly notified) Video Recordings Act 2010. For a brief period, no prosecutions for VRA offences could be brought, although a wide level of voluntary co-operation was noted by the BBFC. However, an attempt to challenge earlier convictions as unsafe, on the basis that the 1984 Act was not in compliance with EU law and thus invalid, was unsuccessful: *R* v. *Budimir & Rainbird* [2010] EWCA Crim 1486, joined with *Interfact* v. *Liverpool City Council (no 2)* [2010] EWHC 1604 (Admin)

58 Video Recordings (Exemption from Classification) Bill: HC Deb 12 January 2010, vol. 503, cols 560–2.

59 Digital Economy Act 2010, s 40(3A), adding new s 2(4) to the Video Recordings Act 1984.

not so extreme as to lose its exemption, but would have been the subject of a restrictive age classification (e.g. 15) had the exemption not applied.[60] Members of Parliament typically pointed to music DVDs (on the grounds that music videos contained violent or sexual imagery or themes) and sports (e.g. 'ultimate fighting' competitions). Some sought the complete removal of the exemption system. However, the result of the short debates was that a new power to amend the exemption categories by secondary legislation was granted to the Secretary of State.

In the British constitutional tradition, this power to amend primary legislation by way of secondary legislation – the use of 'Henry VIII' clauses – is not unusual, although it is unorthodox or simply unconstitutional elsewhere, and not without controversy in the UK.[61] It is now the case that the parameters of the system of video-specific criminal law prior censorship are the subject of limited parliamentary scrutiny (a 'positive assent' requirement in the amended VRA[62]). While this is stronger than the normal treatment of regulations (only subject to annulment), it is difficult to see why a decision with such an impact on freedom of expression could not be considered and made in a more public and legitimate fashion. The question of whether classification is required, and the related issue of sanctioning non-compliance through criminal law, is at the heart of the Act rather than a point of detail needing to be updated regularly. This point was grasped, to a limited extent, by the DCMS in its 2012 consultation on the exercise of this new power, where it distinguished between the complete removal of exemptions (a matter for Parliament) and reducing the scope of an exemption (possible under the new procedure).[63] What it failed to appreciate is that, for a creator whose work would move from 'exempt' to 'subject to classification', the impact on their freedom of expression would be the same in both cases (although the lesser deference to parliamentary sovereignty in the latter case might make a challenging the decision more feasible).[64]

The power was exercised in 2014 (the only occasion so far), with support from the BBFC. The Government acknowledged that a driving force was the criticism of music videos expressed in the controversial Bailey Review,[65]

60 HL Deb 8 March 2010, vol. 718, cols 23–5.

61 E.g. Lord Judge, 'Ceding power to the executive: the resurrection of Henry VIII' (Speech at King's College London, 12 April 2016) www.kcl.ac.uk/law/newsevents/newsrecords/2015–16/Ceding-Power-to-the-Executive--Lord-Judge--130416.pdf (arguing that these clauses are unnecessary, undermine parliamentary sovereignty, and should not be used); *Laurentiu* v. *Minister for Justice* [1999] 4 IR 26 (compatibility of such clauses with the constitutional provisions on the powers of the legislative branch in Ireland).

62 Video Recordings Act 1984, s 22A(3).

63 Department for Culture Media and Sport, 'Consultation on exemptions to the Video Recordings Act and on advertising in cinemas' (2012) www.gov.uk/government/uploads/system/uploads/attachment_data/file/73028/VRACinemaads_consultation_May2012.pdf [2.14–15].

64 See *R (Public Law Project)* v. *Lord Chancellor* [2016] UKSC 39 [24–6] (on judicial review of the exercise of delegated powers to amend primary legislation).

65 Department for Education, *Letting children be children: report of an independent review of the commercialisation and sexualisation of childhood* (Cm 8078, 2011); see also Feona Attwood and others, 'Engaging with the Bailey Review: blogging, academia and authenticity' (2012) 3 *Psychology and Sexuality* 69.

regarding matters of sex, sexualisation, gender stereotyping and violence.[66] The change made was to lower the threshold for the exemption, thus bringing more works within the VRA's requirement for classification. There are some similarities between the new definition of what is exempt and the approach now taken in respect of video games under the parallel system for games classification. A new list of 15 possible grounds for loss of exemption incorporates all the former grounds, but adds a number of matters which clearly fell well outside the former rules, such as swearing, promoting the use of alcohol or tobacco, and words intended or likely to cause offence (e.g. regarding race or sexual orientation).[67] Of course, few if any of these criteria would cause a work to be refused classification; the difference is that there is now a requirement to seek classification and to abide by the relevant age certificate (likely to be 12, 15 or 18 given the nature of the criteria; the former criteria meant that the (rare) loss of exemption was typically a precursor to classification at 18 or even R18). The changes also bring within the classification system 'extra' documentaries and the like included along the main feature film on a disc, which until 2014 were likely to have been exempted.[68]

BBFC online and music videos

One final point regarding video highlights the flexibility of classification, but also the limitations of the VRA. As noted above, video recordings of music have typically been the subject of an exemption from classification, although the 2014 changes reduced the scope of that exemption. Whatever way the line was drawn, however, it clearly encompassed videos or DVDs which comprised a compilation of the shorter-form music videos associated with individual tracks or singles in the music industry.

Such videos are, however, now available in other formats. From the 1980s, music videos were seen on television, including the emerging class of channels led by MTV. More recently, though, the Internet has proven to be a good home for music videos. Initially, even when full-length film was a hard sell due to the cost and speed of access or download, music videos were a more attractive proposition due to the self-contained nature of a video, and the running time of about three or four minutes (see Chapter 6 for discussion of an unexpected consequence of this short duration). Online platforms such as YouTube became

66 Department for Culture, Media and Sport, 'Consultation on exemptions to the Video Recordings Act and on advertising in cinemas: government response' (2013) www.gov.uk/government/uploads/system/uploads/attachment_data/file/202904/Government_response_VRA_and_Cinema_Ads__FINAL_approved_version.docx (n 63) [8].

67 Video Recordings Act 1984 (Exempted Video Works) Regulations 2014, SI 2014/2097, adding new s 2(1ZA) to the Video Recordings Act 1984.

68 Pett (n 54) 85. DVD extras are an important part of the marketing and positioning of DVDs as 'multilayered packages': Pat Brereton, *Smart cinema: DVD add-ons and new audience pleasures* (Palgrave Macmillan 2012) 199.

home to a diverse range of videos (not always uploaded by someone with authorisation to do so, though the music industry soon recognised the value of monetising online music videos), and mobile phones and smartphones, alongside computers, were used to access and watch music videos.

As with the general principle of the non-application of the VRA to downloaded or streamed content (discussed in more detail in the next chapter regarding games), so it was with music videos. But the comparative significance of online within the genre (as argued above), and the wider criticism of the 'unregulated' nature of music videos (which gave rise to the call to reduce the scope of the exemption) meant that the regulation of 'online music videos' took on particular importance. The response has been a voluntary scheme, administered by the BBFC with clear support from Government. The first iteration involved three major record companies (Sony, Universal and Warner) supplying music videos to the BBFC (i.e. outside the context of classifying a given DVD) for an advisory rating. The record companies identified those videos that would be expected to be rated at 12 or above; this of course is also the approximate threshold for the loss of the VRA exemption. Subsequently, two major sites providing access to music videos (the generalist YouTube, and the music-focused Vevo) began to make use of the ratings, and further labels joined the scheme.[69] To some extent, the sites verify age, although only at the 18 boundary and driven by the user's own identification of their age when registering for a free user account.

Taxation

Film production attracts tax relief, but the way that this is done implicates aspects of distribution and exhibition, and therefore illustrates the significance of the choice of medium once more. Indeed, tax relief makes up a clear majority of the public funding enjoyed by film,[70] so the question of which films qualify is of some significance. In this section, we will investigate the way in which lines are drawn within the original scheme for film, as well as its extension to other media in more recent years. My particular concern is to investigate whether the favourable treatment of theatrical exhibition against other forms of communicating audiovisual content is justifiable.

The special tax treatment of film production (initially promulgated in 1992 and 1997)[71] arose out of the practice whereby production expenditure is typically

69 British Board of Film Classification, *Annual report and accounts 2015* (2016) 16; Department for Culture, Media and Sport, 'Action to protect children from viewing age-inappropriate music videos online' (2015) www.gov.uk/government/news/actiontoprotectchildrenfromviewingage inappropriatemusicvideosonline

70 In 2014/5, tax relief of £251m constituted 60% of the £414m of public money spent on film; the balance included National Lottery funding for films (15%), the BBC (10%) and the devolved institutions (8%): British Film Institute (n 21) 232–3.

71 Finance (No 2) Act 1992, s 42 (primarily supporting major productions), and the more extensive provision in Finance (No 2) Act 1997, s 48. An earlier tax scheme for capital allowances had operated from 1979 to 1984: Margaret Dickinson and Sarah Street, *Cinema and state: the film industry and the government 1927–84* (British Film Institute 1985) 247.

incurred long before income is a realistic prospect, due to the nature of filmmaking. However, concerns were expressed by the Treasury and by tax authorities about the appropriateness of its use, leading to changes that were intended to close 'loopholes'. The result was the current scheme, adopted in the Finance Act 2006. The new scheme consisted of a 20% credit (subsequently raised to 25%) which is paid directly to a film production company (normally a special purpose vehicle), considered to be a more direct form of support less susceptible to use in tax planning for wealthy individuals.[72] It operates as an additional deduction for expenditure, possibly payable as a credit depending on the profit or loss of the project in question. As such, its characterisation as a State subsidy to private enterprise (in a particular sector and not available to all) is appropriate.[73] The new scheme was also required to comply with EU law,[74] which required the test to be stated in avowedly cultural terms (i.e. as opposed to industrial).[75] Films require certification by a designated authority (before 2011, the UK Film Council; now the British Film Institute), which includes a points-based assessment of its 'British' nature.

In 2002, the scheme for tax relief was amended so as to confine its application to films 'genuinely intended' for theatrical release,[76] and similar provision continues to be made in the current scheme.[77] The problem with the open-ended application appears to have been its use for a range of television productions and

72 Although this is still a matter of controversy, e.g. *Eclipse Film Partners* v. *HMRC* [2016] UKSC 24; Vanessa Houlder, 'Film investors face "life-changing" bills for tax avoidance' *Financial Times* (London, 19 November 2016) 1.

73 See further Christoph Beat Graber, 'State aid for digital games and cultural diversity: a critical reflection in the light of EU and WTO law' in Christoph Beat Graber and Miri Burri-Nenova (eds), *Governance of digital game environments and cultural diversity* (Edward Elgar 2010).

74 The European Commission carries out its functions in relation to Article 107 TFEU, which makes it possible for State aid to promote culture (where it does not 'affect trading conditions and competition in the Union to an extent that is contrary to the common interest'). At the time, the matter was governed by the 'Cinema Communication': European Commission, 'Communication on certain legal aspects relating to cinematographic and other audiovisual works,' COM (2001) 534. Subsequently, the Communication was updated: European Commission, 'Communication from the Commission on State aid for films and other audiovisual works' [2013] OJ C332/1. The UK criteria are set out in Films Act 1985, sch 1, as amended by the Films (Definition of 'British Film') (No. 2) Order 2006, SI 2006/3430 and Films (Definition of 'British Film') Order 2015, SI 2015/86. The significance of Schedule 1 as containing the conditions for tax relief is emphasized in *Peakviewing (Interactive)* v. *Secretary of State for Culture, Media & Sport* [2002] EWHC 1531 (Admin).

75 See for example the Regulatory Impact Assessment for SI 2006/3430 (n 74):

> In this regard culturally British films can be regarded as merit goods that the market often fails to provide at the optimum level … the aim of support is to address the market failure in the supply of culturally British films by way of an incentive for specific behaviour – the production of culturally British films.

However, the scheme needed some revisions before it was sufficiently cultural to satisfy the European Commission: John Hill, 'Living with Hollywood: British film policy and the definition of 'nationality' (2016) 22 *International Journal of Cultural Policy* 706, 713–14.

76 Finance Act 2002, s 99.

77 Corporation Tax Act 2009, s 1196; previously, Finance Act 2006, s 39.

short video clips, meaning greater relief being granted than anticipated.[78] Indeed, the definition of theatrical release is even narrower than the Licensing Act's: 'exhibition to the paying public at the commercial cinema'). This move reintroduced a distinction between cinema films and 'straight to video' or 'made for TV' films.

This distinction is a controversial one, especially in media studies. Changes in how major theatrical releases are produced and marketed in the 1990s demonstrated the strong influence of the straight-to-video sector,[79] causing a blurring of the distinction between them. In more recent years, it was argued that straight-to-video release is a particular opportunity for independent films and new directors, as film festivals become less open to emerging work,[80] and the established profile of movies deliberately made for television.[81] When mainstream work neglects direct-to-video works, this can mean than that work favoured by marginalised social groups is further marginalised.[82] Incidentally, the 'straight to video' sector in the UK is disproportionately British-produced.[83]

In 2013, additional schemes for three further forms of production – 'high-end television', animation, and video games – came into force. (The last of these is discussed in Chapter 4). This round of law reform did not amend the film scheme, although it was quite clearly based upon it, and therefore illustrates some of the potential differences between film and other media, from the point of view of tax relief.

The intention that tax relief should promote 'quality' production arises more directly in the new schemes; this is particularly clear in the case of the television relief. This reinforces the unstated assumption of the film scheme, although in a less problematic way, because it appears on the face of the statute. It still uses proxies, though; the concept of high end television is operationalised as productions with expenditure of £1m per hour, with a further limitation to certain genres: a definition of dramatic productions (including comedy), and, after consultation, documentaries.[84]

It is also useful, however, to compare the way in which the film and non-film schemes are defined in technological terms. The film scheme, as set out above, uses intention to exhibit as a threshold for support. On the contrary, the television

78 Andrew Davis, 'A kick in the fiscals' *Financial Times* (London, 30 April 2002) 16.

79 Rebecca Feasey, 'Sex, controversy, box-office: from blockbuster to bonkbuster' in Julian Stringer (ed.), *Movie blockbusters* (Routledge 2003) 168.

80 Aaron Barlow, *The DVD revolution: movies, culture, and technology* (Praeger 2005) 22.

81 Kerry Segrave, *Movies at home: how Hollywood came to television* (McFarland 1999) Chapter 6.

82 James Walters, 'A taste for leeches: DVDs, cultural hierarchies and queer consumption' in James Bennett and Tom Brown (eds), *Film and television after DVD* (Routledge 2008).

83 Oxford Economics, 'More than a support act: the true value of video entertainment in the UK' (2011) www.bva.org.uk/files/u1/Oxford-Economics-Value-of-video.pdf

84 HM Treasury, *Creative sector tax reliefs: response to consultation* (2012); Aredhel Darnley, 'Creative sector tax reliefs – Treasury proposals elicit detailed responses as DCMS consults on cultural tests' (2013) 24(1) *Entertainment Law Review* 6. See now Corporation Tax Act 2009, s 1216AB(3) (drama or documentary); s 1216AB(5) (minimum duration 30 m – or more precisely, made for a 30 m slot, as a television programme for a 30 m slot is normally a few minutes shorter due to advertising breaks); s 1216AB(6) (£1 million average expenditure per hour); s 1216AC(2) (definition of drama); all as inserted by Finance Act 2013, sch 16.

and animation schemes are directed at works intended for *broadcast* to the general public;[85] the application of this rule to animation was the subject of some criticism during the consultation process, on the ground that it could discourage technological innovation.[86] That said, this concept is much broader than the film relief, although admittedly set out in medium-specific terms (which prompted a further, quixotic provision that 'television includes the Internet'[87]).

The result is that the question of public support via tax relief depends on a series of questions about form and genre. For instance, a non-animated one-off drama made for DVD release does not qualify for relief as a film, but would if it was animated and intended for TV broadcast, or cost over £1m to make and was similarly intended. These changes therefore highlight the significance of distribution and exhibition to what is supposed to be a relief regarding production. An update to the Film Policy Review provides a partial explanation; that the new relief recognises 'further convergence' between film and high-end television[88] – although the lack of a justification for supporting all (exhibited) film, but only some television and no direct-to-video production demonstrates, as ever, that convergence is more likely to be partial, and even introduce new fissures and assumptions while ostensibly abolishing past distinctions. Although beyond the scope of this chapter, the subsequent introduction of tax relief for theatre and then for orchestras demonstrates both the significance of this form of public support, as well the duplication of concepts from medium to medium, followed swiftly by the further emergence of questions around how to define the newly favoured medium and the parameters of special conditions for it.[89]

Copyright

Copyright underpins a number of aspects of the distinctiveness and the business models of film. (Video in particular has also been the basis of a famous turning

85 Corporation Tax Act 2009, s 1216CA(1), inserted by Finance Act 2013, sch 16. As with film, the emphasis is on intention and demonstrating such through (e.g.) financial planning: Aredhel Johnson and Harriet Revington, 'Creative sector tax reliefs: HMRC publishes guidance on animation and high-end TV reliefs' (2014) 25 *Entertainment Law Review* 246.

86 HM Treasury (n 84) [2.18] and [2.21].

87 Corporation Tax Act 2009, s 1216AA(3), inserted by Finance Act 2013, sch 16.

88 Film Policy Review Panel, 'It's still about the audience: two years on from the Film Policy Review' (n 21) 18.

89 For instance, in respect of orchestras, a debate arose on how to define the size and composition of an orchestra; the initial proposal of 14 members across the four familiar instrumental sections of brass, woodwind, strings and percussion, which would have excluded (e.g.) some chamber groups and brass bands, was then amended to one for a looser requirement for 12 members with at least one of the sections being used during most performances. Nonetheless, a definition that excluded groups mostly performing 'pop and rock music' continued to be favoured. HM Treasury, *Orchestra tax relief: response to the consultation* (2015) [2.6–14]. The result was Corporation Tax Act 2009, s 1217RA(3) (inserted by Finance Act 2016, sch 8) where the figure of 12 was used, although glossed instead with a requirement that in 'none of the musical instruments to be played, or a minority of those instruments, [be] electronically or directly amplified'. Another example is how a rule applying a greater credit to touring theatres than performances in one location (Corporation Tax Act 2009, s 1217K(4), inserted by Finance Act 2014, sch 4) was, after consultation, *not* duplicated in the otherwise quite similar scheme for orchestras.

point in copyright law – the recognition that recording television broadcasts on video for later watching is lawful.)[90] One example which will be discussed in the next section of this chapter is the question of windowing. Conventionally, films have been distributed through a system of 'windows': cinema, video and TV in that order, with set intervals between each and further separation as between different types of TV, e.g. subscription movie channels vs free-to-air TV. The ability of creators or their representatives to control the exhibition and distribution of films is built upon the exclusive rights set out in copyright law, and built into the conditions under which works are made available.[91]

On the other hand, the extent to which copyright law allows for the purchaser of a copy of a work to make further use of it without recourse to the rightsholder also had an impact ('exhaustion' or the 'first sale doctrine'). In the US, for instance, this meant that rightsholders had limited power over the emergence of a rental market, but tried to manage it for some time by setting the sale price at a level that would make it attractive only to video stores rather than consumers.[92] In more recent times, attempts to design 'rental' systems for Internet use, relying on related aspects of the first sale doctrine, have been the subject of a number of adverse legal findings;[93] these cases see a conflict between the concept of the film (and related business models) and the use of the specific technologies of the Internet.

Windowing also has a territorial dimension, in that copyright law enables the adoption of differing release strategies across different jurisdictions. Indeed, DVD releases are normally 'locked' to a specific region, and the system for identifying region-coded DVDs within hardware is only effective because copyright law offers protection for technological protection measures and against their circumvention.[94]

Of course, including film within copyright law in the first instance was not without its problems. In the UK, films were originally regarded as a type of dramatic work. In 1956, film was recognised as a separate type of work for the purposes of copyright law.[95] This however meant that a film-specific concept of authorship needed to be recognised; the rights were those of the 'person by whom the arrangements necessary for the making of the film are undertaken'.[96] This is now simplified through a reference to the 'producer' as the author, although the 'principal director' is now also treated as an author.[97]

90 *Sony* v. *Universal* (1984) 464 US 417.

91 See for instance Copyright, Designs and Patents Act 1988, s 18A (renting to the public) and s 19 (showing the work in public).

92 Joshua M. Greenberg, *From BetaMax to Blockbuster: video stores and the invention of movies on video* (MIT Press 2008) 85.

93 *Warner Bros* v. *WTV Systems* (2011) 824 F Supp 2d 1003 (Central District of California); see critique in Tryon, *On-demand culture: digital delivery and the future of movies* (n 22) 52–4.

94 Copyright, Designs and Patents Act 1988, pt VII.

95 See discussion in Anne Barron, 'The legal properties of film' (2004) 67(2) *Modern Law Review* 177.

96 Copyright Act 1956, s 13.

97 Copyright, Designs and Patents Act 1988, s 5(2).

Film as a medium

The legal distinctions discussed in this chapter must be assessed in light of the changing market for film, and indeed in the context of the Toronto School approaches to assessing the characteristics of a medium, as set out in Chapter 2. In 1985, the British Film Institute's Film Year campaign, 'Cinema – the best place to see a film', had the theme (at a time when video tapes were coming into favour) of 'celebrating film in its first and natural home – the cinema'.[98] A generation later, a report for the UK Film Council argued that 'over 2 in 5 of the general public agree that the cinema remains the best place to enjoy watching films'.[99] Of course, this means that a majority of the general public do not agree that the cinema is the best place to enjoy watching films. Indeed, at a European level, nearly 40% of the population never visit a cinema at all.[100] Furthermore, when looking at volume rather than preference, it emerges that (using a measure of the 'last 10 films you saw'), cinema accounts for 11%, and a much wider range of films are available on DVD than in cinemas.[101] DVD, in particular, has also been the source of significant Hollywood income as an after-market for films already seen in cinemas,[102] although in the last couple of years, these revenues have fallen quite dramatically, without an immediate replacement from other sources such as video-on-demand.[103]

'Windowing' is being challenged by simultaneous release across a number of outlets,[104] an unsuccessful studio-led trial of 'premium VOD',[105] disputes over early DVD release[106] and the development of new non-theatrical services by exhibitors themselves.[107] In the US, the typical window between theatrical

98 The history of this campaign is set out in Hanson (n 4) 123.

99 Harris Interactive, 'Portrayal v. betrayal: an investigation of diverse and mainstream UK film audiences' (*Report for UK Film Council*, 2011) www.bfi.org.uk/sites/bfi.org.uk/files/downloads/uk-film-council-portrayal-vs-betrayal-case-study.pdf

100 European Commission, 'European film in the digital era: bridging cultural diversity and competitiveness' COM(2014) 272, 5.

101 Andrew Higson, *Film England: culturally English filmmaking since the 1990s* (IB Tauris 2011) 23. See also BOP Consulting (n 45) 1 (three-quarters of the films watched in the UK are watched on television).

102 John Belton, 'If film is dead, what is cinema?' (2014) 55 *Screen* 460, 461.

103 Elizabeth Jane Evans and Paul McDonald, 'Online distribution of film and television in the UK: behavior, taste, and value' in Jennifer Holt and Kevin Sanson (eds), *Connected viewing: selling, streaming, and sharing media in the digital era* (Taylor & Francis 2014) 160.

104 Tryon, *Reinventing cinema: movies in the age of media convergence* (n 24) 105–7 (Steven Soderberg's *Bubble* as an example; the film was released on DVD and cable VOD on the same day as it was released in cinema). Simultaneous release can now mean TV or online release at the same time as a film festival premiere, i.e. even earlier again: Jeremy Kay, 'Crossover traffic' *Screen International* (November 2013).

105 Tryon, *On-demand culture: digital delivery and the future of movies* (n 22) 38–9.

106 Adam Dawtrey, 'An Alice in Wonderland nightmare as Disney battles the cinemas' *Guardian* (London, 24 February 2010) 22. A cinema chain threatened to boycott the release of *Alice in Wonderland* as an objection to Disney's intentions to shorten the four-month window between cinema and DVD to 3 months. However, all major UK exhibition chains ultimately agreed to show the film and accept Disney's actions.

107 Charles Gant, 'Video on demand: kill or cure for arthouse cinemas' *Guardian* (London, 5 April 2012) 14.

release and DVD release fell from 167 days to 132 days during the period 2000–2010[108] and continues to shorten.[109] Thus, the role of theatrical release itself becomes less clear. Indeed, in the context of the tax scheme, intention may be difficult to establish; it has been suggested that a film intended for wide theatrical release that ends up going straight to DVD may qualify, while one intended for television that ultimately receives a theatrical release may not be.[110] Works that might have been considered unsuccessful or forgotten reappear, not just on television but online and in less obvious venues such as in-flight entertainment.[111] Some national film bodies, most notably the National Film Board in Canada, have emphasised non-theatrical distribution over a long period.[112] Theatrical release is therefore properly thought of as just one part of a multifaceted map of distribution and exhibition, rather than a gold standard.

This also calls into question whether 'exhibition' and 'video recordings' are the right distinctions in terms of the regulation of content. The Licensing Act 2003 did include one change of note, in specifically mentioning a 'film classification body' (the authority designated under the VRA – i.e. the BBFC), instead of 'such other body as may be specified in the licence', as was the case under the Cinemas Act 1985. However, it did not change the position whereby local authorities continue to play a role in regulating cinemas (and therefore film). With the BBFC functioning without difficulty as a designated national authority in the case of video recordings, both the indirect designation of the BBFC and the residual role for local authorities can be questioned. Indeed, as Barendt argues, the current approach could lead to disparities in the exercise of Article 10 freedoms depending on the decisions of local authorities;[113] recent scholarship points to how the exercise of the statutory power by local authorities often (though not always) restricted the exhibiting of a film that had been classified by the BBFC.[114]

Meanwhile, changes in technological offers and audience behaviour are easily observed – meaning that although distinctions such as cinema exhibition versus video distribution might have been justifiable, even a medium-led regulatory approach cannot be assumed to continue in effectiveness without further scrutiny. While the VHS sector was dominated by feature films, the DVD market

108 Elissa Nelson, 'Windows into the digital world: distributor strategies and consumer choice in an era of connected viewing' in Jennifer Holt and Kevin Sanson (eds), *Connected viewing: selling, streaming, and sharing media in the digital era* (Taylor & Francis 2014) 65.

109 Tryon, *On-demand culture: digital delivery and the future of movies* (n 22) 9.

110 Adrian Shipwright, 'Finance Act notes: films and sound recordings' (2006) 5 *British Tax Review* 517, 523.

111 Barbara Klinger, 'Cinema's shadow: reconsidering non-theatrical exhibition' in Richard Maltby, Melbyn Stokes and Robert Allen (eds), *Going to the movies: Hollywood and the social experience of cinema* (University of Exeter Press 2007) 275.

112 Zoë Druick, *Projecting Canada: government policy and documentary film at the National Film Board of Canada* (McGill-Queen's University Press 2007) 17.

113 Barendt (n 35) 132.

114 E.g. Sian Barber, 'Exploiting local controversy: regional British censorship of Last Tango in Paris (1972)' (2016) 36(4) *Historical Journal of Film, Radio and Television* 587.

saw both films and 'TV box sets' being popular. The technological feasibility of making a whole TV series available in a small size at a reasonable cost of production is an example of a key factor. This has been argued to blur the distinctions between the film and TV industries.[115] One scholar explained how the VHS and in particular DVD market offered the individual 'unpatrolled physical access to the cinema'[116] – in this case, 'the cinema' meaning the works rather than the premises. Indeed, the domestic viewer can watch a work distributed via DVD, broadcasting or the Internet on a large screen with high-quality surround sound,[117] in a way that is arguably more 'special' than the modern multiplex[118] (although, some cinemas now try to provide a very different experience, with gourmet food and premium pricing[119]). Some still highlight the 'anticipation, the dark, the majesty of the big screen and the devotion of unbroken time to the viewing experience'[120] in the cinema (as compared with clips on YouTube), or 'the scale and drama of the big screen showing, and the "night out" effect of going to the movies'.[121] In scholarly work, film studies is more likely to be concerned with cinema spectatorship than with video distribution,[122] and McLuhan, of course, compared cinema with television within his hot/cool framework.[123] Yet there is little sign of a slowing down in the promotion of home- and Internet-based forms of dissemination. Furthermore, non-theatrical platforms such as in-flight entertainment have offered a different model of viewing (quite early in the windowing system), including the use of headphones which make the experience quite different to that of the cinema.[124] Even the cinema itself is a place where the appropriate use of second screens (i.e. mobile phones) is being slowly worked out.[125]

115 Derek Kompare, 'Publishing flow: DVD box sets and the reconception of television' (2006) 7 *Television and New Media* 335, 338.

116 Barbara Klinger, *Beyond the multiplex: cinema, new technologies, and the home* (University of California Press 2006) 57.

117 Barrie Gunter, *Television versus the internet: will TV prosper or perish as the world moves online?* (Chandos 2010) 40–6.

118 Barlow (n 80) 15; on the contested meanings of the multiplex, see Mark Jancovich and Lucy Faire, 'The best place to see a film: the blockbuster, the multiplex, and the contexts of consumption' in Julian Stringer (ed.), *Movie blockbusters* (Routledge 2003).

119 Ryan Gilbey, 'Banish the truffle oil!' *New Statesman* (London, 17 April 2012) www.newstatesman.com/blogs/film/2012/04/banish-truffle-oil

120 Nicholas Rombes, *Cinema in the digital age* (Wallflower 2009) 24.

121 Film Policy Review Panel, 'It's still about the audience: two years on from the Film Policy Review' (n 21) 4.

122 Caetlin Benson-Allott, *Killer tapes and shattered screens: video spectatorship from VHS to file sharing* (University of California Press 2013) 19.

123 See further discussion of how this distinction may be challenged as cinemas change: Nick Stevenson, 'Marshall McLuhan and media and cultural studies' in Paul Grosswiler (ed.), *Transforming McLuhan: cultural, critical, and postmodern perspectives* (Peter Lang 2010) 21.

124 Stephen Groening, '"No one likes to be a captive audience": headphones and in-flight cinema' (2016) 28 *Film History* 114.

125 Dan Hassoun, 'Engaging distractions: regulating second-screen use in the theater' (2016) 55 *Cinema Journal* 89 (highlighting the tension between a prohibitive approach and one which utilizes the presence of such devices as an opportunity for advertising or interaction).

Assumptions about exhibition are even built into the system of VAT. This is demonstrated by a CJEU finding of March 2010 that a coin-operated 'cubicle' for private viewing of films (perhaps unsurprisingly of an adult nature) did not benefit from EU law on the (reduced) rate of VAT for cinema admissions.[126] The full provision provides a useful insight into the context for offering special treatment to cinema; it covers 'admissions to shows, theatres, circuses, fairs, amusement parks, concerts, museums, zoos, cinemas, exhibitions and similar cultural events and facilities', as well as 'reception of broadcasting services'.[127] We see here the grouping of cinema within a set of entertainment facilities (primarily with a physical dimension), but alongside an identical designation for non-physical entertainment in the form of broadcasting. The Court of Justice referred to the category in which cinema falls as having a common feature of being 'available to the public on prior payment of an admission fee giving all those who pay it the right collectively to enjoy the cultural and entertainment services characteristic of those events and facilities'. This broad statement suggests that the distinction is between one business model (general admission to a site or to a particular screen) and another (free admission, individual and customised per-use fee) rather than one which is specifically about film or music or a particular form of communication. Moreover, it constructs film audiences as engaged in unique 'communal' activity rather than individual, small-scale watching. We could even consider coin-operated cubicles can be considered a rather primitive version of what we now know as video-on-demand. However, Belavusau has suggested that the basis of this case may also be judicial unease regarding the position of pornography, a long-standing issue of exceptionalism.[128]

The Film Policy Review Panel noted how 'crowded' the theatrical sector is (in terms of films seeking exhibition),[129] encouraging the exploration of a wider range of business models[130] and that 'an increasing number of works … will never reach a cinema screen or for which the cinema might not be the preferred or most ideal destination'.[131] The European Commission similarly observes that 'small, niche productions' might fare better if distribution efforts were focused on video-on-demand and emerging business models.[132] It is hard to reconcile these recommendations with the arguably unnecessary and inappropriate protection given to a particular type of exhibition through tax credits, especially where the official aims of the provision are to support the cultural goals of a strong domestic production sector (despite well-placed political cynicism as to whether these goals are simply industrial policy in disguise).[133]

126 Case C-3/09 *Erotic Center* v. *Belgium*.

127 Directive 77/388/EC of 17 May 1977 on the harmonisation of the laws of the Member States relating to turnover taxes [1977] OJ L145/1 (as amended), Annex H, Category 7.

128 Uladzislau Belavusau, 'Sex in the Union: EU law, taxation and the adult industry' [2010] 4 *European Law Reporter* 144.

129 Film Policy Review Panel, 'A future for British film' (n 23) 12.

130 Ibid. 27.

131 Ibid. 30.

132 COM (2014) 272 (n 100) 8.

133 Hill (n 75) 714.

A study of the work of the UK Film Council and Government policy towards film rightly noted that an influential report ('Digital Britain') glossed over the policy challenges of convergence, 'not least what is meant by the term "film" in a digital era increasingly characterised by "screens", "platforms" and "content"'.[134] This is true, and indeed is also reflected to some extent in the use of terms within the relevant statutes.

However, it is necessary to go further. I argue that the degree of scrutiny applied to particular genres (and it is hard to deny that particular genres are associated with alternative content, i.e. the 'high' culture of the opera house and London theatre) makes a statement around harm and legitimacy that will have ramifications for cinema content regulation as a whole. Similarly, an unacknowledged cultural hierarchy appears to be in place in the area of tax relief. Particular types of exhibition (and audience) attract special legal treatment. These distinctions were perpetuated (or perhaps muddled further) by the later introduction of various 'creative sector' reliefs, despite the Review Panel's optimistic claim that this reflects the trend towards convergence. This imprecise overlap between legal categories and between law and the market (including consumer expectations) demonstrates the weakness in assigning a statutory privilege to one form over another, particularly at a time when a range of forms of both distribution and exhibition are available for the same underlying creative works. This is of a piece with the continued effective regulation of content and of *production* through legislation ranging from the Licensing Act (in respect of cinemas) to the tax provisions, which all utilise aspects of *distribution* or *exhibition* as a threshold for the application of the law.

Klinger observes (in reference to academic work in film studies) that 'the big-screen performance is marked as authentic, as representing bona fide cinema, while the small screen by comparison is characterised as inauthentic and ersatz'.[135] Indeed, Belton concludes his analysis of whether cinema has a future as a concept by defining it as 'the projection on a screen of life-size – or bigger than life-size images before an audience; everything else is movies'.[136] This favouring of the big screen could well describe aspects of the legal approach too. Furthermore, the legal concepts can affect the way in which those involved in funding and making films approach the question of exhibition – therefore reinforcing and embedding a hierarchy that was barely discussed within the law-making process. This is ultimately a problem of the incomplete and inadequate attention to the reasons for regulating by medium in some areas and regulating more generally in others.

134 Gillian Doyle and others, *The rise and fall of the UK Film Council* (Edinburgh University Press 2015) 8.

135 Klinger, *Beyond the multiplex: cinema, new technologies, and the home* (n 116) 284; see also Benson-Allott (n 122) 23 (pre-recorded video thought of even by 'visually oriented new media' scholars as 'the bastard child of cinema and television'). Though note that, on the contrary, Rosenbaum argues that academics, especially while teaching, are *too* willing to substitute (e.g.) a DVD for 'watching a film' (by which he means in the cinema): Jonathan Rosenbaum, *Movie wars: how Hollywood and the media conspire to limit what films we can see* (A Capella 2000) 88.

136 Belton (n 102) 470.

4 Games

Introduction

In this chapter, I consider the legal status of games from the same perspective as the preceding chapter – that is, content regulation, tax relief, and copyright.[1] Again, the consideration of content regulation encompasses distribution models which challenge the statutory categories, such as online games. Copyright is the subject of a more extensive discussion, in light of the significance of software to the sector. The concluding section considers games as a medium, with special emphasis on how games are compared with film, including in the policy-making and regulatory processes.

Content regulation

Statutory regulation of video games

Concerns over violence in games predate formal content regulation. In the UK, Parliament first grappled with the topic in 1981, through consideration of a Private Members Bill (the deliciously named 'Control of Space Invaders and Other Electronic Games Bill 1981'), which did not become law.[2] Earlier again and before any legislation on games, the Atari game *Death Race* (1976), a version of the 1975 movie *Death Race 2000*, provoked concerns and was ultimately withdrawn – the first game to be 'pulled' from the shelves[3] despite the

1 This chapter is informed by research carried out as part of CREATe, the RCUK-funded Centre for Copyright and New Business Models in the Creative Economy, AHRC Grant Number AH/K000179/1, with co-investigator Keith M. Johnston and research associate Tom Phillips. For further information on the project, including the outcomes of workshops organised under its auspices, see *inter alia* Daithí Mac Síthigh, 'Multiplayer games: tax, copyright, consumers and the video game industries' (2014) *European Journal of Law and Technology* 5; Tom Phillips, '"Don't clone my indie game, bro": informal cultures of videogame regulation in the independent sector' (2015) 24 *Cultural Trends* 143.

2 HC Deb 20 May 1981, vol. 5, col. 287.

3 Ian Bogost, *Persuasive games: the expressive power of videogames* (MIT Press 2007) 200; Terri Day and Ryan Hall, 'Déjà vu: from comic books to video games: legislative reliance on "soft science" to protect against uncertain societal harm linked to violence v. the First Amendment' (2010) 89 *Oregon Law Review* 415, 417.

very abstract 'gremlin' characters that players had the chance to kill.[4] To a lesser extent, sexual themes have also been the basis of controversy, or at least prurient news coverage.[5]

Video games were, from 1984, classified in the UK by the British Board of Film Classification (BBFC), under the authority of the Video Recordings Act (VRA) discussed in Chapter 3. The Act requires the classification of video works (including some video games), and includes, as already discussed, criminal offences of the sale or supply of an unclassified work, the sale or supply of a work beyond its classification (e.g. a work rated suitable for 18 and above, sold to a person under 18),[6] and false labelling (e.g. with the wrong classification).[7]

In its original form, the VRA referred to video games as a type of video work, but applied only to works on 'disc or magnetic tape'.[8] In 1993, the BBFC advocated a number of amendments to the original VRA. One was to add 'chip, cartridge, card' and 'any other recording medium hitherto or yet to be invented' to section 2(a) of the Act.[9] The eventual change adopted by Parliament was to replace 'disc or magnetic tape' with 'disc, magnetic tape, or any other device capable of storing data electronically'.[10] It was widely noted at the time that these amendments meant that games (or indeed video works more generally) on a 'memory chip, plug-in cartridge or board or similar'[11] could now be the subject of regulation under the VRA. This change preserved the ability of the BBFC to regulate some emerging formats, although (as discussed below) it is not applicable to games played online or downloaded from the Internet for offline use.

However, even where the form of distribution was within the scope of the VRA, the majority of games remained 'exempt' from regulation (i.e. classification by the BBFC was not required). This was because a general exemption applied to video games under section 2(1)(c), although the exemption could then be lost if the game fell within a list of categories in sections 2(2) and 2(3). As with the similar exemption for works in music, religion, sport, and the like (as discussed in the previous chapter), the exemption did not apply to works which depicted ('to any significant extent') human sexual activity, acts of gross violence towards humans or animals, and criminal activity that is likely to encourage the commission of offences. The result was that it was only the most violent or

4 Nick Montfort and Ian Bogost, *Racing the beam: the Atari Video computer system* (MIT Press 2009) 125; Bill Loguidice and Matt Barton, *Vintage games: an insider look at the history of Grand Theft Auto, Super Mario and the most influential games of all time* (Focal 2009) 197–8.

5 Tanya Krzywinska, 'The strange case of the misappearance of sex in video games' in Johannes Fromme and Alexander Unger (eds), *Computer games and new media cultures* (Springer 2012).

6 Various multimedia complications under the VRA were encountered, such as covermounted discs on magazines (which may mean that the retailer is susceptible to a VRA offence if selling it to an underage purchaser): *Harrow LBC* v. *WH Smith* [2001] EWHC Admin 469.

7 Video Recordings Act 1984, s 12 (labelling) and s 13 (false indication).

8 Video Recordings Act 1984, s 1.

9 James Ferman, 'Computer pornography: memorandum of evidence to Home Affairs Committee', reprinted in British Board of Film Classification, *Annual report 1993* (1994).

10 Added by the Criminal Justice & Public Order Act 1994.

11 James Norton, 'Digital media works' (1995) 13 *International Media Law* 59.

controversial of games that were subject to the criminal law restrictions on sale and supply under the VRA. The number of works subject to the VRA did grow, however. Before 1995, few works were submitted;[12] by 1999, only 21 works were classified (and these were mostly CD-ROM erotica rather than games per se).[13] However, BBFC legal advice in 2005 on 'DVD-style' material within games brought about a sharp rise to 252.[14] Over the following years, around 200 games were classified each year.

The issue of violence has, unsurprisingly, been at the heart of the small number of legal disputes regarding BBFC decisions. In the *Carmageddon* case, the Video Appeals Committee (VAC) ruled that the 'original' version of the game was not exempt (i.e. required classification in order to be sold or supplied), but could be classified at 18 (with a parental lock).[15] The driving/demolition derby game – where bonus points were awarded for 'killing' pedestrians and animals – was initially refused classification by the BBFC. The game came as somewhat of a shock to the BBFC, which expressly repudiated earlier optimistic comments about game violence being 'more like a game of ping pong than a bloody battle'.[16] The VAC took Article 10 of the European Convention of Human Rights into account (noting that the then-Human Rights Bill would soon be applicable). In a split decision, it relied on arguments such as the game being a 'fantasy game' where the blood was 'a bad joke but nevertheless a joke' and – making interesting assumptions about the relationship between hardware and software – that the game could only be played on the more adult PC rather than a widely used console (as adults are reluctant to let their children loose on such an expensive piece of machinery as a computer).

The wider circumstances of the case are also interesting. The Video Standards Council (which, as discussed below, acted as a self-regulatory body in respect of the wider video games sector) strongly defended the game, while the majority of the BBFC's own consultative body (the Video Consultative Council) disagreed

12 Julian Petley, 'Head-on collisions: the BBFC in the 1990s' in Edward Lamberti (ed.), *Behind the scenes at the BBFC: film classification from the silver screen to the digital age* (BFI 2012) 132.

13 British Board of Film Classification, *Annual report 2001* (2002) 22.

14 British Board of Film Classification, *Annual report 2005* (2006) 63–6; games including full-motion video clips 'which are not an integral part of a game's narrative action and development' or other promotional videos such as trailers and advertisements were considered non-exempt for the purposes of the VRA.

15 Video Appeals Committee decision re 'Carmageddon', reprinted in British Board of Film Classification, *Annual report for 1997/98* (1998) Appendix IV. See also Damian Tambini, Danilo Leonardi and Christopher Marsden, *Codifying cyberspace: communications self-regulation in the age of Internet convergence* (Routledge 2008) 212; Geoffrey Robertson and Andrew Nicol, *Media law* (5th rev edn, Penguin 2008) 840–1.

16 British Board of Film Classification, *Annual report for 1995/96* (1996) 18; British Board of Film Classification, *Annual report for 1996/97* (1997) 8. The BBFC was however already alert to the issue; director James Ferman noted in 1993 that 'until video discs came along, the characters in computer games were cartoon figures; the resolution was very poor. I suspect that, even a year from now, they will be very different from what they are now': Alwyn Turner, *A classless society: Britain in the 1990s* (Aurum 2014) 135.

with the VAC's decision to classify it.[17] There were two versions of the game available – the original version, and a 'zombie' version with green gunge instead of red blood.[18] The latter was available, with a voluntary rating of 15, as the lack of gross violence against humans or animals meant it fell within the VRA exemption[19]) but an additional 'splat pack' could be downloaded from the Internet to 'convert' it back to the original.[20] Beyond this, though, all concerned recognised that the decision would set an important precedent. A number of games including the original *Grand Theft Auto* were delayed approval pending the *Carmageddon* result, but were subsequently classified at 18.[21]

The other fully argued case, regarding *Manhunt 2*, went as far as the High Court[22] – the first, and so far only, decision of the VAC regarding games to reach this stage. The VAC had overruled the decision of the BBFC to refuse to classify *Manhunt 2*, and the BBFC in turn made the application for judicial review. This concerned a revised version of the game, as an earlier version had also been rejected but not appealed.

The High Court found that the VAC had made an error of law in interpreting section 4A of the VRA, placing insufficient emphasis on the harm that may be caused to those likely to view the game in question (in effect, agreeing with the BBFC's initial approach), and quashed its decision to classify *Manhunt 2.* Ultimately the VAC (on further consideration) still approved the game after applying the revised legal test, and it was released with a classification of 18 rather than refused classification.[23] The delays to the release of the game and the initial refusal of the BBFC did, however, contribute to the industry's calls for a change to the system of regulation, as ultimately expressed in the 2010 amendments to the VRA discussed in this chapter. This may be a good example of the law of unintended consequences, in that (as Barker has recently shown)[24] the BBFC was trying to demonstrate a new toughness, motivated in part by a desire to reassure Government and Parliament that it would continue to be an appropriate regulator for games.

Because the majority of games were exempt from the application of the VRA, self-regulatory systems took on particular importance. In Europe, the industry-led scheme has been known since 2003 as Pan-European Game Information (PEGI). It developed out of an earlier set of ratings, known as ELSPA (after the Entertainment and Leisure Software Publishers Association), which had been

17 British Board of Film Classification, *Annual report for 1996/97* (n 16) 45–6.
18 Steven Poole, *Trigger happy: the inner life of videogames* (Fourth Estate 2000) 218.
19 Petley (n 12) 133.
20 'Board's reply to VAC Appeal 11', reprinted in British Board of Film Classification, *Annual report for 1996/97* (n 16) Appendix VI.
21 'The link between video game violence and aggression: a critical summary of current research', reprinted in British Board of Film Classification, *Annual report 1998* (1999) 12.
22 *R (BBFC)* v. *Video Appeals Committee* (2008) EWHC 203 (Admin).
23 British Board of Film Classification, *Annual report 2007* (2008) 94.
24 Martin Barker, '"Knowledge-U-Like": The British Board of Film Classification and its research' (2016) 13 *Journal of British Cinema and Television* 121, 131.

developed by ELSPA and the UK-based Video Standards Council (VSC) in 1994. PEGI is now managed by the VSC and the Netherlands Institute for the Classification of Audio-visual Media (NICAM). In the case of consoles, manufacturers have long required the use of BBFC or PEGI ratings (in practice meaning a high profile for the latter, given the small number of games classified by the BBFC), and many retailers similarly required some form of rating.[25] In practice, while the BBFC was reviewing about 200 games a year (as noted above), over 1,000 were being classified under the PEGI system.

The Digital Economy Act 2010 brought about two major changes to game content regulation, amending the VRA to narrow the scope of the exemption from classification, and providing for the creation of a new games-specific classification authority. Concerns had been expressed on a regular basis regarding the two systems and possible discrepancies, such as the idea that parents may assume that the PEGI ratings relate to ability rather than suitability.[26] The games industry had also long criticised the VRA, arguing that the system was slow and clumsy and that it would be better to give legal standing to the PEGI system.[27] In political terms, two influences were Tania Byron's 2008 review for the Department of Education on the 'protection of children in the digital world'[28] and a House of Commons committee report on 'harmful content', published in the same year. The two reports differed, though, in their recommendations; Byron suggested a hybrid system,[29] while the Culture, Media and Sport Committee[30] preferred the use of the BBFC system for all games for those aged 12 and over. The BBFC itself favoured the extension of the VRA to a wider range of games;[31] the European Commission favoured the PEGI system and presented it as a desirable goal for member states to consider.[32]

After a consultation exercise,[33] it was decided to give statutory force to aspects of the PEGI system, and this was brought about by way of amendments to the VRA contained in the Digital Economy Act, after worryingly limited

25 Department for Children, Schools and Families, 'Safer children in a digital world: the report of the Byron Review' (2008) http://data.parliament.uk/DepositedPapers/Files/DEP2008–0831/DEP2008–0831.pdf [7.10].

26 Damiano Felini, 'Beyond today's video game rating systems: a critical approach to PEGI and ESRB, and proposed improvements' (2014) 10(1) *Games and Culture* 106, 113 (on consumer confusion between game ratings and the typical use of age labels on toys to indicate complexity); Department for Children, Schools and Families (n 25) [7.25]; Slesenger Research, 'Classifying games: qualitative research findings' (2008) www.bbfc.co.uk/sites/default/files/attachments/Classifying%20Games%20-%20Qualitative%20Research%20Findings%20(January%202008)_0.pdf 31–2.

27 Entertainment and Leisure Software Publishers' Association, *Playing for success* (1998) 4–5, 18–19.

28 Department for Children, Schools and Families (n 25).

29 Ibid. [7.47–49].

30 House of Commons Culture, Media and Sport Committee, *Harmful content on the Internet and in video games* (HC 353, 2007–2008) 203.

31 British Board of Film Classification, *Annual report 2007* (n 23) 4–5.

32 European Commission, 'Communication on the protection of consumers, in particular minors, in respect of the use of video games' COM(2008) 207.

33 Department for Culture, Media and Sport, 'Video games classification: a consultation' (2008) http://dera.ioe.ac.uk/8338/5/VideoGames2008.pdf

Parliamentary consideration.[34] The VRA now provides for the designation of more than one authority. The BBFC continues to be the classification authority in respect of video works, but the VSC was designated in 2012 in respect of video games and performs its video game functions under the name 'Games Rating Authority' (GRA),[35] using the PEGI labels and criteria. The narrower basis for exemption from the VRA essentially means that games classifiable under PEGI at 12 or above now require statutory classification. The remaining exemption can be varied in future by statutory instrument (subject to the affirmative resolution procedure), so as to afford 'flexibility to provide for any future developments and new games with different content';[36] the weaknesses of this system discussed in the previous chapter, regarding limits to parliamentary scrutiny, are equally applicable here.

In the United States, self-regulation has been the main form of regulation of games, through the Entertainment Software Rating Board (ESRB). Controversies over games such as *Death Race* (as noted above) and the horror-style *Night Trap* (1993) are argued to have influenced the development of a self-regulatory system as a necessary alternative to any proposed statutory system.[37] In 2005, California attempted to introduce a statutory system for the regulation of games (regulating the sale of certain games to under 18s) not dissimilar to the VRA, but it was ultimately found to be unconstitutional. In *Brown* v. *Entertainment Merchants' Association*[38] the Supreme Court took a strong line in finding that games were protected in full by the First Amendment.[39] As such, the California plan has been abandoned, and the ESRB system continues to be the main means by which video game content is 'regulated' in the US, although the concurring and dissenting opinions at the Supreme Court did include some criticism of the effectiveness of labelling.

As with film, the history of regulation includes a series of questions about the regulation and definition of the medium, as well as whether it is appropriate to create specific rules within a medium. The nature of games as software, though

34 This Bill was first considered by the House of Lords, with comparatively short debates on these sections (the focus of the debate was on the copyright provisions also contained in it). Subsequently, it was the subject of the 'wash-up' procedure before the 2010 General Election, with the House of Commons not even considering amendments to the sections on games in a very short committee stage taken in the House.

35 See Digital Economy Act 2010 (Appointed Day No. 2) Order 2012, SI 2012/1164 (commencement); Video Recordings (Labelling) Regulations 2012, SI 2012/1767 (labelling); see also the formal designation of the GRA by the Secretary of State (House of Commons Votes and Proceedings, 10 May 2012).

36 House of Lords Delegated Powers & Regulatory Reform Committee, *2nd report of session 2009–10* (HL 24, 2009–2010) [72, 75].

37 Van Burnham and Joey Anuff, *Supercade: a visual history of the videogame age, 1971–1984* (MIT Press 2001) 139, 159. This has not passed without criticism, for instance the contention that the ESRB takes a more relaxed approach to war and boxing games than to other genres: Stephen Kline, Nick Dyer-Witheford and Greig De Peuter, *Digital play: the interaction of technology, culture and marketing* (McGill-Queen's University Press 2003) 134.

38 (2011) 564 US 786, (2011) 131 S Ct 2729.

39 See discussion below.

(to which we will return soon), has meant that technological change has perhaps had a more immediate impact on the effectiveness of the existing law.

Regulation of downloaded and online games

Downloaded and online games fall outside the scope of the Video Recordings Act. This has taken on more significance in recent years, not just because of technological change (ease and speed of downloading), but also because of the emergence of the casual gaming sector, which is primarily online or downloaded, typically for browser-based play or smartphone and tablet apps. This is, of course, not an entirely new sector,[40] although Juul characterises downloadable games as a major trend in the modern casual gaming 'revolution'.[41]

The appeal of an app-based game such as Angry Birds (even to recently retired prime ministers)[42] highlights the emergence and normalisation of smartphones as gaming devices. Juul's discussion of casual gaming predated the growth in popularity of iPhone games, although he identified the similar platform of online Flash games. Games and entertainment became the most popular categories in the iOS App Store some years ago.[43] Furthermore, games on social networking sites are also significant, especially as regards the marketing and discovery of new games[44] and the move to a service- rather than product-based business model.[45]

The difference between game apps (or similar) and console games is more legally salient than previous divergences in the sector, such as comparing console and PC games with handheld games.[46] In those cases, the same regulatory regime applied, although of course questions can be asked about how well it mapped onto different formats. For apps, as for browser-based games, however, the inapplicability of the VRA is obvious. Even if a game contains the exact same features and gameplay as an equivalent game supplied on disc or other physical medium, the BBFC (and now the GRA) have no statutory jurisdiction.[47] Beyond

40 Loguidice and Barton (n 4) 291 (*Tetris* as a foundation of casual gaming); James Newman, *Videogames* (2nd edn, Routledge 2013) 51 (highlighting the launch of the PlayStation as a step towards a different style of gaming); James Newman, *100 videogames* (British Film Institute 2007) 128, 194–6 (short games preinstalled, such as *Minesweeper* on Windows and *Snake* on Nokia mobile phones); Osamu Inoue, *Nintendo magic: winning the videogame wars* (Vertical 2009) 24 (role of Nintendo's Wii and DS in 'expanding the gaming population').

41 Jesper Juul, *A casual revolution: reinventing video games and their players* (MIT Press 2010) 5, 131. See further Randy Nichols, *The video game business* (British Film Institute 2014) 67–9.

42 Matt Rudd, 'There's no escape' *Sunday Times* (London, 12 February 2012) Magazine 20.

43 Tom Chatfield, *Fun Inc.: why gaming will dominate the twenty-first century* (Pegasus Books 2010) 213.

44 Nicholas Lovell, *The curve: turning followers into superfans* (Revised edn, Penguin 2014).

45 Chatfield (n 43) 34.

46 Kate Berens and Geoff Howard, *The rough guide to videogaming* (2nd edn, Rough Guides 2002) 3 (excluding handheld games from a guide to gaming, on the basis that the player experience was not comparable).

47 See further Daithí Mac Síthigh, 'The regulation of video games: past, present and future' (2010) 21 *Entertainment Law Review* 298.

the VRA, the Audiovisual Media Services Directive excludes, through recital 18, activities including private correspondence, ancillary animations on websites, 'games of chance', and 'online games' from the requirement on EU member states to regulate television and on-demand audiovisual media services.[48]

Yet the question of downloaded games and the law is not a new issue either. The BBFC worried about the prospect of games delivered 'in digitised form down a modem from outside national frontiers' in 1993,[49] and by 1997 was publicly highlighting the availability of an unclassified game (*Schoolyard Slaughter*) through download.[50] 'Importing' of games through the Internet without BBFC or PEGI scrutiny was also emphasised by the BBFC in its first annual report of the new millennium.[51]

Some existing systems have been extended to capture new platforms, especially self-regulatory systems. The voluntary, European Commission-supported PEGI Online system has for some years included online versions of existing console games,[52] and in 2012 it began to offer 'PEGI for Apps' as a further service. In the US, the ESRB suggested in 2010 that its system should be used for games in the App Store,[53] but this proposal was not taken up. In 2011, it reached an agreement with CTIA (a trade association for mobile phone carriers), providing for the use of ESRB ratings, generated through a questionnaire, on carrier game stores (and Microsoft's), and later on various other, console-led platforms. However, this did not apply to the iOS App Store or to other app stores beyond the participating parties – such as the Google Play store.

In 2015, however, Google, Microsoft and Nintendo joined the International Age Rating Coalition (IARC) scheme, using both generic categories and existing local systems (e.g. non-statutory regimes such as PEGI and ESRB, and statutory schemes such as the Australian Classification Board) in the applicable territories. A single questionnaire generates both generic and local ratings. Interestingly, it applies to apps more generally and not just to game apps – an extension of the work of some of the participating 'game' rating bodies.

The shift to Internet downloads reduced the influence of mobile-specific rating bodies, such as the Independent Mobile Classification Body (IMCB).[54] The IMCB supported the 'rating' of certain mobile content as unsuitable for under 18s, by reference to its own policy on standards (although the actual rating was carried out by

48 Directive 2010/13/EU of 10 March 2010 on the coordination of certain provisions laid down by law, regulation or administrative action in Member States concerning the provision of audiovisual media services [2010] OJ L263/15; the Directive is discussed in more detail in Chapter 6.

49 British Board of Film Classification, *Annual report 1993* (n 9) 21.

50 British Board of Film Classification, *Annual report for 1996/97* (n 16) 23.

51 British Board of Film Classification, *Annual report 2001* (n 13) 66.

52 Christopher Marsden, *Internet co-regulation: European law, regulatory governance and legitimacy in cyberspace* (Cambridge University Press 2011) 157–61.

53 Daniel Terdiman, 'Will Apple offer ratings for iPhone games?' (*Cnet.com*, 10 June 2010) http://news.cnet.com/8301–10797_3–10262087–235.html.

54 See discussion in Marsden (n 52) 143–5.

content providers), and mobile carriers used these ratings to support blocking certain content until the user's age had been verified. Its system did not cover material generally available on the Internet, as it is focused on content provided directly through carriers rather than merely through the use of a carrier-provided data connection. Now, this function is carried out by the BBFC as a non-statutory system (by agreement with the mobile carriers), and encompasses what is now called 'commercial content' (i.e. that provided by the carriers, normally through contracts with others) as well as 'Internet content', which is filtered by the carriers. The commercial content is rated using the BBFC's categories (as discussed in Chapter 3), although the Internet content is simply designated as 18 (i.e. requiring age verification) or under 18 (unfiltered).[55]

Beyond statutory and non-statutory classification, though, individual intermediaries such as web hosts and platform managers can also play an influential role in controlling access to and use of games.[56] Apple's app rating scheme for its App Store, which operates automatically on the basis of information supplied by the developer, utilises four categories: 4+, 9+, 12+ and 17+; Apple devices support parental controls (linked to these ratings), and developers must comply with strict conditions as to the content of apps, which are assessed through prior scrutiny of all submitted apps. This approach is not without precedent. For instance, Nintendo took a deliberate decision to develop the Nintendo Entertainment System (NES) as a family-friendly console with significant restrictions in its early days of any depiction of drugs, 'foul language', smoking and alcohol.[57] It can be observed that Apple's approach echoes this – although Nintendo has reduced its restrictions over time,[58] to the extent that the controversial *Manhunt 2* (at first, refused classification in the UK, as discussed above) was available on its Wii.

In terms of content restrictions in the iOS App Store, it can be noted that Apple applies a wide range of restrictions. Some relate to the use of the hardware,[59] and others to usefulness.[60] Most controversially, Apple has taken a hard line against sexual content in apps,[61] even to the extent of reviving a century-old

55 However in the case of network EE, the BBFC also supports a 'Strict' filter at the equivalent of a 12 rating.

56 I have made this argument in more detail in Daithí Mac Síthigh, 'App law within: rights and regulation in the smartphone age' (2013) 21(2) *International Journal of Law and Information Technology* 154. See more recently Frank Pasquale, *The black box society: the secret algorithms that control money and information* (Harvard University Press 2015) 61–4; Angela Daly, *Private power, online information flows and EU law: mind the gap* (Hart 2016).

57 Dominic Arsenault, 'The Nintendo Entertainment System' in Mark Wolf (ed.), *The video game explosion: a history from PONG to PlayStation and beyond* (Greenwood 2008) 111; Nichols (n 41) 36–8.

58 Kline, Dyer-Witheford and De Peuter (n 37) 130.

59 Guideline 2.4, prohibiting the use of the phone's location features to control vehicles or aircraft.

60 Guideline 2.11, allowing duplicates to be rejected; guideline 2.12 providing for 'not very useful' apps or those not providing any 'lasting entertainment value' to be rejected.

61 Jenna Wortham, 'Apple bans some apps for sex-tinged content' *New York Times* (New York, 23 February 2010) B1.

cause célèbre, that of Joyce's *Ulysses*.[62] It also excludes apps that are 'defamatory, offensive, mean-spirited, or likely to place the targeted individual or group in harms way'[63] (although 'professional political satirists and humorists' are exempted from this prohibition) and 'excessively objectionable or crude content'.[64] In-game 'enemies' cannot be real governments or corporations.[65] Apple also responds to political controversy by introducing new stipulations, such as proscribing apps which provide access to information on drink-driving checkpoints in the US.[66]

Again, the wide range of specific measures developed in relation to downloaded and online games, and even the fact that we can identify this category, means that an aspiration to regulate all audiovisual content is very far removed from reality – when even within the narrower games sector, a single regime remains very far away. This is not to say that some simplification is neither possible nor desirable, but the barriers to a converged regulatory system are not trivial, and sometimes entirely defensible.

Taxation

In this section, I will assess aspects of the (successful) campaign by video game industry bodies for a game development tax credit, with an emphasis on how the credit compares with that in other fields, and how its boundaries have been drawn. Initially, some in the games industry were sceptical of seeking support in this fashion, out of concern that it would lead to an emphasis on cultural aspects[67] (somewhat ironic, as we will see). However, many were in support, and the major political parties promised the extension of the 2006 film credit to the games sector in the 2010 general election. Following the formation of the Coalition government, though, the new Chancellor did not put forward such a scheme. Instead, he found that the proposal was an example of a 'poorly targeted' form of relief.[68] This drew criticism from representative bodies – not just comparing with other creative sectors (i.e. those discussed in Chapter 3), but comparing the

62 John Naughton, 'Buck naked on your iPad? No way….' *Observer* (London, 20 June 2010) www.theguardian.com/technology/2010/jun/20/james-joyce-ulysses-seen-app. For discussion of the history of the censorship of Ulysses (e.g. restrictions on the sale of the book on the grounds of obscenity), see Edward de Grazia, *Girls lean back everywhere: the law of obscenity and the assault on genius* (Random House 1992) 7–38.

63 Guideline 4.1.

64 Guideline 16.9; see Stuart Dredge, 'Apple bans satirical iPhone game Phone Story from its App Store' (*Guardian Apps Blog*, 14 September 2011) www.guardian.co.uk/technology/appsblog/2011/sep/14/apple-phone-story-rejection

65 Guideline 15.3.

66 Guideline 22.8; see Chloe Albanesius, 'Apple bans DUI checkpoint apps in App Store' *PC Magazine* (9 June 2011) www.pcmag.com/article2/0,2817,2386693,00.asp

67 Aphra Kerr, 'The UK and Irish game industries' in Peter Zackariasson and Timothy Wilson (eds), *The video game industry: formation, present state, and future* (Routledge 2012) 128.

68 HC Deb 22 June 2010, vol. 512, col. 175; Keith Stuart, 'Budget 2010: video games tax relief disappears' *Guardian* (London, 23 June 2010) www.theguardian.com/uk/2010/jun/22/budget-2010-video-games-tax-relief-disappears

position of games development in the UK with the opportunities available in other jurisdictions.[69] Canada was frequently cited. Within the UK, there was also a regional dimension. Around 25% of companies in the UK games industry are located in Scotland[70] (where approximately 10% of the population lives). As such, an additional voice in the debate was the Scottish Affairs Committee of the House of Commons, which recommended that the question of tax relief be given further consideration.[71] Between the claims of private bodies and ongoing political interest, the case for favourable tax treatment for this industry continued to be put well after it appeared that it had been rejected by Government.

In December 2012, a scheme for video game tax credits was announced, alongside the new schemes for high-end TV and for animation. The scheme was modelled on that for film, with two main legislative components. The first was the amendment of the legislation on taxation (the Corporation Tax Act 2009), so as to provide for the tax treatment of video game development expenditure. The second was the setting up of a 'cultural test' which would determine eligibility for the credit. The design of the scheme appears to distinguish between revenue at the point of sale and revenue from subsequent purchases;[72] this is of little relevance to the conventional sale of boxed games for consoles, but a significant matter for those using newer business models.

The Corporation Tax Act is where one might expect to find the definition of a video game. However, no such definition is found. Supporting material confirms that it was the Government's intention that 'video game' take its ordinary meaning.[73] However, having realised the consequences of this (and concerned about meeting the EU requirements discussed below), 'anything produced for advertising or promotional purposes' and gambling are both explicitly excluded from the scheme.[74] There is, of course, the potential for abuse of this broad definition, although for the time being it is interesting to note how the price of state support for the industry includes some structures for 'deserving' and 'undeserving' being set out in legislation, as the medium-based definition originally proposed was considered to be too broad to achieve the Government's goals while complying

69 Keith Stuart, 'Tiga, tax breaks and the future of the UK games industry' (*Guardian – Games Blog*, 10 October 2010) www.theguardian.com/technology/gamesblog/2011/oct/10/tiga-richard-wilson-interview

70 House of Commons Scottish Affairs Committee, *Video games industry in Scotland* (HC 500, 2010–2011) [19].

71 Ibid. [50], [55–7].

72 Corporation Tax Act 2009, s 1217AA (inserted by Finance Act 2013, sch 17), defining completion of a game for the purposes of the scheme of tax credits as when the game 'is first in a form in which it can reasonably be regarded as ready for copies of it to be made and made available to the general public'.

73 HM Treasury, *Creative sector tax reliefs: response to consultation* (2012) [2.61].

74 Corporation Tax 2000, s 1217AA (2) and (3), inserted by Finance Act 2013, sch 17; see criticism in Aredhel Darnley, 'Creative sector tax reliefs – treasury proposals elicit detailed responses as DCMS consults on cultural tests' (2013) 24(1) *Entertainment Law Review* 6, 8. 'Advergames' are indeed a significant link between games and advertising: Jean-Marc Lehu, *Branded entertainment: product placement and brand strategy in the entertainment business* (Kogan Page 2009) 179.

with EU law. The Government also considered whether games containing pornographic content would be eligible for the scheme.[75] In light of consultation responses, its revised position was that games containing pornographic or other extreme material would not be eligible, but this would be determined through self-certification by the applicant rather than a need to apply for formal classification under the VRA.[76] This was however not included in the legislation and although the BFI declares that it will not certify as British those games that would not be classified under the PEGI system,[77] this (as compared with the clear exclusion of gambling and advertising) does not appear to enjoy any statutory support.

The creation of the system for video game tax credits also required European Commission approval, which was also required when the film scheme was adopted in 2006 (as discussed in Chapter 3). The Government put forward a similar points-based eligibility test – the 'cultural test' – for the games scheme. Within the UK's test, points are awarded for various features (e.g. setting, characters, subject matter, language, cultural contribution, the people involved, and support for cultural 'hubs'). A set number of points are needed, with some additional thresholds within sub-categories in place so as to avoid an inappropriate result.

This test is necessary so as to ensure that the scheme promotes cultural objectives rather than protect national industries or distorts open markets within the European Union. Such measures would likely violate Article 107(1) TFEU. However, the same article permits, subject to European Commission scrutiny, certain derogations from this general rule where culture is concerned. 'Aid to promote culture and heritage conservation where such aid does not affect trading conditions and competition in the Union to an extent that is contrary to the common interest' is appropriate, according to Article 107(3)(d) TFEU.[78]

The European Commission initially doubted the validity of the scheme. It noted that a proposed rule on territory (whereby only spending on goods and services used or consumed in the UK is eligible for relief) is specifically authorised in its own Cinema Communication, which sets down general principle for the review of national measures in this sector.[79] While the UK games scheme was modelled on the film scheme (which had indeed been approved), that approval was in the context of the cinema-specific guidance, which was not binding upon the Commission in other sectors. The Commission also pointed to the fear of a 'subsidy race', noting the expressed desire of the UK Government to offer a

75 HM Treasury, *Consultation on creative sector tax reliefs* (2012) [5.17].

76 HM Treasury, *Creative sector tax reliefs: response to consultation* (n 73) [2.63].

77 British Film Institute, 'Video games cultural test guidance notes' (2016) www.bfi.org.uk/sites/bfi.org.uk/files/downloads/bfi-british-film-certification-cultural-test-for-video-games-guidance-notes-2016–03.pdf

78 Other exceptions, not relied on in this case, include aid of a social character, the development of underdeveloped regions, and (where not adversely affecting trading conditions) aid to facilitate the development of particular economic activities or areas.

79 European Commission, 'Communication from the Commission on State aid for films and other audiovisual works' [2013] OJ C322 (see in particular paragraph 24 on application to games).

scheme that is 'among the most generous in the world'.[80] It also queried whether State aid was necessary in a growing market of this nature (as compared with, presumably, failing or declining markets where aid is deemed necessary to fill the gaps left by private investment or consumer payments).

This investigation was the subject of criticism from the UK games industry.[81] However, the fact that schemes in other jurisdictions or for other sectors had been approved could not realistically prevent Commission action, and the general presumption is against state aid (i.e. it is only in a minority of situations that it will be permitted, as an exception to the general rule that state aid to private industry is forbidden). In any event, the final decision of the Commission was to allow the scheme to proceed. It found that the scheme was '(focused) on a small number of distinctive, culturally British games which have increasing difficulties to find private financing',[82] and notes that the territorial restriction had been removed.

Having succeeded in putting forward the cultural case, UK speakers immediately played it down. For instance, the Chancellor argued that the games industry was 'a key industry of the future' and that he wanted 'Britain to be one of its biggest centres', adding again that the 'relief is one of the most generous in the world and will help [SMEs] to grow, creating new jobs for hardworking people'.[83] The minister with responsibility for the creative industries added that 'the government recognises the important contribution the industry makes to the economy and is committed to supporting the industry's continued growth through a range of measures like these new tax reliefs'.[84] Finally, the chief executive officer of industry body TIGA framed the successful campaign as one that will 'create jobs, boost investment and enable the production of more British video games'.[85]

These are remarkable statements in the context of what the European Commission was actually asked to approve and how the initial framing of the scheme (e.g. as the most generous) had caused difficulties during the approval process. There is no mention of the word 'culture' until the final paragraph of the Government's press statement, and that is only in the context of providing a link to the cultural test. The politicians are happy to touch upon more general political language such as 'hardworking people' rather than what it told the Commission

80 SA.36139 'Video games tax relief' [2013] OJ C152 8.

81 UKIE, 'Ukie responds to announcement of European Commission tax breaks investigation' (16 April 2013) http://ukie.info/content/ukie-responds-announcement-european-commission-tax-breaks-investigation; UKIE, 'Ukie welcomes autumn statement announcements of support for business, urges government to push games production tax credits through ' (5 December 2013) http://ukie.org.uk/content/ukie-welcomes-autumn-statement-announcements-support-business-urges-government-push-games-pr

82 European Commission, 'State aid: Commission approves UK video games tax relief plan' (27 March 2014) http://europa.eu/rapid/press-release_IP-14–331_en.htm

83 HM Treasury, 'Video games tax relief passes final hurdle' (27 March 2014) www.gov.uk/government/news/video-games-tax-relief-passes-final-hurdle

84 Ibid.

85 Ibid.

about culture, and the industry representative welcomes jobs and investment and only then Britishness (albeit with no specific mention of culture). Of course, nothing forbids elected public or private representatives from praising industrial growth. Indeed, 'growth and jobs' is a key plank of the EU's overall strategy, and as noted above, Article 107 does provide for some permissible state aid in respect of development. However, the disconnection between the scheme that is designed and defended as a cultural measure and the words (for domestic consumption, of course) of praise for what the Government's subsidy will do *for the industry* is plain to see.

Despite the apparent lack of belief by government in its own cultural claims (or unwillingness to speak about them), there are plenty of reasons why games could and should be plausibly protected by Article 107(3)(d), assuming the other aspects of the test could be met. Although some (such as Apple) continue to exclude games from cultural categories for presentational and (self-)regulatory purposes,[86] commentary and academic analysis of games often includes insights from a cultural perspective;[87] even in the context of discussing the protection of children and harmful content, the cultural dimension is still acknowledged.[88]

Moreover, a mixed-methods study of Japanese culture in Taiwan found positive identification by heavy game users with Japan, with the impact being best described as nation-building rather than nation-branding.[89] Over a long period, games were brought within the famously extensive national cultural policy area in France.[90] Although a cynical observer of the UK government and UK-based games industry would suggest that the cultural test merely cloaks the desire for a subsidy to local industry, the focus of the test on promoting culturally British video games could actually be to the advantage of the UK and to 'British culture'. Of course, some might understand the cultural dimension while still objecting to the need to frame that contribution in terms of national culture. However, the approach of the UK government appears to be one of sidelining a cultural vocabulary entirely.

Copyright

Although it would not be useful to address all of the copyright issues in the games sector here,[91] a discussion of some will illustrate how copyright law also continues to be the site of debate as to the category of games. As Boyden argued,

86 Steven Poole, 'Why does Apple hate video games so much?' *Edge* (June 2013) 32 (criticising the exclusion of games from Apple's less regulated category for submissions to the iOS App Store, which consists of books and music).

87 Jonathan Corliss, 'The social science study of video games' (2011) 6(1) *Games and Culture* 3, 6.

88 Department for Children, Schools and Families (n 25) [6.62].

89 Chi-Ying Chen, 'Is the video game a cultural vehicle?' (2013) 8(6) *Games and Culture* 408.

90 Hugh Dauncey, 'French videogaming: what kind of culture and what support?' (2012) 18 *Convergence: The International Journal of Research into New Media Technologies* 385.

91 A fuller analysis of copyright and games, including some reflections on a survey carried out as part of the CREATe project, is found in Daithí Mac Síthigh, 'The game's the thing: property, priorities and perceptions in the video games industries' in Megan Richardson and Sam Ricketson (eds), *Research handbook on intellectual property in media and entertainment* (Edward Elgar 2017).

studying games (video games and otherwise) at the boundaries of IP law can also lead to a better understanding of the scope and boundaries of copyright itself.[92] For present purposes, I highlight two initial questions of boundary-setting – which law applies and what type of 'work' a game is – and then consider three areas of game-related controversy in copyright law – second-hand sales, digital rights management and 'cloning'.

Turning first to demarcation, we can note two particular areas of interest; the EU's Software Directive (and similar provisions elsewhere), and the definition of works (e.g. literary, artistic, etc.) protected by copyright law. The main contours of EU copyright law are found in two Directives. The Information Society Directive,[93] along with member state provisions including those adopted in the context of international treaty obligations, is the better known system. A second system, however, deals specifically with computer programs – the Software Directive[94] – and requires the protection of computer programs as literary works, with some provisions and exceptions specific to this field.[95] There are a number of inconsistencies between the two regimes,[96] and so it is not surprising that applying the Directives to video games can prove controversial.

The question of which works are protected by copyright law arises because 'games' are not mentioned in the relevant international treaties, e.g. the Berne Convention as amended. This means that in order to be protected, a game needs to be characterised as a type of protected work (such as a program or a film), or aspects of a game need to meet this test (e.g. as an artistic work). Generally, games have been treated either as computer programs (i.e. as discussed above, typically as a type of literary work) or as mixed works.[97] A mixed work can include categorisation as a film,[98] although this can refer only to video-like material.[99] In the UK, film is protected against the copying of a recording rather than reshooting (i.e. using production techniques similar to those used in a previous film);[100] this makes this form of protection less relevant in the types of claim discussed below regarding, for instance, cloning. A mixed approach might

92 Bruce Boyden, 'Games and other uncopyrightable systems' (2011) 18 *George Mason Law Review* 439, 442.

93 Directive 2001/29/EC of 22 May 2001 on the harmonisation of certain aspects of copyright and related rights in the information society [2001] OJ L167/10.

94 Directive 2009/24/EC of 23 April 2009 on the legal protection of computer programs [2009] OJ L111/16 (codifying Directive 91/250/EEC as amended).

95 In some other jurisdictions, including the US, Canada, and Australia, computer programs are treated as a type of literary work, with fewer software-specific provisions in place. See for instance Benedict Atkinson, *The true history of copyright* (Sydney University Press 2007) 381.

96 Marie-Christine Janssens, 'The Software Directive' in Irini A. Stamatoudi and Paul Torremans (eds), *EU copyright law: a commentary* (Edward Elgar 2014) [5.03].

97 World Intellectual Property Organisation, *The legal status of video games: comparative analysis in national approaches* (2013) [14].

98 Paul Gottlich, 'Online games from the standpoint of media and copyright law' [2007] 10 IRIS Plus 8 58–9; *Galaxy* v. *Sega* (1997) 75 FCR 8; *Sony* v. *Stevens* [2005] HCA 58.

99 Stanley Lai, *The copyright protection of computer software in the United Kingdom* (Hart 2000) 89.

100 Simon Stokes, *Art and copyright* (2nd edn, Hart 2012) 180; *Norowzian* v. *Arks* [2000] FSR 363.

also highlight a game as a dramatic work, although again UK law's requirement of unity in this type of work can be a barrier.[101] Treating games as audiovisual works (in addition to rather than instead of software protection) was also a key theme in a series of arcade game cases in the US in the 1980s; this related in part to US-specific rules on registration[102] and to a practice of registering a work in both forms.[103]

The Court of Justice of the European Union (CJEU) has also addressed the status of games, in its decision in *Nintendo* v. *PC Box*.[104] In determining whether the provisions of the Information Society Directive or Software Directive were applicable to a case regarding technological protection measures, the court found it necessary to define games in more detail. It found that games 'constitute complex matter comprising not only a computer program but also graphic and sound elements, which, although encrypted in computer language, a unique creative value which cannot be reduced to that encryption'. Consequently, when graphics and sounds are part of the originality of a game 'they are protected, together with the entire work, by copyright in the context of the system established by' the Information Society Directive. This arguably contradicted the CJEU's earlier recognition of the specialised nature of software copyright in *UsedSoft*.[105] However, it is in line with the way in which accounts of the current games industries highlight the role of creative works (e.g. music) and multidisciplinary creative teams, especially in light of technological advances.[106]

Having considered these preliminary questions of status, we can now consider how copyright law is applied within the sector. The first issue is that of second-hand sales. The CJEU found in *UsedSoft*[107] that the 'exhaustion' right in copyright law (the right to sell a purchased work without restriction) applies to downloaded *software*. This would even mean that the software has ostensibly been licensed rather than sold, the right could apply.[108] However, both *PC Box* and a recent German decision cast doubt on the applicability of *UsedSoft* regarding *games*, and specifically game business models.[109] Notwithstanding these setbacks, the broad principles are being reflected in business practices in

101 David Booton and Angus MacCulloch, 'Liability for the circumvention of technological protection measures applied to videogames: lessons from the United Kingdom's experience' (2012) 3 *Journal of Business Law* 165, 176.

102 *Stern* v. *Kaufman* (1982) 669 F 2d 852 (2nd Circuit Court of Appeal); *Atari* v. *Amusement World* (1981) 547 F Supp 222 (District Court, Maryland).

103 *Williams* v. *Artic International* (1982) 685 F 2d 870 (3rd Circuit Court of Appeal).

104 Case C-355/12 *Nintendo* v. *PC Box* [2014] ECDR 6.

105 Case C-128/11 *UsedSoft* v. *Oracle* [2012] 3 CMLR 44.

106 Newman, *Videogames* (n 40) 33; Nichols (n 41) 128–30.

107 Case C-128/11 (n 105).

108 See generally Andrew Nicholson, 'Old habits die hard?: UsedSoft v. Oracle' (2013) 10 *SCRIPTed* 389 (on the decision and its implications), Reto Hilty, '"Exhaustion" in the digital age' (*Max Planck Institute for Innovation and Competition Research Paper 15–09*, 2015) http://ssrn.com/abstract=2689518 (on the background to and context of the question of exhaustion, and the application of the decision to various formats).

109 Martina Gillen, 'DRM and modchips: time for the Court of Justice to do the "right" thing' (2014) 11 *SCRIPTed* 229; Maša Savič, 'The legality of resale of digital content after UsedSoft in subsequent German and CJEU case law' (2015) 37 *European Intellectual Property Review* 414, 419.

parts of the software industry,[110] and resellers have sought the annulment of clauses in software licensing agreements on *UsedSoft* and unfair competition ground (successfully in some situations).[111]

A second area is digital rights management – specifically the use of technological protection measures in game consoles, which typically prevent the use or playing of unauthorised games and software (also noted in Chapter 3 regarding DVD regions). Console manufacturers have taken civil actions against 'modchipping' in the UK (modifications to consoles to allow for the use of unauthorised software), and supported criminal prosecutions of modchippers, under (the transposed provisions of) both Directives. The distinction between them is important, because criminal sanctions are in place for non-software cases, the exceptions differ,[112] and the burden of proof differs; it is required that a device be 'primarily designed' for the purpose of circumvention under the Information Society Directive (Article 6), whereas the Software Directive refers to a 'sole intended purpose' (Article 7). In practice, console manufacturers emphasise the artistic elements of games (e.g. specific works of art in the form of game graphics) in order to secure the protection of the Information Society Directive. When the CJEU heard its first DRM case (*Nintendo* v. *PC Box*),[113] it found that, because of proportionality, EU law would only protect technological protection measures against circumvention where the objective is to prevent infringing acts[114] and where the circumvention device does not have a commercially significant other use.[115] It seeks evidence of actual use of a device in breach of copyright (potentially a difficult issue),[116] and requires consideration of the effectiveness of measures and the relative costs of different forms of protection.[117]

Finally, consider the matter of cloning ('the intentional copying of sets of game mechanics, with slight alterations to art and design in order to capitalise on a previous games' success.')[118] With 'discoverability' as a real issue in crowded app stores,[119] and the cost of developing casual games being comparatively low in some circumstances,[120] it can be easy for clones to draw users (and money)

110 Robin Fry, 'Reselling software licences' (2015) 26 *Computers and Law* 19.

111 Savič (n 109) 417.

112 Reverse engineering, backup, and interoperability –and a recital on how the right to load and run a program (which would in theory be considered as copying) may neither be prohibited by contract nor require specific authorization.

113 Case C-355/12 (n 104); see discussion in Marcella Favale, 'A Wii too stretched? The ECJ extends to game consoles the protection of DRM – on tough conditions' (2015) 37 *European Intellectual Property Review* 101.

114 Case C-355/12 (n 104) [31].

115 Ibid. [30].

116 Gareth Dickson, 'Game over for excessive TPM?' (2014) 24 *Computers and Law* 5, 7.

117 This casts doubt on some English authorities, such as the findings that the cause of action is a tort of strict liability and that protection need not be totally effective: *Sony* v. *Ball* [2004] EWHC 1739; *Playables* [2010] EWHC 1932 (Ch).

118 Phillips (n 1).

119 Newman, *Videogames* (n 40) 35.

120 Claudio Feijoó, 'An exploration of the mobile gaming ecosystem from developers' perspective' in Peter Zackariasson and Timothy Wilson (eds), *The video game industry: formation, present state, and future* (Routledge 2012) 87.

away from successful games, even for a short period. Yet the issue of what courts once called 'knock-off' games actually emerged much earlier – during the arcade games boom of the 1980s.[121] Developers of successful games repeatedly brought claims of infringement against other developers under US law. These cases required courts to develop copyright law doctrines, in particular the idea/expression dichotomy, and to apply them to the arcade games sector;[122] more recently, these cases have been applied to a Tetris-like app.[123] Even in the UK, the leading authority on this topic (dating from two decades later) happens to be about arcade games. In *Nova Productions*,[124] it was held that no code had been copied and the similarity was essentially one of gameplay or the game mechanics – which are not protected. Drawing on the *Easyjet* precedent (development of similarly functioning new booking software without access to code),[125] Jacobs LJ said that finding for the claimants would mean that 'copyright would become an instrument of oppression rather than the incentive for creation which it is intended to be'.[126] A similar finding, regarding software, was also made in New Zealand in 2014,[127] and the CJEU has expressed some scepticism on whether functionality can be protected by copyright law.[128]

Identifying a suitable legal response to cloning remains difficult,[129] and is surely not helped by the complexity of judicial adjudication on the issues at stake. In the US arcade case of *Data East*, the judges did not play the game, although had access to screenshots; in *Nova Productions*, the judge at first instance played the games and saw videos; screenshots were reproduced in an annex to the decision; in the *Tetris* case, the judge relied on YouTube videos of

121 Writing in 2000, Lai described cloning as a whole segment of the software industry, for the 'production of less expensive look-alike and work-alike versions of popular software': Lai (n 99) 57.

122 E.g. *Atari* v. *North American Philips* (1982) 672 F 2d 607 (some success for the defendant in arguing that features like the score table were beyond the scope of protection, but ultimately a victory for Atari, the makers of Pac-Man, in showing infringement in respect of the characters used); *Data East* v. *Epyx* (1988) 862 F 2d 204 (finding that the US doctrines of merger and scènes à faire supported a finding of no infringement).

123 *Tetris* v. *Xio Interactive* (2012) 863 F Supp 2d 394 (District Court, New Jersey) (e.g. distinguishing the 'purely fanciful' nature of Tetris from the 'sports' cases such as on karate and golf, which come with existing rules, assumptions, and in some cases stock images: at 396 and 408).

124 *Nova Productions* v. *Mazooma Games* [2006] EWHC 24 (Ch); [2007] EWCA Civ 219.

125 *Navitaire* v. *EasyJet* [2004] EWHC 1725 (Ch), discussed at [130–4] (HC) and [45–8] (CA).

126 [2007] EWCA Civ 219 (n 124) [55].

127 *Karum* v. *Fisher* [2014] NZCA 389; see also Ken Moon, 'Another nail in the coffin for non-literal software copyright infringement?' (2015) 10 *Journal of Intellectual Property Law and Practice* 921.

128 Case C-393/09 *Bezpečnostní softwarová asociace* [2011] ECDR 3 (that a graphical user interface can be protected by copyright, but not if it is 'differentiated only by (its) technical function); see also Stokes (n 100) 111; Janssens (n 96) [5.15] (suggesting that this equated to the US 'merger doctrine'); Moon (n 127) 926 (describing the CJEU's approach as merger-like but underpinned by originality rather than the idea/expression dichotomy); Case C-406/10 *SAS Institute* v. *World Programming* [2012] 3 CMLR 4.

129 See further Phillips (n 1).

gameplay, along with screenshots and written material. In all cases, we see the use of varying media in order to try and understand this medium. Moreover, assumptions are made about games as a medium; in *Atari* v. *North American Philips*, the court held that video games, 'unlike an artist's painting or even other audiovisual works, appeal to an audience that is fairly undiscriminating insofar as their concern about more subtle differences in artistic expression'. The shared view of the CJEU and the industry (for different reasons), of emphasising the creative, non-software dimension of games may be an indication of how far we have come.

Games as a medium

The discussion above has highlighted the complexity of games as a medium, but this can be understood in part through analysis of how games are situated against other media, especially film. This arises in relation to content regulation in particular. In this final section, I identify the strengths and weaknesses of relying upon aspects of film law in the assembling of video game law.

Sometimes there can be 'advantages' to following on from film, from the point of view of the game developer. For example, in the constitutional challenge to statutory content regulation in California, the Court of Appeal noted that while the US Supreme Court had not yet addressed video games, 'story-laden video games of the type potentially covered under the Act are similar to movies'.[130] This was significant because, as noted in Chapter 2, film is protected under the First Amendment as speech. When the case reached the Supreme Court, the late Scalia J went to further lengths to compare video games with other forms of expression (from comic books to movies), and even highlights the degree of gore found in the clearly-acceptable Snow White, Hansel and Gretel, and Cinderella, not to mention Homer's *Odyssey*, Dante's *Divine Comedy* and Golding's *Lord of the Flies*.[131] The interactivity of good fiction is used to dismiss the claim that interactive games deserve special legal attention.[132] This placed a heavy burden on California to justify the restriction; the court was not persuaded by the evidence put forward regarding a link between gaming and aggression. This legal reasoning is consistent with some academic views on games, such as the distinction between representational goals (literature, art, and film) and instrumental goals (utilities and tools).[133]

On the other hand, the use of film and other comparators can lead to rather different conclusions. As the House of Commons Committee pointed out in its report on harmful content, film distributors 'accept the requirement for individual assessment for distribution in each country' despite the difficulties it entails,[134] so why could the games industry not do the same? In her review,

130 *Video Software Dealers Association* v. *Schwarzenegger* (2009) 556 F 3d 950, 958
131 (2011) 564 US 786 (n 38).
132 See also discussion in Jennifer Petersen, 'Behind the screen: visuality, law, and new media' (2014) 12 *Popular Communication* 166.
133 Bogost (n 3) 45.
134 House of Commons Culture, Media and Sport Committee (n 30) [199].

Byron suggested that aligning classification systems for games and for film (i.e. extending the statutory regulation of the former) would reinforce her proposal that 'games have to be taken as seriously as films'.[135] However, how the regulation of games might resemble that of film and/or cinema was a persistent theme in press coverage of the regulation of video games.[136] This idea of seriousness or respectability has also troubled some scholars of games (particularly where the more 'cinematic' games are recast as 'interactive cinema'), with allegations of an 'imperialist agenda' on the part of film studies.[137]

Moreover, the political response to video games resembles that seen in the case of the 'video nasties' that so influenced the original adoption of the VRA in respect of video works.[138] The reaction to video games has also been compared with the reaction to controversial young adult literature (which was thought to be as bad as underage drinking),[139] and a ban on pinball in New York which stayed in force for many years.[140] Today, of course, we place little emphasis on literature or pinball as media requiring specific and strong regulation. A further and ironic comment is that of Chatfield, who argued that while video games are powerful, they are 'more so in many ways than either television or film, although not as transforming as the written word'.[141] This situates games between film (the subject of various comprehensive regulatory regimes as discussed in the previous chapter) and print (where we see very little modern-day medium-specific regulation), while suggesting that the little-regulated print is more transformative than the substantially-regulated film field.

There is a further need to be sceptical regarding the transposition of film concepts into the regulation of games, even in terms of the efficiency and accuracy of regulation. During its period as the regulator of video games, the BBFC highlighted a need to be more cautious in classifying games as opposed to video, because of the degree of interactivity.[142] This is not something that appears on the face of the VRA, although it may be justified in part through the 'harm' provisions in the Act. Second, film-like content within a game took on an arguably disproportionate role in the classification process under the VRA. Examples of such content include full-motion video (FMV), pre-rendered graphic animation, and in-game cut scenes, generated 'on the fly' using the same visual references

135 Department for Children, Schools and Families (n 25) [7.33]

136 The phrase 'cinema-style' or 'film-style' was repeated in headlines and in text. See for example James Kirkup, 'Film-style age classifications for online computer games' *Daily Telegraph* (London, 1 August 2008) 12; Seán Poulter, 'Call for cinema-style age ratings on games' *Daily Mail* (London, 27 February 2009) 12.

137 Geoff King and Tanya Krzywinska, *Screenplay: cinema/videogames/interfaces* (Wallflower 2002) 21, 25.

138 Newman, *Videogames* (n 40) 65; Mark Kermode, 'Should we avoid violent video games?' *Guardian* (London, 11 December 2009) G2 15.

139 David Edery and Ethan Mollick, *Changing the game: how video games are transforming the future of business* (FT Press 2009) 25.

140 Jesper Juul, *Half-real: video games between real rules and fictional worlds* (MIT Press 2005) 21.

141 Chatfield (n 43) 57.

142 British Board of Film Classification, *Classification guidelines 2009* (2009).

as gameplay.[143] It became more commonly used as more powerful hardware and storage media with greater capacity became available.[144] The BBFC feared that this would mean the introduction of 'soft' pornographic content in games,[145] although it was violent material that instead became more familiar and more controversial. The most important feature in relation to cutscenes is that the BBFC viewed all such scenes in full. Even in the early days of the classification of computer games, the BBFC requested a video recording of the 'look and feel' of games, along with a synopsis, flowchart, and script.[146] Cutscenes are the 'most obvious links between games and cinema'[147] and it is likely that the BBFC had particular expertise in assessing them, although conceptually, even the use of film-like material can be argued to put the player in the role of a film director rather than a spectator.[148] However, focus groups in a report for the BBFC had 'particularly strong reactions' to videos within games, with parents expressing criticism of rating decisions based on these videos, but then reverting to agreement with the BBFC decision after playing the game as a whole.[149] This is closely related to the important question raised by social science approaches that suggests that in-game violence is primarily perceived as a means to getting to another level, rather than related to real-life experience.[150]

Indeed, it is notable that the question of the status of video within games continues to have regulatory implications, even after the reforms discussed in this chapter. The DEA changes made provision for situations where video and game material were contained in the same product, especially as regards the responsibilities of the two classification authorities.[151] In practice, the Games Rating Authority seeks the input of the BBFC where this situation occurs; prior to 2012, this was not necessary as a single classification certificate was issued by the BBFC for all works, whether video-only, game-only, or a hybrid.[152] This happens on a number of occasions each year; in the most recent year for which details are available (2015), the non-integral video footage contained in or with five games was reviewed by the BBFC on this basis, ranging from *Guitar Hero* (video of

143 Sacha Howells, 'Watching a game, playing a movie: when media collide' in Geoff King and Tanya Krzywinska (eds), *Screenplay: cinema/videogames/interfaces* (Wallflower 2002) 114–16.

144 Loguidice and Barton (n 4) 83; see also Poole, *Trigger happy: the inner life of videogames* (n 18) 90, 108 (video material varying from mere 'tinsel' the game to that which advances the 'plot').

145 British Board of Film Classification, *Annual report for 1995/96* (n 16) 8.

146 Norton (n 11) 60.

147 King and Krzywinska (n 137) 11.

148 Caroline Westbrook, 'Movies? How terribly 80s' *Empire* (January 1995) 128.

149 Slesenger Research (n 26) 67.

150 Department for Children, Schools and Families (n 25) [6.29].

151 Video Recordings Act 1984, s 4ZC, inserted by Digital Economy Act 2010, s 41(1).

152 Although, the question of defining a game still arose because of the different treatment of exemptions: e.g. *Kent County Council* v. *Multi Media Marketing (Canterbury)* [1995] TLR 263 (moving images different to games).

the creation of concert footage) to *Gears of War: Ultimate Edition* (behind the scenes footage, which included gameplay clips).[153] The GRA also allocates responsibility for classification of certain games to the BBFC, namely R18 games (though no such games have been submitted for classification since well before the 2012 amendments) and 'ancillary' games as part of broader video works.[154]

These points regarding the complexity of the film-game relationship, as well as some of the distinctive issues encountered regarding tax credits and copyright, demonstrate the need to consider games as a medium. This is not to say that all games are the same, nor that there cannot be a useful conversation regarding the lessons learned over the course of a century of film censorship or the experience of diverse attempts to support production through the use of public finances. But even in a situation where there is convergence between the markets, or the use of content and brands straddling the categories, one law for both would hardly achieve the range of public policy goals identified in this chapter and the preceding one, and would struggle to get past the assumptions built into many existing provisions. These assumptions are not necessarily dangerous, but they were often formed in good faith based on the experience of one medium, and not intended to be used as the basis for regulating another.

153 British Board of Film Classification, *Annual report and accounts 2015* (2016) 42. In 2014, it was seven games: Video Standards Council, *Annual report and accounts 2014* (2015) 16.

154 The basis for such is Video Recordings Act 1984, s 4ZB, although the allocation is by notice rather than by primary or secondary legislation. See e.g. Video Standards Council (n 153) 15.

5 Radio

Introduction

The underlying basis for requiring the licensing of radio services includes the technological point that frequency planning is necessary in order to ensure that any given service be capable of being received.[1] However, regulatory responses to these technological issues vary, from the primarily private sector service providers in the US, to full or partial public service monopolies in the UK and some Nordic states, to timesharing across political and religious organisations in the Netherlands.[2] Indeed, the regulation of radio broadcasting services has not yet been the subject of EU legislation. This has meant that although there are some common principles of human rights law, through the ECHR, the absence of pan-European standards and the associated interpretations of the CJEU means that the distinctiveness of radio is reinforced, compared with the partially harmonised regulation of television.[3] In line with a non-determinist take on medium theory, then, the identity or specificity of radio is the legacy of technology, politics, international relations, and social factors.

In this chapter, I will discuss the key radio-specific aspects of broadcasting law. This will include the means of transmission (e.g. analogue, digital, Internet), the regulation of localness and format through licensing, and the regulation of content through the Broadcasting Code. The later pages of the chapter then address the changing status of radio and of music and audio media more generally, including services that fall outside of broadcasting law as currently constituted. It must however be noted that radio is an area on which there is a comparatively limited literature, whether in law or in media studies, perhaps reflecting a lack of emphasis even within regulation itself – such as the informal

1 Guy Starkey, *Local radio, going global* (Palgrave Macmillan 2011) 1–5; Eric Barendt, *Freedom of speech* (2nd edn, Oxford University Press 2005) 430–1.

2 Guy Starkey, *Balance and bias in journalism: representation, regulation and democracy* (Palgrave Macmillan 2007) 23.

3 Lorna Woods, 'Legal and extra-legal regulation' in David Goldberg, Gavin Sutter and Ian Walden (eds), *Media law and practice* (Oxford University Press 2009) 346; John Nathan Anderson, 'Radio broadcasting's digital dilemma' (2012) 19 *Convergence: The International Journal of Research into New Media Technologies* 177, 181.

designation of attending to radio issues as a 'Friday afternoon job' within broadcast regulation.[4]

The characteristics of radio remain a subject of debate. In audience research, Ofcom found that the key features of radio, from a listener's perspective, included accessibility, localness, and interactivity. The last of these encompasses a range of less than obvious return paths, such as call-in shows, text message requests, and the on-street and online presences of broadcasters. (Using other technologies to add to the radio experience is not unusual; in the 1920s, broadcasters experimented with the distribution of photographs or slide presentations intended to be used during broadcasts.[5]) Swedish research in 2008 noted a range of positive aspects associated with radio, including the lack of subscription fees, wide geographic and technological access (e.g. ranging sparsely populated areas to on trains and in cars), and the ability to listen while doing something else.[6] This last point is capable of a more provocative construction, as in (for instance) McKibben's highlighting of radio as 'a transmission device, a way to take other art forms (songs, sermons) and spread them out into the world'.[7] Moreover, it recalls what is a continuing debate over how to apply McLuhan's hot/cool framework to present-day radio.[8]

Radio licensing

General issues

Independent local radio in the UK was first authorised by the Sound Broadcasting Act 1972, with rules on content and localness that now seem quite interventionist (though they were not necessarily perceived as such at the time).[9] In the late 1980s, broadcasters were encouraged to develop new services through the 'splitting' of what were, up until that point, single services simulcast on AM and

4 Tony Stoller, *Sounds of your life: the rise and fall of independent radio in the UK* (John Libbey 2010) 327, 346; Starkey, *Local radio, going global* (n 1) 60.

5 Katie Day Good, 'Radio's forgotten visuals' (2016) 23 *Journal of Radio and Audio Media* 364.

6 Swedish Radio and TV Authority, *The future of radio* (2008) 24.

7 Bill McKibben, 'All programs considered' *New York Review of Books* (New York, 11 November 2010) 44.

8 Pierre C. Bélanger and Geoffrey Manchester, '"Beyond the clouds": insider perceptions on the transmutation of terrestrial radio in Canada' (2013) 20 *Journal of Radio & Audio Media* 358, 358 (citing podcasts, online playlists, and the like as evidence for change, although they propose that McLuhan classified radio as cool, whereas the opposite is the case); Kate Lacey, 'Listening in the digital age' in Jason Loviglio and Michele Hilmes (eds), *Radio's new wave: global sound in the digital era* (Routledge 2013) 13 (emphasising the affinity of radio with other electronic media, in order to apply McLuhan's work); Starkey, *Local radio, going global* (n 1) 180 (discussing how, in like of changes in the technology of television, telephone and the Internet, radio listeners now have a passive ('cool') relationship with the medium that differs from what McLuhan observed in the 1960s).

9 Starkey, *Local radio, going global* (n 1) 43.

FM.[10] The Broadcasting Act 1990 charged the (new) Radio Authority with a duty to use all available frequencies, and put in place the framework for the first advertisement of national analogue commercial radio licences (the three licences issued then are the only such licences issued). Further amendments included the Broadcasting Act 1996 (providing for the regulation of digital audio broadcasting (DAB) radio), the Communications Act 2003 (folding the regulation of radio into Ofcom, and a number of other changes), and the Digital Economy Act 2010 (renewal of analogue licences without contest if stations arranged for simulcast on DAB, and changes to localism rules). While the switching off of analogue (AM and FM) radio has been under consideration for some time, the targets for the availability of DAB (which would trigger a move in this direction) have not yet been met.[11]

The licensing of radio in the UK still makes use of the 'beauty contest' model, whereby applicants are judged against the commitments they make in response to a call for applications. This model was a key component of the regulation of commercial television in the UK in the ITV era, but is increasingly irrelevant there (with the exception of the new system for local TV, inaugurated in 2012).[12] It has however also been some time since genuine competition for radio licences has been apparent. In 2015, following a consultation, it was decided by Government that existing analogue licences (national and local) due to expire in 2017 or afterwards, after the earlier renewal under the Digital Economy Act 2010, would be renewed for a further five years.[13] The justification for this move was to support the transition to digital radio (which remains a work in progress with no switchover date set) and to 'provide commercial radio with the stability it needs to support this transition'[14] – again different to television, where the digital transition proceeded with fewer delays and is now complete.

Format

One aspect of this model of regulation is that radio broadcasters must comply with the 'Format' (the capitalization is intentional, as it is how Ofcom uses the

10 Ibid. 109–11.

11 The thresholds in question (announced in 2010) are 50% of all listening being via digital platforms (including DAB), national DAB coverage comparable with FM, and local DAB access for 90% of the population and on major roads. As of 2016, the listening figure is 45.5% (so, not yet sufficient), and the national and local threshold appear to be met, although the statistic for local DAB on major roads is only 76% (albeit higher for some national DAB services). See Ofcom, 'The communications market: digital radio report' (2016) www.ofcom.org.uk/__data/assets/pdf_file/0032/94838/The-Communications-Market-Digital-Radio-Report-2016.pdf

12 On the award of local TV licences, see: Local Digital Television Programme Services Order 2012, SI 2012/292; Martin Moore, 'Plurality and local media' in Steven Barnett and Judith Townend (eds), *Media power and plurality: from hyperlocal to high-level policy* (Palgrave Macmillan 2015); Kerry Traynor, 'Birmingham, Alabama 8; Birmingham, UK 1: local television in the United Kingdom and an ethnographic case study of one service in the north of England' (2015) 6 *International Journal of Digital Television* 163.

13 Legislative Reform (Further Renewal of Radio Licences) Order 2015, SI 2015/2052.

14 HC Deb 14 March 2015, vol. 594, col. 115WS.

term) associated with their licensed service. Hausermann has outlined how the key difference between European and US practices in radio broadcasting is the 'full-service' orientation of European stations, compared with the narrower (often format-driven) tradition in the United States.[15] The UK appears to sit somewhere in the middle, in that full-service stations have long been a part of the commercial radio landscape (especially the initial independent local stations), but narrower Formats have also been a recognisable feature, at least from the late 1980s onwards. In 2001, Formats consisting of a label (e.g. classic rock) and a paragraph of description replaced longer 'promises of performance',[16] and further simplification took place in 2008.

A Format can be amended, in accordance with a procedure set out in the Broadcasting Acts (as amended).[17] An applicant must satisfy Ofcom that the proposed change would not substantially alter the character of service or narrow the range of independent radio services available in the area in question, or that it would maintain or promote competition, or that there is significant demand or support for the proposal in the area. Since 2003, a change in relation to local content is also handled under this route.[18] In some circumstances (i.e. where the application is on the basis of range, competition, or demand/support), Ofcom must carry out a public consultation.[19] Further information on Ofcom's approach can be found in its non-legislative statements,[20] where it is noted that the original award is taken into account, and how caution is necessary to guard against 'format creep', i.e. a series of small changes which, taken together, could constitute a substantial alteration to the Format.

The overarching basis for Format regulation includes s 85(2)(b) Broadcasting Act 1990 (that the regulator must 'do all that they can to secure the provision within the United Kingdom of … a range and diversity of local services') and the general provision in s 3 Communications Act 2003 (including a duty to secure 'the availability throughout the United Kingdom of a wide range of television and radio services which (taken as a whole) are both of high quality and calculated to appeal to a variety of tastes and interests'). Nonetheless, the continuing relevance of Format regulation has been challenged. Ed Vaizey, while the Minister responsible for this area, drew an explicit link between 'the availability of different types of music increase dramatically from a wide variety of sources, including the internet and digital radio' and the need to review (music) Formats, to ascertain whether the radio industry could be given 'greater freedom to adapt

15 Jüerg Häusermann, 'Radio broadcasting: from secret to public to private' in Charley Rowe and Eva Lia Wyss (eds), *Language and new media: linguistic, cultural, and technological evolutions* (Hampton Press 2009) 196.

16 Guy Starkey, *Radio in context* (2nd edn, Palgrave Macmillan 2014) 105.

17 Broadcasting Act 1990, ss 106(1A) and 106(ZA) (as amended by Communications Act 2003).

18 Communications Act 2003, s 314.

19 Broadcasting Act 1990, s 106ZA(1) (added by Communications Act 2003, s 313).

20 Ofcom, 'The regulation of Format changes' (u.d.) www.ofcom.org.uk/__data/assets/pdf_file/0024/87405/The-regulation-of-Format-changes.pdf

to changing consumer tastes'.[21] Curiously, although the Minister said that he had asked Ofcom to carry out this review, there was no mention of the speech in the resulting call for inputs. Ofcom asked for comments on three options: no change, simplifying the range of music Formats, or restructuring more radically (e.g. by reference to audience). Broadcasters differed in their responses – RadioCentre (which represents most but not all of the commercial radio industry) accused Ofcom of over-regulating music and calling for limited regulation of Formats, but smaller operations UKRD and UTV supported the 'no change' option. The question of regulating music is a delicate one, not least because the nature of radio services has an impact on release strategies for recorded music.[22]

Ofcom ultimately concluded that it could make some changes within the current statutory arrangements, but wondered whether Parliament ought to consider 'whether the current framework remains appropriate in light of changes in the market and listener behaviour'.[23] The essence of the new system is that there are fewer, broader Formats (e.g. 'rock' encompassing former formats such as soft rock, classic rock, and contemporary rock; 'mainstream popular music' encompassing 17 different existing formats ranging from 'top 40' to 'varied music').[24] This tension is far from a new one for Ofcom. For instance, the Broadcasting Act 1990 provided that the Radio Authority would seek to license a new independent national commercial radio service consisting 'wholly or mainly, in the broadcasting of music which … is not pop music'.[25] In turn, pop music was defined as including

> rock music and other kinds of modern popular music which are characterised by a strong rhythmic element and a reliance on electronic amplification for their performance (whether or not, in the case of any particular piece of rock or other such music, the music in question enjoys a current popularity as measured by the number of recordings sold).[26]

This broad definition of pop as including anything rhythmic and amplified (including the twist that it not necessarily be popular) was clearly intended to influence the type of applications and thereby the resulting service (which turned

21 Ed Vaizey, 'Digital Radio Action Plan (speech)' *Go Digital Conference* (London, 16 December 2013) www.gov.uk/government/speeches/go-digital-conference-16-december-2013-check-against-delivery

22 Anita Elberse, *Blockbusters: why big hits – and big risks – are the future of the entertainment business* (Faber & Faber 2014) 61.

23 Ofcom, 'Review of music in radio Formats: statement' (2015) www.ofcom.org.uk/__data/assets/pdf_file/0025/51667/statement.pdf [2.9]. Note that this quotation comes from the document's summary; the same text appears later in the document at [5.27], but referring to 'consumer behaviour' instead of 'listener behaviour'.

24 Ibid. [4.27]–[4.29].

25 Broadcasting Act 1990, s 82(2)(a)(ii).

26 Broadcasting Act 1990, s 85(6).

out to be Classic FM),[27] even though the broad thrust of the 1990 Act was purportedly deregulatory.

Local

The concept of local radio can mean at least three things: stations licensed for a locality (recalling the limited transmission range of radio broadcasting and the original approach of licensing one station in each local area under the Sound Broadcasting Act 1972), the carriage of content about local issues (e.g. local news), and the production of content within that locality. The requirements that stations holding local licences (which means the vast majority of radio stations in the UK) produce content in that locality have been the subject of significant changes, through various amendments to the Broadcasting Acts and Communications Act contained in s 34 Digital Economy Act 2010. It is now possible for content to be produced within larger 'approved areas', which are defined by Ofcom, subject to the making of an application to vary the character of the service (not requiring Ofcom to run a consultation on the request). For instance, a station originally licensed to serve Sunderland (population 0.35 million) could apply to produce its local content anywhere within the 'North East England' approved area (population 2 million), which includes Newcastle upon Tyne, Durham and Middlesbrough. This has meant that, in practice, the rebranding of local stations with national brands and what Starkey calls 'simulated localness' has become a major part of UK local radio.[28]

Ofcom also does not regulate the degree to which a service uses automation (such as voice tracking). This technology can potentially create an impression of a more local service than is actually the case, in the mind of the listener.[29] Ofcom does however expect stations to 'be able to react to events on a timely basis when it comes to automated and live programming'. This point recalls an infamous event in US media (retold in a number of works in media studies, such as in the introduction to Klinenberg's *Fighting For Air*[30]), when local radio in North Dakota was unable to respond to a major rail crash due to the degree of automation in use by the stations run by major player Clear Channel (which owned all six commercial stations ostensibly based in the vicinity of the incident).

A non-statutory concept of 'quasi-national' stations has also come about, although Ofcom was originally cautious as it wanted to avoid indirect competition with the licensed independent national stations, and focused on the specialist

27 Stoller (n 4) 204.

28 Guy Starkey, 'Cultural policy in the coalition years: laissez-faire regulation, the public spending squeeze and the drive to digital' (2015) 24 *Cultural Trends* 80, 81.

29 Starkey, *Local radio, going global* (n 1) 159.

30 Eric Klinenberg, *Fighting for air: the battle to control America's media* (Metropolitan Books 2007) 4–11.

nature of regional stations.[31] First set out in Ofcom's 2009 paper on 'Radio in Digital Britain',[32] it provides that where a regional analogue station also provides a national DAB service, they will no longer be the subject of local requirements (material or place of production). The reason for this dispensation is that it allows these services to 'become like national stations' and so provide choice and competition, through having national DAB coverage supplemented by FM services through their regional licences. An exception exists for regional licences in Scotland, Wales and Northern Ireland, which continue to have specific requirements in respect of programming specific to the devolved nation in question.

Challenges to Formats and localness

The question of whether and to what extent localness and Formats should play a continuing role in the regulation of radio has been a significant one in recent years. Localness in particular is, of course, a matter special to radio;[33] it is hard to think of another area of media regulation which has this focus. Formats are increasingly something only found in radio, and give legal power to broader notions of genre found elsewhere. In late 2015, the then-Minister with responsibility for radio, Ed Vaizey, announced that he had asked Ofcom to prepare an 'options paper' on the regulation of Formats and localness, on distinctions between different types of licence (i.e. community vs small-scale commercial), and on the future regulation of DAB radio (e.g. in terms of public service requirements).[34] Ofcom's response of February 2016 highlighted that local content would now be unlikely to exist without regulation, although it thought the emphasis should be on content rather the place of production (except possibly for Scotland, Wales, and Northern Ireland), and did not propose 'levelling up' localness requirements for DAB (discussed below) as compared with the more regulated environment for analogue stations.[35] The new Minister, Matt Hancock, summarised the key points in a September 2016 speech as that various areas for deregulation (including the analogue/digital distinction) had been identified, albeit with a need for continued regulation regarding aspects of news and local content.[36] A consultation is taking place during 2017 – but for present purposes, it is crucial to see how this debate is only happening because radio is regulated as radio rather than as generic media content.

31 Stoller (n 4) 229.

32 Ofcom, 'Radio in Digital Britain' (2009) http://webarchive.nationalarchives.gov.uk/20100304014526/http://ofcom.org.uk/radio/ifi/radio_digitalbritain/digitalbrit.pdf [7.9].

33 See for instance Bélanger and Manchester (n 8) 369.

34 Ed Vaizey, 'Letter to Siobhán Kenny (CEO, RadioCentre)' (4 November 2015) www.gov.uk/government/uploads/system/uploads/attachment_data/file/473720/Radio_letter.pdf

35 Ofcom, 'Radio deregulation: letter to Ed Vaizey MP' (23 February 2016) www.ofcom.org.uk/__data/assets/pdf_file/0030/76908/letter_to_ed_vaizey_mp_230216.pdf

36 Matt Hancock, 'Speech at Radio Festival 2016' (26 September 2016) www.gov.uk/government/speeches/minister-for-digital-and-culture-speech-the-radio-festival-2016

Content regulation

Although Ofcom has now operated a single Broadcasting Code for over a decade, both the Code and the body of decisions issued by Ofcom demonstrate the continued significance of radio-specific content regulation. Some are dictated by the nature of radio listening (e.g. the different approach to the watershed), while others are a result of the outsized significance of music within radio as compared with television.

The watershed point is an interesting, practical one. For television, the requirement for greater restriction of content (in the interests of protecting children) is a simple, binary concept of before vs after 9 pm (although Ofcom does point out that the transition should be gradual rather than abrupt).[37] For radio, however, Ofcom highlights the protected hours ('when children are particularly likely to be listening') as between 6 am and 9 am and between 3 pm and 7 pm during the week, and from 6 am to 7 pm at weekends and during school holidays.[38] This reflects the 'school run' listening pattern for radio, i.e. the greater chance that children will be listening to the radio up to 9 am. This is supplemented by a general presumption that there should not be strong language during the day on radio or television (whether children would be likely to be listening or not).[39]

The music point is a more complex issue. As Street has argued, music 'does not just provide a vehicle of political expression, it is that expression'.[40] The Broadcasting Code is therefore a significant source of the regulation of expression through music, although formally limited to the broadcast of music on radio rather than the underlying lyrics on printed or recorded music. In Ofcom's work, genre has been central to discussions of the appropriate regulatory approach. It has recognised that there are traditions of 'certain genres of music including potentially offensive lyrics in songs' and 'certain genres of music (e.g. Urban and R&B), at times, referencing various adult themes in their songs, such as the taking of drugs and sexual activity'.[41] This is an important acknowledgement, not least because there is some evidence that offensiveness is more likely to be assumed in some genres over others (e.g. rap vs country), even if the lyrics are identical.[42]

The actual regulation of lyrics often falls to radio stations, attempting to predict how Ofcom might react. Unsurprisingly, Street's broader observation

37 Broadcasting Code, s 1.4 (watershed); s 1.6 (transition).

38 Broadcasting Code, s 1.5; Ofcom, 'Offensive language on radio' (2011) www.ofcom.org.uk/__data/assets/pdf_file/0014/40541/offensive-language.pdf 3–4.

39 Broadcasting Code, s 1.16 and s 2.3.

40 John Street, *Music and politics* (Polity 2012) 1.

41 Ofcom, 'Offensive language on radio' (n 38) 6.

42 Andrea Millwood Hargrave and Sonia Livingstone, *Harm and offence in media content: a review of the evidence* (2nd edn, Intellect 2009) 201; Carrie Fried, 'Bad rap for rap: bias in reactions to music lyrics' (1996) 26 *Journal of Applied Social Psychology* 2135; Carrie Fried, 'Who's afraid of rap: demographics and differential reactions to music lyrics' (1999) 29 *Journal of Applied Social Psychology* 705.

that 'much that might be deemed offensive is not censored; often what seems entirely inoffensive is banned'[43] is reflected in Ofcom decisions.[44] The power of the station is also found through the long-running record of BBC decisions to refrain from playing particular songs on the grounds of their lyrics (ranging from *Je t'Aime* to *Give Ireland Back To The Irish*,[45] to (quite improbably) *Ding Dong The Witch Is Dead*, which re-entered the sales charts after the death of Margaret Thatcher in April 2013).

Of course, the regulation of music is clearly divided up by medium. We have already encountered, in Chapter 3, two versions of the regulation of music videos – through the VRA (indeed as extended to remove the broader exemption) for music DVDs and the like, and through the voluntary use of BBFC ratings on sites such as YouTube for standalone videos (and we will meet another in Chapter 6). Alongside the arrangements for radio discussed here, we can also note the special guidance issued by Ofcom regarding music videos on television.[46] Although much of Ofcom's statement relates to clothing, dancing, and sexual images, it does also deal with 'lyrics' – again making the genres point, but also considering the combination of seemingly unsexualised lyrics with particular images. Music lyrics also prompt action under other statutes and beyond statute entirely. The former is illustrated by the use of song lyrics as the basis for a decision to refuse entry to the UK to the artist Tyler, the Creator, on the basis that his lyrics glamorised, in graphic terms, 'violent physical abuse, rape and murder'.[47] The latter is seen in situations where an objection is made to the content of a song and it is resolved to 'ban' it, which as in the case of 'Blurred Lines' (Robin Thicke) (again provoked by allegations that the lyrics endorsed sexual violence) and a number of students' unions, then affects both recorded music in entertainment venues and the carrying of radio stations in (e.g.) shops.[48]

The distinctiveness of radio also emerges outside the Broadcasting Code through the regulation of advertising. For instance, RadioCentre recently argued for relief from EU requirements in terms of terms and conditions in consumer

43 Street (n 40) 12.

44 For instance, of Ofcom's five decisions in 2014 regarding the content of music, three related to older tracks and were argued to have been played in error by very small-scale community or temporary stations (including 'Who Are You' (The Who) and 'Don't Stop' (The Outhere Brothers)), with only two dealing with recently released music (a single expletive in 'Another Love' (Tom Odell) on a local commercial station, and a series of expletives, mostly from Lily Allen, in a concert carried live on BBC Radio 1.

45 Martin Cloonan, *Banned!: Censorship of popular music in Britain, 1967–92* (Arena 1996) 112.

46 Ofcom, 'Observing the watershed on television and music videos' (2011) www.ofcom.org.uk/__data/assets/pdf_file/0030/86781/watershed-on-tv.pdf 10–11.

47 Julianne Escobedo Shepherd, 'Tyler, the Creator on being banned from the UK: "I'm being treated like a terrorist"' *Guardian* (London, 1 September 2015) www.theguardian.com/music/musicblog/2015/sep/01/tyler-the-creator-comments-banned-uk-freedom-of-speech

48 E.g. Amanda Ferguson, 'No Blurred Lines at all as Queen's University students ban Robin Thicke's hit song' *Belfast Telegraph* (Belfast, 21 November 2013) 3.

credit advertisements.[49] The requirement is that 'standard information shall specify in a clear, concise and prominent way by means of a representative example',[50] but RadioCentre contended that this was difficult to do on a short radio advertisement without occupying a significant amount of time. Its case was framed in terms of platform neutrality or avoiding disparate impact, although it could also be seen as a statement of the distinctive qualities and affordances of radio.

Radio and technology

DAB

The most obvious technological change in relation to radio in recent years has been the development of digital radio. In the UK, the system used is digital audio broadcasting (DAB). This has brought about a distinctive regulatory system, and a new source of power through the concept of the multiplex operator. A limited number of multiplexes are available in a DAB system. A multiplex is a bundle of radio services. Ofcom's approach (of competitive licensing for multiplexes, but TV-style standard licences for the individual services) was described as somewhat revolutionary,[51] because the operator would have influence over which services were ultimately available to the public. The initial pair of national multiplexes was held by the BBC and by the Digital One consortium, the sole applicant for the available multiplex. The three independent national radio stations were guaranteed carriage on the multiplex. Local multiplexes were also licensed over the course of a decade (one in each area, with three in London) (and, for a time, regional multiplexes were also part of the mix), and small-scale DAB has more recently been trialled in smaller geographic areas.[52] Licences for individual stations are awarded in standard form, as long as the broadcaster has made provisional arrangements for carriage on a multiplex.

Ofcom has now awarded a further national multiplex licence, after the original awardee (4Digital) failed to launch its proposed service. In assessing the two applicants for this opportunity under the beauty contest model, Ofcom was faced with a choice between a wider range of stations (from the unsuccessful applicant, Listen2Digital) and the use of existing brands (by the successful applicant Sound Digital), which could support the reach and appeal of digital radio. (This question of what to prioritise has also arisen in relation to a multiplex

49 Mark Sweney, 'Cut the "small print" from ends of radio ads, stations to ask Brussels' *Guardian* (London, 14 October 2016) www.theguardian.com/media/2016/mar/14/cut-small-print-from-end-radio-ads-stations-ask-eu

50 Directive 2008/48/EC of 23 April 2008 on credit agreements for consumers [2008] OJ L133/66, art 4(2).

51 Stoller (n 4) 280, quoting David Vick.

52 This is now being put into permanent form through the Broadcasting (Radio Multiplex Services) HC Bill (2016–2017).

operator's ability to focus on the number of stations carried versus the audio quality of individual stations).[53]

A multiplex operator can vary the list of stations it carries;[54] Ofcom can only refuse if capacity to 'appeal to a variety of tastes and interests would be unacceptably diminished'.[55] As is so often the case, the creation of a new power centre by Parliament ultimately creates a paradox when MPs and even Ministers wish to act in respect of a particular public interest. Having laid down their arms in pursuit of one goal, politicians wonder why they are left weaponless in pursuit of another. This is illustrated by a 2015 controversy regarding the availability of one station, Premier Christian Radio. Premier was in dispute with multiplex operator Arqiva regarding its continued carriage on Digital One. Minister Ed Vaizey's comments in Parliament[56] demonstrate the conflict between various goals. Opening by saying that 'technically' he should not intervene (on the grounds that these were commercial decisions) and that he 'wholeheartedly' supported this 'important' radio station, and calling for 'some give and take on all sides', he appealed to Arqiva to 'go beyond purely commercial graft' and to do the right thing. He recognised that multiplex operators have gatekeeper powers and wondered whether Ofcom should have greater power to intervene in disputes of this nature. Premier was given a short extension of carriage on Digital One, and is now carried on Sound Digital (the new second national commercial multiplex).

The Swedish research on radio referred to in the introduction to this chapter included some useful investigations of what listeners hoped that technological change would achieve. This included easier location of channels (i.e. without knowing a frequency), limited textual material (e.g. traffic), and higher quality audio.[57] There appeared to be limited interest in advanced forms of convergence such as the buying of digital music or seeing visual material alongside a broadcast. The UK's implementation of digital radio, as already noted, has seen a trade-off between increasing variety (to some extent) and quality, with the broad thrust of regulation favouring the former.

Alternatives to (broadcast) radio

Technological change is also noteworthy in so far as it supports the development of alternatives to (analogue and digital broadcast) radio. This point is recognised,

53 Anderson (n 3) 183; Richard Rudin, 'The development of DAB digital radio in the UK: the battle for control of a new technology in an old medium' (2006) 12 *Convergence: The International Journal of Research into New Media Technologies* 163, 171.

54 Communications Act 2003, s 315; Broadcasting Act 1996, s 54(6B).

55 Broadcasting Act 1996, s 54(6A). See also Stephen Lax and others, 'DAB: the future of radio? The development of digital radio in four European countries' (2008) 30(2) *Media, Culture and Society* 151, 161–2 (highlighting the 'light touch' approach and how it has facilitated the extension of London analogue stations into national brands through carriage on local DAB multiplexes); Rudin (n 53) 173 (summarizing the criticisms of multiplex operators as gatekeepers).

56 HC Deb 11 February 2015, vol. 592, col. 926.

57 Swedish Radio and TV Authority (n 6) 46.

for instance, by Ed Vaizey in his 2013 speech on radio (discussed above in the context of changes to music Formats). Vaizey committed to a closer look at 'other rules and regulations that exist around radio, to ensure they are fit for purpose in a digital age'.[58] This is of course a similar argument as seen across this book – that technological and market changes, often outside of the particular regulated domain, spark a reassessment of the approach to regulation within that domain.

In respect of radio, that question is complicated by the way in which radio is difficult to separate from the music industry. Bull's analysis of 'iPod culture' sets personal music players against radio broadcasters, one against the other, in an evocative fashion; 'no longer prey to the whims of corporate radio, our sonic envelopes, our cathedrals of sound, exist in the personal play list of the iPod.'[59] On the contrary, Black argues that the Internet radio space, at least in its earlier days, saw the continued dominance of the established broadcasters.[60] One thing that can be observed, however far one thinks technological change is affecting the significance of broadcast radio, is that the development of new services far outside the industrial context of radio can be the source of this pressure.[61] Moreover, as the development of those services was often a concerted effort to provide a legal alternative to online downloading services, they already engage a number of different policy and economic goals. Nonetheless, if music selection behaviour is studied, as it was by Krause *et al.* in 2014, broadcast radio is still a significant way in which music is heard,[62] though less so for younger listeners.[63] Furthermore, new devices may be used for accessing broadcast radio; the iPod Nano, for instance, included an FM tuner when its fifth version was launched in 2009,[64] and third-party peripherals made it possible to access broadcast radio on other devices. Some controversy has flowed from the presence of suitable hardware within a number of smartphones, which has not been enabled for use by manufacturers.[65]

There are at least three overlapping categories of service or hardware that are relevant to this discussion of alternatives: Internet streaming, podcasts, and online music services.

58 Vaizey, 'Digital Radio Action Plan (speech)' (n 21).

59 Michael Bull, *Sound moves: iPod culture and urban experience* (Routledge 2007) 2

60 David Black, 'Internet radio: a case study in medium specificity' (2001) 23(3) *Media, Culture and Society* 397, 403–4.

61 Ofcom, 'Radio deregulation: letter to Ed Vaizey MP' (n 35) 1, 17,

62 Amanda Krause, Adrian North and Lauren Hewitt, 'Music selection behaviors in everyday listening' (2014) 58 *Journal of Broadcasting and Electronic Media* 306, 310.

63 Ibid. 312.

64 John Plunkett, 'Apple's new iPod Nano is great news for radio – but not for DAB' *Guardian* (London, 10 September 2009) www.theguardian.com/media/organgrinder/2009/sep/10/ipod-nano-digital-radio

65 Jonathan P. Pluskota, 'The perfect technology: radio and mobility' (2015) 22 *Journal of Radio and Audio Media* 325, 334.

Radio and the Internet

Streaming

The Internet has proven, to some extent, to be a platform for extending the reach of existing licensed services (although, of course, with the relevant regulators having no jurisdiction and often well beyond the geographic area as originally envisaged by the licence applicant).

The key source of legal control of Internet radio, whether in the form of simulcast of a broadcast service or a service native to the Internet, has been copyright law.[66] This arose in the earlier days of the field, where there were frequent disputes between online services and collecting societies representing the interests of artists and record companies. In particular, the long-standing special position of broadcast radio in the US (whereby stations were not required to make performance right payments to the holders of mechanical rights i.e. record companies, but only to the holders of publishing rights, i.e. publishing companies on behalf of songwriters and composers) was not extended to online services. This was varied to some extent by legislative change, addressing the arguments that for some services, calculating fees on the basis of royalties, expenses, or a flat rate would be more appropriate than doing so per song.[67]

Despite these issues, though, Internet radio (more properly characterised as various audio streaming protocols) has had some successes, though even the terminology has been controversial.[68] Initially, a key selling point was the wide range of stations available, including automated and music-only stations (many not broadcast) with quantity and range well beyond DAB or satellite.[69] But an early criticism of Internet radio – that it was not sufficiently portable to deserve the name radio[70] – is also being addressed, through easier computer-based access and access through devices not normally perceived as computers. The first is seen where a user has a single point of access to a high number of streams, such as TuneIn (which also offers a premium service as TuneIn Premium for £6 or $8/month),[71] or through the directory of radio stations on iTunes. In the UK, the 'Radioplayer' project provides a convenient cross-platform app- or web-based front end for radio stations (BBC, commercial and community), restoring the idea of flicking through stations long familiar to radio listeners, with a small amount of additional material (track information of the type already available on DAB, photographs and web links, etc.). Radioplayer is

66 See further Chris Atton, *An alternative Internet* (Edinburgh University Press 2004) 122.

67 17 USC 112; 17 USC 114.

68 Black (n 60).

69 Bill McKibben, 'Radio free everywhere' *Atlantic Monthly* (December 2007) www.theatlantic.com/magazine/archive/2007/12/radio-free-everywhere/306433/; Marc Fisher, *Something in the air: radio, rock, and the revolution that shaped a generation* (Random House 2007) 297–310; Atton (n 66) 116–18.

70 Black (n 60) 401.

71 Brian Barrett, 'Internet radio is fixing to make a comeback' *Wired* (September 2015).

available in other markets e.g. Ireland, Germany, and Norway. In the US, Clear Channel's iheartradio app bundles together Clear Channel services by genre rather than location.[72] The second point (non-'computer' access) is addressed through the availability of consumer devices in the UK are also available for Internet radio or as a combined DAB/Internet device. These devices access online streams through an Internet connection in the same way that a laptop would, but are presumably suitable for consumer use in a way that a laptop might not (e.g. in a kitchen, for inexperienced users). Beyond this, smartphones make useful devices for mobile access to radio through an Internet connection; as asked in a *New York Times* article on broadcast radio and new devices, 'why include tuner technology to play a few dozen stations when you can harness thousands of radio stations over the Internet?'[73] However, the limited use made of smartphone features could be a barrier to appealing to younger audiences, who are argued to see a blank/static screen associated with a stream as unattractive;[74] nonetheless, the relationship between screen use and audio/radio is deepening.[75]

Within the wider audio streaming landscape, we can see the emergence of a number of different business models. An example of a 'station'-based model is the provision of access to a range of Internet audio streams, typically with a subscription option in order to listen without advertising. An example of this model is Canadian-based Calm Radio, which offers over 200 'stations'. Another is access to premium content; Major League Baseball's 'Gameday Audio' offers access to the broadcasts of baseball games (heard on local radio stations in relevant markets, but accessible to a global audience through this format rather than the station's own stream, which is typically silenced while games are being broadcast). A recently emerged platform is that of Facebook Live Audio,[76] which built on an existing system for video streaming to allow audio streaming via the site.

Online music services

Early online music services focused on providing semi-customised streaming services. Pandora (initially available in the US and subsequently in Australia and New Zealand) makes use of user preferences (liking and disliking songs) to provide a personalised stream, funded through advertising or subscription.

72 www.iheartradio.com. See further Bélanger and Manchester (n 8) 367.

73 Eric Taub, 'When the Web is in reach, so is a radio universe' *New York Times* (New York, 31 December 2009) B7.

74 Paul Robinson, 'Can radio outsmart the smartphones?' *Broadcast* (19 March 2013) www.broadcastnow.co.uk/opinion/can-radio-outsmart-the-smartphones/5053094.article

75 Michele Hilmes, 'The new materiality of radio: sound on screens' in Jason Loviglio and Michele Hilmes (eds), *Radio's new wave: global sound in the digital era* (Routledge 2013) 44.

76 Marc Schneider, 'Facebook debuts live audio broadcasts' *Billboard* (21 December 2016) www.billboard.com/articles/business/7632362/facebook-debuts-live-audio

In recent years, the best known 'alternative' to radio, especially outside the US, is catalogue-based online music services such as Spotify or Apple Music. Again, Spotify is available free (with advertising) or with a subscription; Apple Music is only available by subscription. The primary model is that of a catalogue or jukebox of music (organised by album but accessible by artist, playlist, etc.), and although doubted at first, royalty payments now make an appreciable contribution to record industry profits.[77]

Interestingly, these services also see the appeal of the conventional radio station. Apple, for instance, gave a high promotional profile to its 'Beats One' service, which is to all intents and purposes an Internet-only radio station with presenters/DJs described, inevitably, as curators. More generally, online music services often adopt the language of radio,[78] recognising the dual role as provider of access to music and as a 'discovery service' for new or less familiar tracks.[79] This can be observed through changes such as the resources dedicated by Spotify to creating and curating playlists, and the commensurate attention paid by record companies to securing inclusion of their work on influential playlists.[80]

Ofcom argues that, if the regulation of Formats within DAB radio were lessened or removed, online music services would provide an alternative to the types of specialist service that might no longer be provided by broadcast radio stations.[81] Ofcom thought that the same would be true, to some extent, for the regulation of independent local radio. Although this may be the case, access to specialist content through broadcast radio does still carry a certain cachet. Unlicensed radio in London has demonstrated the appeal of being available on FM; a BBC report in 2015 highlighted the reputational and cultural significance of broadcasting (even without a licence) above and beyond what could be gained from online streaming.[82]

Podcasts

A final model is that of the podcast. This format, in existence from the early 00s,[83] though coming to mainstream attention through support from Apple (e.g. ease of access to services through iTunes from 2004 onwards, and, much later, a

77 Hannah Ellis-Petersen, 'Music streaming hailed as industry's saviour as labels enjoy profit surge' *Guardian* (London, 30 December 2016) www.theguardian.com/technology/2016/dec/29/music-streaming-industry-saviour-labels-spotify-apple-music

78 E.g. in names and in promotional taglines; see Mark Glantz, 'Internet radio adopts a human touch: a study of 12 streaming music services' (2016) 23 *Journal of Radio and Audio Media* 36, 40.

79 Bélanger and Manchester (n 8) 367.

80 Ellis-Petersen (n 77).

81 Ofcom, 'Radio deregulation: letter to Ed Vaizey MP' (n 38).

82 BBC, 'Newsnight' (26 August 2015)

83 Such as the 'iPodder' software for access to podcasts. See further Andrew J. Bottomley, 'Podcasting: a decade in the life of a "new" audio medium' (2015) 22 *Journal of Radio and Audio Media* 164.

standalone Podcasts app[84]), utilises two straightforward web technologies – RSS feeds (the once much-vaunted ability to 'push' content to users rather than wait for them to 'pull' it from a server, though in practice it is often a schedule of checking rather than a truly continuous interaction) and audio files such as MP3. Apple's 2014 creation of a separate and more obvious app for podcasts from iOS 8 onwards, in place of a sub-section of its music app and store, brought further attention to the field, as did the popularity of particular podcasts, such as *Serial*.[85]

The existence of podcasts during this period has provided an alternative model of distributing audio content, including documentaries and speech-based programming of the type familiar to radio listeners. Podcasts are said to have the advantage of little or no advertising, and the ability to listen any time;[86] they certainly share some features with radio, but may be thought of more accurately as 'radio-esque'.[87] While podcasts do have some association with online subcultures and participatory culture, Markman and Sawyer argue that the podcast-only sector (i.e. not derived from broadcast) is 'dominated by technologically savvy, educated, older, professional males' and has seen limited crossover into fields beyond audio.[88] Moreover, as in other areas of online content, the role of the gatekeeper cannot be ignored. Services for accessing podcasts (podcatchers) act as intermediaries. In the case of Apple, criticisms have included the lack of access to data about listeners and the transparency of the highlighting of featured feeds.[89] Tellingly, the BBC's plans to expand its online on-demand access to radio material (outside the UK) was explained as a plan to create the 'Netflix of the spoken word'.[90] An alternative model in technological terms was the copy-protected download, as used by services such as Audible (primarily audiobooks but including some radio programmes).

The relationship between radio broadcasting and podcasting is also interesting. In 2012, one-third of the top 100 podcasts on Apple's service originated from broadcasters. By the end of 2016, this had remained more or less the same, although in the UK, more than half of the top 20 were broadcast-originated.[91] In

84 Jeremy Wade Morris and Eleanor Patterson, 'Podcasting and its apps: software, sound, and the interfaces of digital audio' (2015) 22 *Journal of Radio and Audio Media* 220, 223.

85 Sarah Larson, '"Serial": the podcast we've been waiting for' (*New Yorker*, 9 October 2014) www.newyorker.com/culture/sarah-larson/serial-podcast-weve-waiting

86 Kris M. Markman and Caroline E. Sawyer, 'Why pod? Further explorations of the motivations for independent podcasting' (2014) 21 *Journal of Radio and Audio Media* 20.

87 Richard Berry, 'Will the iPod kill the radio star? Profiling podcasting as radio' (2006) 12 *Convergence: The International Journal of Research into New Media Technologies* 143, 155–6.

88 Markman and Sawyer (n 86) 24, 30.

89 John Herrman, 'Podcasts surge, but producers fear Apple isn't listening' *New York Times* (New York, 8 May 2016) BU1.

90 Hannah Gannagé-Stewart, 'BBC plans "Netflix of spoken word"' *Broadcast* (23 November 2016) www.broadcastnow.co.uk/news/bbc-plans-netflix-of-spoken-word/5111585.article

91 11 of the top 20, 34 of the top 100, and 66 of the top 200 (author's count as of 31 December 2016). Note that the 'chart' is a synthesis of subscriptions, downloads and ratings, rather than a true measurement of audience share: Matt Deegan, 'YouTubers doing podcasts and the iTunes chart' (*Matt Deegan Writes*, 15 December 2016) www.mattdeegan.com/2016/12/15/youtubers-podcasts-itunes-chart/

some cases, broadcasters started with extracts or highlights, moving on to full programmes at a later stage.[92] In turn, as in other fields discussed in this book, popular podcasts can become 'part' of the broadcast landscape through rebroadcast or acquisition,[93] and broadcasters can create podcast-only content in order to reach new audiences.[94] Nonetheless, there can also be tensions between the models. US public radio network NPR committed *not* to promote podcasts on air, in order to address the objections of local affiliates, who saw direct listeners access to podcasts as a threat to the donations that sustain public radio in the US.[95] Some of NPR's podcasts are created *as podcasts*, i.e. featuring established NPR journalists, but only available through this format. NPR's app NPR One (combining streams, podcasts, and catch-up content) now directs US-based listeners to donate to their local public radio station or another local station of their choice, and is beginning to solicit donations (to NPR itself) from international listeners.[96]

Although for many years the podcast appeared to take on the characteristics of an on-demand or download model, later developments have challenged this. For instance, the Stitcher 'smart radio' app allows users to stream podcasts (or to mark them for offline listening, which is akin to downloading), especially through a 'create your own' function (a playlist, essentially) branded as 'stitch(in) the content you want into personalised, always-current stations'.[97] Spotify now offers 'audio shows' (i.e. podcasts) as part of its streaming-focused service.

Conclusion

This chapter has explored two different aspects of the regulation of radio as a medium. The first was the degree to which radio law is distinctive to radio. Examples of this distinctiveness relate to the nature of the licensing process (e.g. Formats and localness), but also to the particular significance of music, the need to adapt rather than duplicate better-known rules applicable to television, and the differently configured digital transition. The answer to this first question is therefore

92 Christopher Cwynar, 'More than a "VCR for radio": the CBC, the Radio 3 podcast, and the uses of an emerging medium' (2015) 22 *Journal of Radio and Audio Media* 190, 192.

93 Bottomley (n 83) 167.

94 Canadian public broadcaster CBC experimented with online forms, with the 'Radio 3 Podcast' being the linchpin of its 'Radio 3' project. Unlike Radio 1 and Radio 2, Radio 3 is not available through broadcast radio in Canada; the brand refers to a website, podcasts, and a more radio-like service available online and by satellite (since 2015, operating without presenters). See Cwynar (n 95); Mark Teo, 'CBC Radio 3's new format replaces hosts with musicians' (*Aux.tv*, 9 March 2015) www.aux.tv/2015/03/cbc-radio-3s-new-format-replaces-hosts-with-musicians/

95 Hilmes (n 75) 51.

96 Mike Janssen, 'NPR Board approves donations from overseas NPR One listeners' (*Current*, 29 November 2016) http://current.org/2016/11/npr-board-approves-donations-from-overseas-npr-one-listeners/

97 www.stitcher.com. See also Lacey (n 8) 15.

relatively clear; radio continues to be a medium governed by some rules only relevant within the radio sector and is likely to continue to be regulated in this fashion, even if the substance of some rules will change. The second question does not yet have a clear answer. How do the various forms of communication discussed in the later pages of the chapter relate to radio – or indeed to other topics discussed in this book, such as video-on-demand? The question takes on added urgency when the co-dependence of radio and the music industry is taken into account. As ever within medium theory, the existence of 'alternatives' also has a potentially disruptive impact on the regulation of established radio services, although this is not a one-way street, given the influence of certain aspects of radio as a medium on some of the new online services discussed here.

6 Video on demand

Introduction

Video on demand (VOD) services emerged as a controversial regulatory category in European Union media law in the first decade of the twenty-first century. In the present decade, we have also seen the rise in significance and popularity of particular VOD services delivered via the Internet – especially Netflix and its competitors. Not surprisingly, the regulatory questions have not been fully resolved, and consumer migration towards VOD services has brought some of the unresolved issues into sharper focus. In this chapter, I will interrogate the regulatory category for VOD created by the 2007 Audiovisual Media Services Directive (AVMSD), primarily through an assessment of the work of the UK regulators Ofcom and the Authority for Television on Demand (ATVOD), in order to identify both the medium-specific aspects of VOD regulation, and the difficulties that have been encountered in defining this medium (especially where concepts from other media are used to define it). After reviewing the basic legal conditions, I consider the work of the regulators regarding three aspects of the definition of on-demand services: principal purpose, comparability and editorial responsibility. After some further remarks on related concerns (branding and distribution) and on recent developments (sexually explicit services), I offer some broader conclusions on the contested relationship between VOD, television, and other media. This will illustrate, in the case of an emerging medium, why the understandable temptation to write rules based on what we already know and understand about another medium can have unexpected consequences.

VOD and the law

The Audiovisual Media Services Directive[1] provides for two regulatory schemes for audiovisual services in European Union member states. The first is a revised

1 Directive 2010/13/EU of 10 March 2010 on the coordination of certain provisions laid down by law, regulation or administrative action in Member States concerning the provision of audiovisual media services [2010] OJ L263/15. The Directive was actually adopted in 2007 as a set of amendments to a 1989 Directive (which had already been amended in 1997), so the 2010 version is a consolidation of all three instruments.

version of that required by the 1989 Television Without Frontiers Directive, and applies to 'linear' or 'television' services. The second is a new development, and goes above and beyond the very minimal regulatory control of 'information society services' (online content in general) under EU law. This second category is 'on-demand audiovisual media services', or what lawmakers called 'non-linear' services in earlier drafts.

In the UK, the Directive was transposed by amending the Communications Act 2003. The key provision is new section 368A(1), which includes a stipulation that the regime applies to services where the 'principal purpose is the provision of programmes the form and content of which are comparable to the form and content of programmes normally included in television programme services'. (This is one of five cumulative criteria, all drawn from the Directive with some slight rewording; others include there being editorial responsibility and the service falling under UK jurisdiction.)

From 2010 to 2015, Ofcom designated a co-regulatory body (the Authority for Television on Demand, ATVOD) as the regulator of on-demand services. (Ofcom now carries out the regulatory functions itself.) ATVOD's initial task was to consider whether a service falls within the 'scope' of the law. If this was the case, the service provider was obliged to 'notify' the regulator and pay a fee. Ultimately, non-compliance with the regulatory system is a criminal offence. However, an initial failure to do so would be met with ATVOD's publication of a 'Scope Determination', which could be appealed to Ofcom. Ofcom could confirm the decision, substitute its own decision (i.e. find that the service was not within the scope of the law) or refer the matter back to ATVOD for further consideration. Both Scope Determinations and Ofcom decisions (when Determinations have been appealed) are published online. This matter of scope has been one of the two main themes of the regulation of VOD in the UK; the second is the considerable attention paid to adult services, which Petley has discussed in detail.[2]

ATVOD's first years also coincided with a period of intense political interest in alternative regulatory models. This was an issue when the Directive was drafted and agreed; the result was the promotion of co-regulation. Furthermore, ATVOD was one of the models discussed during the Leveson Inquiry. As such, and despite the recent change by Ofcom in carrying out this work itself, analysis of the Scope Determinations and the decisions on appeal, particularly regarding the test for 'TV-like' services, can also provide useful information for those considering the next steps in the regulation of other forms of communication.

Identifying on-demand services

Recital 24 of the Directive has been considered at length in scope determinations and appeals. It glosses the definition of on-demand services through the concept

2 Julian Petley, 'The regulation of pornography on video-on-demand in the United Kingdom' (2014) 1 *Porn Studies* 260.

of regulated on-demand services being defined in part by how similar to television they are:

> It is characteristic of on-demand audiovisual media services that they are 'television-like', i.e. that they compete for the same audience as television broadcasts, and the nature and the means of access to the service would lead the user reasonably to expect regulatory protection within the scope of this Directive. In the light of this and in order to prevent disparities as regards free movement and competition, the notion of 'programme' should be interpreted in a dynamic way taking into account developments in television broadcasting.

The UK resisted an earlier concept of non-linear services which did not contain this gloss, which had been proposed (in 2005) by the European Commission,[3] and this 'TV-like' language reflects the influence of the UK's participation in the negotiations and its intention to limit the scope of the new law.[4] Unsurprisingly, Ofcom approached its new task as being about the regulation of services rather than the 'underlying platforms', and argued that the statutory criteria should be applied strictly, and in particular, no more widely than should be the case according to the AVMSD and the revised Communications Act.[5] This reflected the overall intention that the scope of the UK implementation should be narrow.[6]

The Audiovisual Media Services Directive, and its contested concept of on-demand services, reflected concerns about changes in the television and Internet sectors nearly a decade ago. Yet even while it was being debated, user behaviour and the technologies available on mass markets were changing; hybrid practices such as time-shifting through digital video recorders were emerging, undermining the linear/non-linear distinction.[7] The Directive was amended during its consideration by the European institutions, with the main change being the extended definition of TV-like in Recital 24. These definitions themselves contributed to an overall lack of clarity in the Directive.[8] The European Commission itself noted, in its first review of the new Directive in 2012, that 'the regulatory framework set by the AVMSD will have to be tested against evolving viewing

3 Eva Lievens, 'Harmful new media content: the latest regulatory trends' (2006) 11 *Communications Law* 113, 114.

4 Natasha Good and Stuart Goldberg, 'European reaction to the proposed new Audiovisual Services Directive' (2006) 11 *Communications Law* 183, 184.

5 Ofcom, 'The regulation of video-on-demand services' (2009) www.ofcom.org.uk/__data/assets/pdf_file/0020/36407/vodstatement.pdf [3.13].

6 Ibid. [2.08].

7 Rachael Craufurd Smith, 'Media convergence and the regulation of audiovisual content' (2007) 70 *Current Legal Problems* 238, 250–3.

8 Caroline Pauewls and Karen Donders, 'From Television Without Frontiers to the digital Big Bang: the EU's continuous efforts to create a future-proof internal media market' in Robin Mansell and Marc Raboy (eds), *Handbook of global media and communication policy* (Blackwell 2011) 533.

and delivery patterns'.[9] A recent interpretation of the comparability provision of the AVMSD by the Court of Justice of the European Union took a particularly broad approach to its scope.[10]

Three questions of interpretation dominated scope determinations during ATVOD's operations, and although formed out of the legislative requirements, also serve to illustrate key features of medium-specific regulatory systems. The first was how to identify the 'principal purpose' of a service; if its principal purpose was anything other than the provision of programmes, it fell outside the regulatory system. The second, which was only considered in cases where the principal purpose was the provision of programmes, was whether those programmes met the 'comparability' test (i.e. compared with television). The last, which tended to be at issue in cases where purpose and comparability were not in doubt, was who had editorial responsibility for the service (and therefore was obliged to carry out the duties set out in statute, such as notification). Each of these three questions is discussed in this chapter, as well as some broader issues regarding branding and distribution.

The 'principal purpose' test

In the early days of the new regulatory system, ATVOD had to reach a number of decisions regarding audiovisual material published on the website (or, in one case, on YouTube) of an established newspaper or magazine. All cases were defended and appealed. In effect, they were all disposed of in a single Ofcom appeal decision, as, following this decision, the Scope Determinations in all the other cases were withdrawn by ATVOD.

This Ofcom decision, which concerned *Sun TV*, was published in 2011 and sets out Ofcom's broad approach to principal purpose. It concerned the question of whether videos published on the *Sun*'s website met the statutory requirements for regulation as an on-demand service.[11] 'Electronic versions of newspapers' are noted as beyond the scope of the Directive (recital 28). This does not however mean that all regulation of services offered by newspapers is impossible; as Ofcom said in its first statement on VOD, a services does not 'fall outside of the criteria merely because of the industry sector from which the organisation providing that service is drawn'.[12] Consequently, Ofcom's Scope Guidance noted the exclusion of electronic versions of newspapers and magazines, but that this exclusion did not cover 'any on-demand programme services offered by newspapers and magazines'.[13] The *Sun TV* decision, though, turns on the language of the amended Communications Act.

9 European Commission, 'First report on the AVMS Directive' COM (2012) 203, 10.

10 Case C-374/14 *New Media Online* v. *Bundeskommunikationssenat* [2016] 2 CMLR 14.

11 See further Irini Katsirea, 'Electronic press: "Press-like" or "television-like"?' (2015) 23 *International Journal of Law and Information Technology* 134.

12 Ofcom (n 5) [3.75].

13 Ibid. Annex 1 [3.2].

Principal purpose was enough in this case; as the principal purpose was not satisfied,[14] comparability was not considered (because it is only if both components are satisfied that the service is within the scope of the law).

The decision was noteworthy for how it closes off a whole sector, as well as setting out the first part of Ofcom's overall approach to scope. Ofcom set out characteristics for the interpretation of the statutory provisions on principal purpose, which were that a relevant service would be more likely to have its own homepage, to have a separate section of a website where the audiovisual material is catalogued and accessed, to be styled/presented as a television channel, to have more than bite-sized clips, to have limited or no links between audiovisual and other material, to have more audiovisual than written material (with the audiovisual material being the primary means), and overall not said to be integrated into nor ancillary to another service. Ofcom also takes a 'step back' for a broad assessment, with particular reference to recital 24 (quoted in full above).

The 'comparability' test[15]

Ofcom's general approach

The *Sun TV* decision provided a clear statement regarding principal purpose, and few disputes have arisen since. However, establishing what is meant by comparability took much longer to establish. Reviewing these decisions requires that the Directive's concept that 'television-like' services have a particular identity be unpacked. In particular, with the growth in the number and range of channels in the television sector, is it difficult to identify the distinctive features of *television* for the purposes of assessing whether other services are *television-like*?

It was already clear in the earlier wave of cable and satellite (linear) expansion that while some new channels used the 'programming forms and scheduling strategies' of the established broadcasters, other channels (such as rolling news and home shopping channels) took new and sometimes radically different approaches.[16] This meant, for example, that the viewer of a purely linear service would already be exposed to a range of forms. Even something as simple as addressing the camera conveys a very different meaning in dramatic cinema as compared with advertising or news.[17]

Indeed, even if there are clear forms associated with (linear) television, those forms can be combined with more recent developments in other sectors, even if

14 Ofcom also found that ATVOD did not rely on sufficient evidence to determine that the service was within the scope of the Act. It went on to consider the matter based on its own review of the evidence.

15 A more detailed discussion of the data on the use of the comparability test will be found in Daithí Mac Síthigh, '"TV-like": aesthetics, quality and genre in the regulation of video-on-demand services' (2017) 14(3) *Journal of British Cinema and Television*.

16 Robert Allen and Annette Hill, 'Modes of television' in Robert Allen and Annette Hill (eds), *The television studies reader* (Routledge 2004) 163.

17 Jeremy Butler, *Television: critical methods and applications* (4th edn, Routledge 2012) 118.

the end result is then broadcast on television. For example, the TV programme DiggNation (a spin-off of the Digg website) was described as 'a text of both television and participatory culture', drawing from TV tropes of direct address, front-lighting, autocues and title sequences, and participatory forms of low production values and no initial title sequence.[18] These features of participatory culture resemble Christian's definition of the 'digital aesthetic' as including 'the exhaustive use of the close-up' and 'the use of direct address and subjective camera, styles based in webcams and YouTube';[19] this may also be linked to the ongoing debate on the impact of digital technology on film aesthetics.[20]

With this uncertainty in mind, it should also be noted that the consideration of what can broadly be termed production features is novel for a scholar of regulation. It is, of course, not a feature of the regulation of television (or indeed radio) in the UK, nor film (with rare exceptions as noted in Chapter 3 e.g. as regards animal welfare). A service can be made up of the most incoherent of editing, use substandard equipment and ignore established forms such as title sequences. Nonetheless, if it is broadcast as a linear service on cable, satellite or the Internet, it is regulated in the same fashion as other programmes distributed in that fashion. Indeed, the European institutions specifically rejected language relating to 'professional' status (as a means to define the scope of regulation) when considering the Directive.[21] Furthermore, the core concept of 'television' as the services regulated by the Directive and its predecessor is of audiovisual media services 'provided by a media service provider for simultaneous viewing of programmes on the basis of a programme schedule' – excluding the possibility of taking the nature of or the means of access to the service into account when determining whether to regulate it. As such, there is an inherent uncertainty in the legal test that a service be 'TV-like' in order to be within the scope of on-demand regulation.

Ofcom's first significant comparability analysis is found in *Viva TV* (2012), a decision on the regulation of a music video service. Earlier, though, it had been found that a direct read-across from what is actually broadcast on television was not the right legal test; in *Demand Adult* (2011) and *Climax* (2011), on-demand providers had contended that because they provided material that would not be lawful to show on UK television, comparability was impossible.[22]

The analytical approach now taken by Ofcom is best understood by referring to later decisions (i.e. applying the key tests to new factual scenarios). A representative

18 James Bennett, 'Architectures of participation: fame, television and web 2.0' in James Bennett and Niki Strange (eds), *Television as digital media* (Duke University Press 2011) 388.

19 Aymar Jean Christian, 'Joe Swanberg, intimacy, and the digital aesthetic' (2011) 50 *Cinema Journal* 117, 118; see also Jon Dovey, 'Time slice: web drama and the attention economy' in Paul Grainge (ed.), *Ephemeral media: transitory screen culture from television to YouTube* (British Film Institute 2011) 146.

20 See for instance Orit Fussfeld Cohen, 'The new language of the digital film' (2014) 42 *Journal of Popular Film and Television* 47, 48.

21 Craufurd Smith (n 7) 268–70.

22 Petley (n 2) 294–6.

example is *Everton TV* (2013). Ofcom considered the relevance of the 'complete narrative' of some clips, '"TV-like" elements such as branded opening and closing sequences' and production values 'consistent with linear television sports reports, including professional camerawork and internal editing'.[23] However, it noted contrary evidence including the absence of 'linking elements such as a studio based introduction' or 'reflections from commentators to provide an over arching narrative'.[24]

It can be seen that reaching a decision on regulation includes identifying factors like credits and quality, followed by a decision on what makes the factor in question TV-like, and finally an application of this to the specific service under review. Recurring features highlighted in Ofcom decisions have included titles and credits, quality, and duration.

Titles and credits

In decisions regarding two BBC YouTube 'channels' (*Top Gear* and *BBC Food*) published in January 2013, which ultimately went in favour of the BBC (i.e. overturning ATVOD's initial determination that the services were subject to regulation as on-demand services), the lack of traditional start-of-programme titles and end-of-programme credits is noted. (The reason for the lack of such features is clearly that the material is typically taken from the middle of a previously broadcast programme; in the case of *BBC Food*, this was a range of food-related programmes from across the BBC.) Ofcom therefore found that credits are one aspect of TV-like production, arguing that:

> It accordingly contained the kind of camera work, sound and internal editing as would be expected in a clip of material produced as part of a longer programme for BBC linear television. Nevertheless, in terms of form, Ofcom finds it significant that other production elements associated with linear formats, such as opening and closing credits were not present.[25]

Similarly, Ofcom noted in other decisions the presence of brief opening and closing credits,[26] the use of library music as part of opening sequences[27] and the presentation of participant/character names.[28] It had also drawn attention to the presence[29] or absence[30] of production credits.

23 *Everton TV* (26 June 2013) [94]. References are to the titles and dates of Ofcom decisions, which are not given a unique identifier, but can be accessed at www.ofcom.org.uk
24 Ibid. [96].
25 *BBC Food* (18 January 2013) [46–7]; see also *BBC Top Gear* (18 January 2013) [45–6].
26 *Channel Flip* (14 December 2012) [60].
27 *Business Channel* (18 January 2013) [38].
28 *Daisy Rock* (17 September 2015) [59].
29 *Demand Adult* (13 May 2011) 6; *Climax* (13 May 2011) 8.
30 *UCSC* (14 August 2014) [57].

These are however questionable assumptions. Titles can have an 'expressive function',[31] and might identify the assumptions of the author or the intended audience.[32] But is there a direct relationship between television and titles or credits? I doubt this, for three reasons now discussed: changes, exports, and functions.

Eastman and Neal-Lunsford argue that credits and interstitials were the subject of changes in the 1990s, as the 'actual and perceived time between programmes' shrank.[33] Butler has observed more recent changes in the use of credits, including (i) departures from conventional US forms (teaser, theme/credits, break, programme, end, break, theme/credits), (ii) truncated or absent theme tunes, and (iii) additional post-credits dialogue.[34] Moreover, practices reflect different markets; the 'changeover' at the top of an hour means that the assembly of such material is different in the US, and the more relaxed regulation of advertising also affects the decisions of a channel on how to arrange programmes, breaks, and the like.[35] In turn, when US programmes are exported, fades (instead of end credits) are introduced for some markets, and the pattern of advertising breaks is different (e.g. not normally immediately after opening credits or before closing credits).[36]

One can finally note that while credits on television might resemble tuning up at a concert or playing an anthem at a sports game[37] (with longer credits being the 'audiovisual equivalent of hardback binding on a book'[38] or intended to convey something of cinema practices[39]), while also realising that just as concert, sporting and publishing practices can evolve, so can television production.

31 Jason Jacobs, 'Issues of judgement and value in television studies' (2001) 4 *International Journal of Cultural Studies* 427.

32 David Kociemba, '"Actually, it explains a *lot*": reading the opening title sequences of Buffy the Vampire Slayer' (2006) 6 *Slayage: The Journal of the Whedon Studies Association*; Jonathan Gray, *Show sold separately: promos, spoilers, and other media paratexts* (New York University Press 2010) 73.

33 Susan Tyler Eastman and Jeffrey Neal-Lunsford, 'Coping with grazing: prime-time strategies for accelerated program transitions' (1995) 39 *Journal of Broadcasting and Electronic Media* 91. Many thanks to Keith M. Johnston for pointing me towards this work (and a number of the other sources discussed in this section).

34 Butler (n 17) 296. See also Annette Davison, 'The end is nigh' (2014) 8 *Music, Sound, and the Moving Image* 195, 196; John Ellis, 'Interstitials: how the "bits in between" define the programmes' in Paul Grainge (ed.), *Ephemeral media: transitory screen culture from television to YouTube* (British Film Institute 2011) 61 (on voiceovers and split-screen promotions over final credits).

35 Catherine Johnson, *Branding television* (Routledge 2012) 135; Ellis (n 34) 59.

36 Denise Bielby and C. Lee Harrington, *Global TV: exporting television and culture in the world market* (New York University Press 2008) 137.

37 Gray (n 32) 74–5.

38 Ellis (n 34) 61.

39 Glen Creeber, *Small screen aesthetics: from TV to the Internet* (Palgrave Macmillan 2013), citing *Twin Peaks* (90) and *Band of Brothers* (95) in particular; see also Enrica Picarelli, 'Aspirational paratexts: the case of "quality openers" in TV promotion' (2013) 3 *Frames Cinema Journal*.

Ofcom gave partial and belated recognition to this point in its 2015 *Mistress R'eal* decision, where it noted that although credits were absent from the videos in question, this also described some comparable programmes in the same genre (adult content) on a linear (broadcast) service.[40]

Quality

In the pair of BBC decisions discussed above, Ofcom also noted the relevance of production quality. This point has arisen in nearly all of Ofcom's comparability decisions. In discussion of sexually explicit services, it points to whether the audio is of professional quality and whether sets are professionally lit.[41] In the *Frankie & Friends* decision, the use of sets is highlighted as a factor against regulation;[42] in others, Ofcom highlights how entire videos take place in a single location[43] or with a continuous shot. A useful contrast can be seen in non-adult cases, between the *Channel Flip* decision (where Ofcom noted the use of a single camera, simple graphics and short monologues to camera[44] in ultimately finding that the service was not TV-like) and the *Business Channel* decision (where the use of cutaways, library music, and a structure – introduction, piece to camera, voiceover, interview, conclusion – were part of Ofcom's reasoning in finding the service TV-like).[45] Finally, Ofcom has shown itself to be concerned with fictional form. In its first cases on sexually explicit services, it highlighted how the use of a dramatic conceit in videos contributed to a service being TV-like.[46] In later decisions, it continued to be exercised about the presence[47] or absence[48] of a narrative conceit. In the two cases where the 'narrative' is allegedly absent, Ofcom also notes that the dialogue appears unscripted.

These cases all point to the same conclusion; high quality is a factor, for the regulator, in favour of determining whether a service is TV-like and thus sufficiently comparable to meet the regulatory test. As with titles, though, does this equating of quality and television stand up? Does Ofcom rely on an accurate picture of what 'television' is?

Again, I doubt it, because of the range of choices open to television producers (in theory and in practice), and the interchangeability of some production practices between broadcast television and the Internet. Television producers draw from a wide range of production options for features such as lighting – e.g. saturated colour, clean (no shadow) lighting, deliberate 'flatness'.[49] They may do this

40 *Mistress R'eal* (28 October 2015) [41].
41 *UCSC* (n 30) [60]; *Mistress R'eal* (n 40) [45]; *Frankie & Friends* (14 August 2014) [67].
42 *Frankie & Friends* (n 41) [66].
43 *UCSC* (n 30) [60].
44 *Channel Flip* (n 26) [58], [64].
45 *Business Channel* (n 27) [37–8].
46 *Demand Adult* (n 29) 6–7; *Climax* (n 29) 8.
47 *Frankie & Friends* (n 41) [64]; *Daisy Rock* (n 28) [61–2].
48 *Mistress R'eal* (n 40) [43]; *UCSC* (n 30) [60].
49 Karen Lury, *Interpreting television* (Hodder Arnold 2005) 39–40.

to signal something (such as the seriousness or otherwise of the content) through their choice of shots and graphics, or to appeal to a particular audience.[50] Even within broadcast television, there is no single approach to technical quality, and it has changed over time.[51] Low quality video may signify 'authenticity and an indexical reproduction of the real world' or 'not quite television',[52] while framing and (poor) audio quality can emphasise liveness.[53] 'Soft-core reality video' bridges gaps between mainstream and pornographic television forms,[54] while reality TV integrates amateur recordings and the like into a programme[55] (and may indeed be quintessentially unscripted). Some channels broadcast videos originally uploaded to the Web,[56] while amateur videos uploaded to the Internet can use production tropes and clichés once associated with television.[57]

Ofcom draws some support from the research on on-demand services it commissioned from Essential Research, in that audiences were said to be sceptical about the quality of web video,[58] with obvious consequences for what is deemed to be 'TV-like'. However, this may prove to be a weak foundation, as the exposure of younger users in particular to YouTube videos is argued to be affecting the expectation of how 'visual stories' look, compared with those whose primary experience is that of television and cinema.[59] As such, if Ofcom intends to rely on the research findings for the proposition that web video is of lower quality, and continue to argue that quality is relevant to determining regulatory jurisdiction

50 Jonathan Bignell, *An introduction to television studies* (3rd edn, Routledge 2013) 96.

51 For instance, changes in camera size and shape in the 1940s and 1950s are argued to have had an impact on television aesthetics, as did changes in sound recording technology, and (in later years) the use of lighter digital cameras: Creeber (n 39) 20, 36, 51.

52 Jon Dovey, 'Camcorder cults' in Robert Allen and Annette Hill (eds), *The television studies reader* (Routledge 2004) 557; Bignell (n 50) 187.

53 Jeremy Butler, *Television style* (Routledge 2010) 15.

54 Vicki Mayer, 'Guys Gone Wild? Soft-core video professionalism and new realities in television production' (2008) 47 *Cinema Journal* 97, 98.

55 Rosamund Davies, 'Digital intimacies: aesthetic and affective strategies in the production and use of online video' in Paul Grainge (ed.), *Ephemeral media: transitory screen culture from television to YouTube* (BFI 2011) 219 (on how home video in the 1980s had different aesthetics and home video to professional – a distinction that has lessened in importance over time); Benjamin Wiggins, 'The culture industry, new media, and the shift from creation to curation; or, enlightenment ss a kick in the nuts' (2014) 15 *Television and New Media* 395, 398; Creeber (n 39) 74 (on the Japanese origins of the use of 'private clips' in television programmes in the 1980s, picked up in the US and UK shortly thereafter).

56 William Uricchio, 'The recurrent, the recombinatory and the ephemeral' in Paul Grainge (ed.), *Ephemeral media: transitory screen culture from television to YouTube* (British Film Institute 2011) 32; Henry Jenkins, *Convergence culture: where old and new media collide* (New York University Press 2006) 240.

57 Niels van Doorn, 'Keeping it real: user-generated pornography, gender reification, and visual pleasure' (2010) 16 *Convergence: The International Journal of Research into New Media Technologies* 411, 420–3.

58 Essential Research, 'On-demand services: understanding consumer choices' (2012) www.ofcom.org.uk/__data/assets/pdf_file/0025/28906/research_report.pdf 37.

59 Butler, *Television: critical methods and applications* (n 17) 138.

(through what I contend is an incomplete concept of what makes for television), it must surely be prepared to revisit that research on a regular basis.

Duration

The third issue arising in Ofcom decisions on comparability, to some extent, is that of duration. The research it commissioned identified length as 'perhaps the most important element, and something that immediately sprung to mind'[60] in defining programmes. In its BBC decisions, Ofcom noted and relied upon the duration of the individual clips on the YouTube channels in question, and compared them with the length of the source programmes (i.e. Top Gear and various food programmes). Ofcom also noted with approval the findings of the 2012 research (which had included Top Gear clips in its material), explaining that while users 'found the quality and content of the clips to be very much reminiscent of linear television programmes, they distinguished services where the length and volume (i.e. quantum) of material was different'.[61] In the *Channel Flip* decision (frequently cited as a precedent in subsequent cases), Ofcom agreed with the research participants that duration was 'particularly important'; it highlighted the short duration of the three to four minute clips that made up the bulk of the service, as compared with the typical duration of programmes within the genre (comedy and light entertainment).[62] In a later decision, without further reference to the 2012 research, Ofcom highlighted the short duration of most of the videos on the *Everton TV* website (the majority being under five minutes in duration), arguing that these works 'would have been more likely to form parts of sports report or highlights programming rather than being programmes in themselves'.[63] Moreover, Ofcom also dismissed an argument that the YouTube playlist function (where a series of clips can be watched in sequence) changed the analysis of length, because the result was a disjointed presentation.[64]

However, in an earlier appeal decision in *Viva TV*, the arguments of the service provider regarding the length of music videos as a reason not to find the service in scope were unsuccessful.[65] This reflected a point noted in earlier Ofcom documentation, that music videos could not be excluded because they were already the core programmes of music TV (linear) channels. In short, because a music channel may be made up of wall-to-wall videos, each video can be conceived of as a programme.[66] As such, an on-demand service made of

60 Essential Research (n 58) 28.
61 *BBC Food* (n 25) [57]; *BBC Top Gear* (n 25) [56].
62 *Channel Flip* (n 26) [59].
63 *Everton TV* (n 23) [95].
64 *BBC Top Gear* (n 25) [47]; *BBC Food* (n 25) [41].
65 *Viva TV* (22 February 2012) [56], [59].
66 Though note that programmes on music channels, albeit influenced by aspects of music video aesthetics (see Creeber (n 39) 59), may have a more conventional form and duration.

music videos contains similar programmes to a music television channel. (A path not taken was the idea that what appears on a schedule (e.g. a three-hour block of chart hits) could be characterised as a better fit for 'programme' than an individual video, although this might founder on the narrative coherence argument, as with the 'disjointed playlist' argument in the BBC cases.) Any residual doubts about the significance of genre in deciding what weight to place on duration are addressed by Ofcom's decisions on sexually explicit services. It was only in later decisions in this field that this emerged as an issue – usually at the instigation of the service provider. For instance, one provider cited the Essential Research findings in support of its argument that its use of short videos (averaging under eight minutes) was a factor against being found within scope.[67] However, Ofcom responded by quoting a statement originally made in parentheses in *Channel Flip* ('short form content may be more likely to be typical in some genres, such as children's programming and adult content programming') in support of its finding that the shorter duration of videos was indeed TV-like in the adult genre.[68] Similar arguments are found in the 2015 *Daisy Rock* decision. Even within the genre, though, Ofcom was prepared to acknowledge, in a more recent decision, that particular videos were 'relatively brief even in the context of adult content'.[69]

Therefore, it can be observed that the relevant question (as Ofcom sees it) is relative rather than absolute length, i.e. the relationship between TV and on-demand programme length *in the genre in question.* Yet the research it commissioned did not really address this point. Music videos and entertainment programmes (and perhaps sports) might address the point in part, but other areas will be more troublesome. What is the duration of a film; is it the two hours or more of the modern blockbuster, or also something from the well-established 'film short'[70] genre? Typical programme length on linear TV services varies between services (e.g. ITV and BBC) and between jurisdictions or markets.[71] Some web content is short for technological reasons (e.g. in the earlier days of AV-enabled mobile phones),[72] but it could also be short in duration for aesthetic reasons – such as addressing audiences who are familiar with tweets and browser-based games[73] – intended to complement a

67 *UCSC* (n 30) [18].

68 Ibid. [55–6].

69 *Mistress R'eal* (n 40) [40].

70 Barbara Klinger, *Beyond the multiplex: cinema, new technologies, and the home* (University of California Press 2006) 192–3.

71 John Ellis, 'Television production' in Robert Allen and Annette Hill (eds), *The television studies reader* (Routledge 2004) 277.

72 Judith Nicholson, 'The third screen as cultural form in North America' in Barbara Crow, Michael Longford and Kim Sawchuk (eds), *The wireless spectrum: the politics, practices, and poetics of mobile media* (University of Toronto Press 2010) 81–2.

73 Max Dawson, 'Television's aesthetic of efficiency: convergence television and the digital short' in James Bennett and Niki Strange (eds), *Television as digital media* (Duke University Press 2011) 214.

work as paratext.[74] Moreover, the importance of short content on linear services is recognised in respect of services such as the Disney Channel.[75] The risk for Ofcom, as with the discussion of titles and of quality, is that relying upon the limited research it commissioned and its own media studies-influenced glosses and assumptions (e.g. on genre) leads to a misunderstanding of television, and therefore an inability to operationalise the comparability test.

Editorial responsibility

The third type of dispute is characterised by a type of risk shifting. In these situations, there is no doubt that the service is within the scope of the regulatory system, but *who* has editorial responsibility and, as such, should notify the service to ATVOD (or now, Ofcom) is in dispute. The cases are spread across platforms (cable, satellite, IPTV, and mobile) and typically involve a choice between editorial responsibilities lying with the platform operator or with the service provider responsible for the content.

In one appeal, ATVOD had determined that three services provided by Viacom companies (Comedy Central, MTV and Nickelodeon) were the editorial responsibility of those companies, rather than the cable service Virgin Media. For present purposes, this can be discussed as fixing responsibility on a 'low level' rather than the 'high level' service. (These labels are used because the Viacom service is presented to the consumer within the Virgin platform.) In the other, ATVOD had determined that content originating from those companies was the editorial responsibility of Sky ('high level'). Ofcom confirmed ATVOD's decision in the Virgin case and vacated it in the Sky case;[76] subsequently, ATVOD determined that editorial responsibility for the Sky services also lay with the Viacom companies. In two further decisions, ATVOD found that the 'low level' provider was subject to its regulatory system (the earlier case of ITV Archive on Virgin Media, and the more recent decision in On Demand on 3 Mobile). The exception is a decision regarding BBC Worldwide on Mediaset, where the 'low level' determination of ATVOD was rejected by Ofcom.[77] However, the particular circumstances of Mediaset (a non-UK IPTV service) appeared to be a key feature, and compared with the extensive steps taken by UK 'high level' providers to avoid liability, meant that it was of little value as a precedent.

The risk-shifting steps are primarily contractual provisions, and have (as anticipated)[78] been demonstrated in the decisions to be significant. For example, in the

74 Chuck Tryon, *Reinventing cinema: movies in the age of media convergence* (Rutgers University Press 2009) 87; Paul Grainge, 'Introduction' in Paul Grainge (ed.), *Ephemeral media: transitory screen culture from television to YouTube* (British Film Institute 2011) 11.

75 Jennifer Gillan, *Television brandcasting: the return of the content-promotion hybrid* (Routledge 2014) 157.

76 *Viacom* (19 January 2012); *BSkyB* (21 July 2012).

77 *BBC Worldwide* (27 April 2012).

78 Ofcom (n 5) [3.44]

Viacom on Virgin Media case, the contract between the parties included a stipulation that Viacom had editorial responsibility and was obliged to notify ATVOD. In the Viacom on Sky case, there were also contractual provisions, but doubt was caused by clearer Sky branding and some flexibility on the part of Sky (in particular, capacity limits). It can be difficult for the observer to understand the decisions. While both ATVOD and Ofcom should be praised for transparency in general, the extensive redaction masks the reasons for some decisions. For example, the BBC Worldwide/Mediaset appeal decision has extensive redaction of terms.

The Ofcom decisions confirm an understanding that emerged from the initial designation process, against the liability of 'high level' providers. A ministerial statement setting out the course of action made it clear that 'access providers' would not be covered;[79] content providers expressed their dissatisfaction in their responses to Ofcom's consultation.[80] In the final statement, catalogue design, PIN management, age warnings and logos were noted as unlikely to constitute editorial responsibility.[81] As with many of the issues that have been considered by ATVOD and Ofcom, the reference in the Directive to editorial responsibility was inserted between the original Commission proposal and the final approval of the Directive, in response to fears that the draft would bring too many services within its scope.[82]

However, the decisions did disclose some problems with the drafting of the new Communications Act provisions. It was alleged that ATVOD had combined two separate tests ('a person who has editorial responsibility for it' and 'it is made available by that person for use by members of the public'). Ofcom's interpretation is that the essence of the second provision is to highlight the requirement that the service be made available to the public. This means that while there can be more than one party satisfying the latter test, there would only be one party with editorial responsibility. The elegance of the drafting may have (unintentionally) caused some doubt.[83] A clearer approach would be to separate the tests. What we learn from the issue of the statutory language, as well as the broader discussion on editorial responsibility, is that the nature of the market and technology for VOD needs to be understood, if a determination on editorial responsibility is to be possible.

Further issues

Branding

The Essential Research work also identifies 'where the content originated' as a factor, which demonstrates the importance of recognisable TV 'brands' in the

79 HC Deb 11 March 2009, vol. 489, col. 15WS.

80 Ofcom (n 5) [3.39].

81 Ibid. [3.83].

82 In the Commission's background material for the draft Directive, the focus does appear to be on high rather than low level services (in the examples given): European Commission, 'Impact Assessment on proposed AVMS Directive' SEC(2005) 1625 [3.1.3].

83 It appears as if the specific language was chosen to avoid doubt associated with an earlier draft referring to 'widely available': Ofcom (n 5) [3.67].

on-demand sector. It is also identified as the third element that defines a programme ('to be produced by a broadcaster they were familiar with').

This feature demonstrates how the intentions of broadcasters can diverge from the perceptions of audiences or the actions of regulators. The distribution of content by broadcasters through services like YouTube and iTunes is one of the means by which 'the television industry has attempted to position itself'[84] within emerging popular services which appeal to some users. Others have acquired YouTube content producers, as part of a broader strategy of diversification in the face of shifting audiences.[85] Some broadcasters use online services (particularly the US service Hulu) in a way that plays down the 'channel' brand in favour of a given 'programme',[86] but placing and maintaining channel identification (as an on-screen ident or by other means) continues to be important for others. Major broadcasters in the UK have taken a strategy of extending brands to new digital channels (e.g. ITV2), and ensured brand visibility across various platforms (BBC, and in respect of YouTube, ITV and Channel 4)[87] and through characterising on-demand services as 'extension services'.[88] In general, for the established (corporate) producers of audiovisual content, 'more than anything else on the Internet, online access to video strikes at the beating heart of the entire entertainment business'.[89]

As such, proposals made by the House of Lords Communications Committee, in its 2013 report on 'media convergence', were particularly striking. It argued that existing licences should be amended so as to 'ensure that standards similar to those set out in the Ofcom Broadcasting Code, amended for the relevant environment, would apply to any service using the same channel name or brand as a licensed broadcast service'.[90] Although the Committee described the current position as an 'anomaly', it would create an arguably equally anomalous gulf between the regulatory treatment of broadcaster-run on-demand services (a substantial part of those services currently regulated) and the remaining services. Whatever one might say about the merits of the linear/non-linear distinction, applying the very detailed rules of the Broadcasting Code (far above and beyond EU requirements) to one group of on-demand services and the light touch of the Directive to another group, merely based on the brand, would be a completely new approach to regulation.

84 Johnson (n 35) 44.

85 Stuart Dredge, 'Disney's YouTube deal is a real game changer' *The Observer* (London, 30 March 2014) Review 21.

86 Johnson (n 35) 55; Jennifer Gillan, *Television and new media* (Routledge 2010) 3.

87 Johnson (n 35) 74, 129.

88 Elizabeth Jane Evans and Paul McDonald, 'Online distribution of film and television in the UK: behavior, taste, and value' in Jennifer Holt and Kevin Sanson (eds), *Connected viewing: selling, streaming, and sharing media in the digital era* (Taylor & Francis 2014) 162.

89 Robert Levine, *Free ride: how the internet is destroying the culture business and how the culture business can fight back* (Bodley Head 2011) 138.

90 House of Lords Select Committee on Communications, *Media convergence* (HL 154, 2012–2013) [51].

Distribution

The Directive requires in recital 24 that the 'nature and the means of access' to a service be taken into account in determining whether a service ought to be regulated under the on-demand regime. One example might be screen size – which can clearly inform production decisions. It may already be the case that different types of content can be more 'suited' to a different type of screen.[91] Small screens may offer a difference in experience, as discussed in Chapter 3. A visceral, expensively produced blockbuster film may be better suited to a cinema screen and powerful multi-speaker wall-mounted sound system than a screen on a handheld device and a tinny, internal speaker. In television, aspect ratios in particular have been the subject of change over time, particularly as the ratio of production may not match the distribution and reception options of providers and viewers.[92] Now, successive innovations in screen design make the 'home cinema' an option for some; many channels in the UK are available in 'high definition' and even 3D. On the Internet and over mobile data networks, some service providers offer high speed connections – but there are plenty of users still using slower services less well suited to audiovisual material. (Well-designed Web services will vary the quality of the video served to the user based on the detected connection quality and device, and user-set preferences.)

The result is a situation where correlating size and being 'TV-like' is a fruitless, circular exercise. In particular, can these matters be reliably identified (in determining whether a service is TV-like), when it is so difficult to identify the distinctive nature and means of access to television and to on-demand services to begin with? In particular, the degree to which user expectations are affected by actions taken by service providers is unknown but potentially significant. Such actions could include the similarity between YouTube and the 'DVR-mediated television experience',[93] Virgin Media's allocation of a channel number in its electronic programme guide to YouTube (which is in truth no more than a link to its customised YouTube app/interface), and the integration of linear and VOD searches on Samsung devices.

VOD service providers originally based on a model of distributing films and previously broadcast TV programmes are also becoming first publishers of new content, as Netflix famously did in respect of *House of Cards*[94] or obtaining exclusive syndication rights for material initially broadcast on premium channels;[95] its

91 Tryon (n 74) 84–5.

92 Lury (n 49) 23.

93 William Uricchio, 'The future of a medium once known as television' in Pelle Snickars and Patrick Vonderau (eds), *The YouTube reader* (National Library of Sweden 2009) 33. On the relationship between the DVR and other changes in audiovisual content distribution, see James Walker and Robert Bellamy, 'DVRs and the empowered audience' in John Allen Hendricks (ed.), *The twenty-first century media industry* (Lexington 2010).

94 Mark Sweney, 'Netflix bets $100m on digital appetite for remakes' *The Guardian* (London, 2 February 2013) 14.

95 Chuck Tryon, *On-demand culture: digital delivery and the future of movies* (Rutgers University Press 2013) 26.

competitor Amazon Prime Video (formerly LoveFilm) does similar, e.g. *Mr Robot*. YouTube funded 'Original Channels' between 2011 and 2013 (through paying an advance in place of later advertising revenues),[96] which were, in the most part, run by broadcasters and independent producers. (Recall that YouTube uses the old-fashioned language of 'channel' to describe a group of on-demand videos uploaded by a user.)[97] Meanwhile, the BBC now shows some programmes through its on-demand iPlayer service before linear transmission, and its BBC Three service changed from being a television channel available on Freeview and other platforms to an on-demand service in 2016.

Re-regulation: R18 and age verification

The implications of the attempt to provide for the light-touch regulation of on-demand services came into sharp focus once the Directive had been transposed and the new co-regulatory system was up and running. The new system may have introduced a new form of regulation and an obligation to pay fees to a regulator, but for critics of the availability of sexually explicit material, its significance was not wholly clear. It is clear from the text of the Directive that the threshold for regulation would be different, depending on whether the service fell into the television or on-demand category. Whereas television services are not permitted to carry programmes 'which might seriously impair the physical, mental or moral development of minors', on-demand services are merely required to prevent the same minors from (normally) seeing or hearing such content.[98] A lower threshold (likely to impair development) applicable in the case of television (requiring the use of scheduling or technical measures to ensure, again, that minor do not normally see or hear the programme in question) has no equivalent provision in the rules for on-demand services.

ATVOD and Ofcom took the approach that on-demand services were required to use access control for content that would, if it had instead been distributed on video, be classified by the BBFC at R18.[99] This was not entirely obvious, as the

96 Dino Grandoni, 'YouTube's original channels are a risky bet, but Google doubles down' (*Huffington Post*, 12 November 2012) www.huffingtonpost.com/2012/11/12/youtube-original-channels_n_2117717.html; Amy Turner, 'Famous for 15 seconds' *Sunday Times* (London, 11 March 2012) Magazine 12, 14.

97 Philip Napoli, *Audience evolution: new technologies and the transformation of media audiences* (Columbia University Press 2011) 127.

98 AVMS Directive (n 1), Articles 27 and 12; in the UK, see Communications Act 2003, s 368E(2).

99 Works rated at R18 can only be exhibited in licensed sex cinemas and sold or supplied as a video recording in licensed sex shops; see Local Government (Miscellaneous Provisions) Act 1982, sch 3, art 3 (and equivalent provisions in Local Government (Miscellaneous Provisions) (Northern Ireland) Order 1985, sch 2, art 3) and Video Recordings Act 1984, s 12 (UK-wide) respectively; see further Chapter 3. The regulatory category is echoed in an emerging genre of works, which work within the parameters of what is unsuitable at 18 but still meets the criteria for lawful distribution at R18, and addresses the perceived interests of British audiences: I. Q. Hunter, 'Naughty realism: the Britishness of British hardcore R18s' (2014) 11 *Journal of British Cinema and Television* 152.

equating of R18 with the Directive's concept of serious impairment of development required some interpretation of the statutory language. Indeed, Ofcom had long held that R18 content was caught by the lower threshold (although in fact this meant a total ban, as Ofcom simultaneously held the view that no effective means of access control was available in respect of television). Nonetheless, the regulators concluded (in disagreement with regulators in some other EU member states) that R18 content did meet the higher threshold.[100] This was then reinforced by the amendment of the on-demand regulatory system (i.e. above and beyond the initial minimalist transposition of the Directive) in 2014. These changes gave statutory force to the link; Ofcom now has the power to enforce access control in the on-demand sector where the content is equivalent to R18 or if the content had already been rated by the BBFC at R18 when released as a video recording (termed 'specially restricted material' in the amendments. Moreover, the legislative changes provide for a complete prohibition on the inclusion of material refused classification by the BBFC or, again, which would have been so refused had it been submitted for classification; this goes beyond the UK's requirements under the Directive but shares with the other aspect of the amendments the deliberate use of VRA standards in a new context (or, as the Government put it not entirely fairly, resolving a 'regulatory inconsistency with hard-copy material').[101] These changes did draw some criticism including on the grounds that the new requirements drove users to use sites hosted beyond the UK (without access control).[102]

This use of a VRA concept as a template for regulating an aspect of the TV-derived on-demand regulatory system, in turn, became a template for a broader project of Internet regulation very shortly afterwards. A legislative proposal signalled in 2015,[103] consulted upon in early 2016[104] and included in the Digital Economy Bill in 2016[105] would, if adopted, provide for a broader requirement to apply access control on online access to sexually explicit material (i.e. websites not caught by the regulation of VOD). On this occasion, the comparators

100 Ofcom, 'Sexually explicit material and video-on-demand services' (2011) www.ofcom.org.uk/__data/assets/pdf_file/0023/23738/explicit-material-vod.pdf

101 Department for Culture, Media and Sport, 'Impact assessment: R18 content access controls' (2014) www.gov.uk/government/uploads/system/uploads/attachment_data/file/225877/R18_content_access_controls.pdf

102 Amelia Gentleman, 'Sex doesn't sell: the decline of British porn' *Guardian* (London, 6 October 2014) www.theguardian.com/culture/2014/oct/05/sex-sell-decline-british-porn-xbiz-regulations-children

103 Prime Minister's Office, 'Curbing access to pornographic websites for under 18s' (30 July 2015) www.gov.uk/government/news/curbingaccesstopornographicwebsitesforunder18s (specifically, 'the Prime Minister is determined to introduce age verification mechanisms to restrict under 18s' access to pornographic websites and is prepared to legislate to do so if the industry fails to self regulate').

104 Department for Culture, Media and Sport, 'Child safety online: age verification for pornography' (2016) www.gov.uk/government/uploads/system/uploads/attachment_data/file/541366/AV_ConsultationDCMS_20160216_Final__4_.pdf

105 Digital Economy HC Bill (2016–2017).

included the VRA, the regulation of television, the newly adopted VOD provisions, and even the (essentially non-statutory) practices of newsagents regarding the display of pornographic magazines on high shelves. A shift in emphasis, though, was the inclusion of sub-R18 content within the scope of the new proposals (a subset of content that the BBFC would classify at 18, i.e. sex works) – including a new requirement for access control for such content on regulated VOD. Indeed, despite the rhetoric of *equivalence* being used once more, the net result would be the creation of a new statutory category of pornography, based on aspects of BBFC practice, with *medium-specific* prohibitions and sanctions included (though stretching across photographs, video, and even sound), all to be enforced by a 'age verification regulator' (or regulators) to be designated at a later stage by statutory instrument.[106] The Bill has been amended during parliamentary consideration; as introduced, it would have provided for the regulator to compile a list of non-compliant websites and supply it to payment providers and ISPs. By the time it had cleared the House of Commons, it also included provision for ISPs to be ordered to block specific websites at the instruction of the regulator.

VOD, programmes and the idea of television

The concepts of 'programme' and 'TV-like' are potentially in conflict. The multiplicity of versions of a film on DVD and other platforms causes instability in the definition of a single 'text';[107] similarly, video is 'interwoven into other modes of representation such as film and television'[108] and television 'borrows audio-visual content from a range of other places'.[109] The shift in the rhetoric of the media industries from programme to content[110] and continued variety in scheduling practices[111] also undermines the discrete and identifiable notion of a programme. Ofcom recognised this in part through its caution in *Viva TV* against ATVOD's consideration of the 'dramatic conceit' of a music video, on the grounds that the genre does not require it.[112] (This itself may change; music videos today have a 'natural home' online[113] and there is a great deal of variety, not least in what drives viral success.)[114] But how does one prove a genre-based

106 This is likely to include the BBFC and at least one other body.

107 Klinger (n 70) 72.

108 Michael Strangelove, *Watching YouTube: extraordinary videos by ordinary people* (University of Toronto Press 2010) 172.

109 Bignell (n 50) 14.

110 John Caldwell, 'Convergence television: aggregating form and repurposing content in the culture of conglomeration' in Lynn Spigel and Jan Olsson (eds), *Television after TV: essays on a medium in transition* (Duke University Press 2004) 49.

111 Gillan, *Television brandcasting: the return of the content-promotion hybrid* (n 75) 86.

112 *Viva TV* (n 65) [57–8].

113 Maura Edmond, 'Here We Go Again: music videos after YouTube' (2014) 15 *Television and New Media* 305, 305.

114 Ibid. 315.

argument to a regulatory body? The Directive provides, in defining 'programme', that 'examples of programmes include feature-length films, sports events, situation comedies, documentaries, children's programmes and original drama' (Article 1(b)). Is a sitcom defined by its comedy, or by the formal analysis of its camera positioning and catchy title sequence? Does documentary not include a very wide range of approaches in production, across a spectrum of quality if one can even be defined? If formal analysis is appropriate, are focus groups such as those carried out by Essential Research (with a group of 92 people across 14 groups and eight interviews) the most appropriate method?

Categorising some (but, crucially, not all) new services as TV-like is therefore an inappropriate use of a *theoretical proposition* (on-demand services are not TV nor a replacement for TV but build upon the past work of TV) as a means for dividing on-demand services into categories *for regulatory purposes*. Doing so at a time when TV itself is still a major (and changing) sector – i.e. challenging that proposition – makes this work even more difficult again. The consideration of user responses (across the board) may also serve to distract rather than assist the regulator, even though the Directive specifically highlights in recital 24 that consumer expectations are a factor in regulation (whether a user could 'reasonably ... expect regulatory protection within the scope of this Directive'). While the drafters of laws might imagine that both 'old' and 'new' laws are widely understood, this can prove to be nothing but wishful thinking. This was unintentionally highlighted in earlier research commissioned by Ofcom on the regulation of on-demand services, where it was reported that participants (wrongly) assumed that previously broadcast content was regulated when it was available on on-demand.[115] This research was carried out *before* the Directive came into force in the UK – that is, while these services were *not* subject to existing regulation, and therefore the vast majority misunderstood the actual legal requirements. This is a further reminder of the limitations of focus group research for regulatory purposes, especially when the concept of television is being closely studied by those in the field of television studies using a more appropriate mixture of research methods.[116]

Assumptions made about genre are capable of being read in a number of different ways. Of course, the interest shown by the regulator in the relationship between genre and production can be recognised as a welcome acknowledgement of the complexity of televisual texts. However, the results can affect the potential uses of the new platform. There is, for instance, a long history of emerging platforms being a venue for pushing the boundaries of what is acceptable in regulatory terms. Early cable-only and pay-TV services in the United

115 Essential Research, 'The regulation of video-on-demand: consumer views on what makes audiovisual services "TV-like"' (2009) www.ofcom.org.uk/__data/assets/pdf_file/0018/16218/vod.pdf 46

116 For an illustration of methodological diversity, see Sarah Cardwell, 'Television aesthetics' (2006) 1 *Critical Studies in Television* 72.

States such as HBO and Showtime presented material that was more explicit than what would then have been permitted on network television.[117] The use of genre-based arguments in a way that leads to differential outcomes (without even considering the further impact of the approach taken to sexually explicit material, as Petley explains),[118] could put today's projects under surprisingly intense regulatory scrutiny.

In turn, few of the difficulties experienced in applying the Directive to on-demand services would come as a surprise to the scholar of technological change or to anyone versed in the Toronto School's work. In particular, new technologies often build on previous technologies, rather than representing complete novelty.[119] The conceptual difficulties presented by those unclear definitions also confirms the need to study those evolving patterns more carefully. Indeed, defining a regulatory category by how the targeted activities are similar to another category immediately poses questions of the relationship between those categories, and how both similarity and the 'template' category are to be utilised to a sufficiently robust standard.

117 Avi Santo, 'Para-television and discourses of distinction: the culture of production at HBO' in Marc Leverette, Brian L. Ott and Cara Louise Buckley (eds), *It's not TV: watching HBO in the post-television era* (Routledge 2008) 23; Marc Leverette, '"Cocksucker, Motherfucker, Tits"' in Marc Leverette, Brian L. Ott and Cara Louise Buckley (eds), *It's not TV: watching HBO in the post-television era* (Routledge 2008) 125.

118 Petley (n 2) 294–7.

119 Will Straw, 'Embedded memories' in Charles Acland (ed.), *Residual media* (University of Minnesota Press 2007) 11.

7 Premium rate services

Introduction

Premium rate services form a discrete regulatory category under UK law. Indeed, it is a fairly rare example of a national regime within the telecommunications sector, given the degree of harmonisation that has resulted from EU directives. The system being considered here, though, both pre-dates harmonisation and is much closer to 'content regulation' than the majority of regulatory instruments concerning telecommunications.

The regulatory body is the Phone-paid Services Authority (PSA), which was originally known as ICSTIS – the Independent Committee for the Supervision of Standards of Telephone Information Services. In 2007, it was renamed as Phone-payPlus, and its current name was adopted in November 2016.[1] This chapter is primarily a study of documents authored or commissioned by the PSA; there is very little academic work on the topic, but the distinctiveness of PRS and the regulatory mechanisms applicable in the sector (and the various ways in which there is the potential for overlap with differently constituted regulatory systems) makes it appropriate for inclusion in the present study. The PRS system is reviewed through attention to its origins, key principles, emerging areas of focus and enforcement. A final section identifies the areas where PRS regulation overlaps with other areas of law, such as broadcasting. This leads to a conclusion that the very specific regulatory system for PRS has been surprisingly effective, although its medium specificity may be a reason for this success as well as the source of a number of challenges.

Origins

In essence, premium rate services are those services provided by phone (including now, SMS) where the user pays for the service (e.g. the content) through their phone bill. The original business model here was making use of higher tariffs, where the price paid by the customer to their phone provider (for a call to

1 For convenience, I refer to the authority as the PSA throughout this chapter, but give the author of documents as the name in use at the time of publication of the document in question or where otherwise required.

a particular number) would be split between that provider and the content provider.[2] In the case of SMS, premium rate services are typically delivered via shortcodes (e.g. 70000) with prices varying from a few pence up to £10.

In the 1980s, this emerged as a meaningful market. As with many new markets, it was not long before the potential for abuse or exploitation became apparent. The response was the establishment, by BT (and its then-small competitors), and Oftel (Ofcom's predecessor), of ICSTIS.[3] ICSTIS put together a code of practice, and Oftel added a condition to telecommunications operator licences requiring them to ensure that service providers complied with the code and contributed to the funding of ICSTIS.[4]

One issue that was apparent at the inception of PRS, but has become more notable as other forms of access to content have gone in the opposite direction, is the relative anonymity of PRS use, and, to a similar extent, issues of security. There is no need to register with a service provider, nor to share credit card or bank account details. As online markets have developed, the data trail related to service use has become richer and deeper – but in the eyes of some, this heightens the risk of choosing, for instance, to use a social networking site or to pay for digital content through a website.

A point that is not unrelated to the above is that, famously, PRS include certain types of sexually explicit services, although (unusually in the landscape of twenty-first century pornography), aural rather than visual for many years. In the 1980s, callers could pay to listen to 'soft porn messages from busty barmaids and sexy strippers', sometimes being in practice what the first chair of ICSTIS described as 'people grunting over the phone with all kinds of weird noises'.[5] More recently, PRS have included the download of images and (now) short video clips (often through SMS shortcodes and subscriptions), which has facilitated further access to explicit material.

Regulation

General approach

Under this original ICSTIS system, compliance with the code of practice was built into licences. This is a recognisable model of regulation, and is, for

2 Recent reforms to the regulation of phone tariffs mean that there is now a clearer separation between the 'access charge' (the cost of the call or message itself, paid to the user's phone company) and the 'service charge' (the additional component, paid to the receiving communications provider and typically forwarded in part to the content provider): Ofcom, 'Service charge caps for 09 and 118 services' (2012) www.ofcom.org.uk/__data/assets/pdf_file/0031/47767/condoc.pdf

3 Christopher Marsden, *Internet co-regulation: European law, regulatory governance and legitimacy in cyberspace* (Cambridge University Press 2011) 133.

4 Ian Walden, Chris Edwards and Nigel Savage, *Information technology and the law* (Palgrave Macmillan 1990) 183.

5 Shyama Perera, 'Phone watchdog warns porn lines' *Guardian* (London, 22 March 1989) 2 (reporting on launch of the first ICSTIS code of practice).

instance, how the Broadcasting Code and various other obligations are put into practice today. Nonetheless, it became unsuitable for premium rate services when, as part of the above-mentioned harmonisation of telecommunications law in the EU, the very concept of the telecommunications licence was abolished (in 2002/2003). From then, providers of what are now termed electronic communications networks and services are the subject of a general authorisation regime. As such, the regulatory obligations are now enforced through s 120 Communications Act 2003. However, the PSA Code of Practice[6] itself is required by statute rather than contained in the statute; it is drawn up by the PSA, and approved by Ofcom in light of the criteria set out in s 121. The PSA is designated by Ofcom as the regulator of PRS; within the PSA system is a Tribunal, which deals with the more serious cases and determines penalties for violations of the Code.

The statutory definition of a PRS is the provision of content by means of an electronic communications network (e.g. a live or recorded chat service) or allowing an electronic communications service user to make use (by means of that service) of a facility available to users of that service (e.g. a telephone voting service). There must be a charge for the service, paid in the form of a charge for use to the provider of the electronic communications service through which the service is provided. This means that (for instance) if a chat service is accessed through a regular telephone call and the service paid for by credit card, it is not a PRS.

Within the definition of PRS, some services are defined by Ofcom as 'controlled PRS' in the PRS Condition. This means that s 120 applies to them, and they are then regulated by the PSA's code. Other PRS (i.e. within section 120 but outside the direction) may be within the scope of the Act but not considered controlled PRS, in which case code compliance is voluntary.

There are five types of controlled PRS currently subject to regulation through the Condition: a service with a charge of >10 p/m, services accessed through certain prefixes (087, 090, 091, 118) with a charge of >5 p/m, and three services of any charge: chatline, sexual entertainment service or internet dialler software. A service accessed through an international call is not a controlled PRS.[7]

The parties covered by s 120 are referred to in the Code as network operators and level 1 and level 2 providers, in descending order of specificity. A network operator is typically the ECN (fixed or mobile phone company). A level 1 provider is an intermediary, such as the person who operates a particular SMS shortcode. Finally, a level 2 provider is responsible for the content. The Condition requiring compliance with the PSA system originally applied only to controlled PRS providers who were also providers of an ECS/ECN. Regulation of other

6 http://psauthority.org.uk/-/media/Files/PSA/For-Businesses/Your-phone-paid-service/Code-of-Practice/PSA_Code_of_Practice_14th_Digital.ashx?la=en.

7 This was the subject of some controversy in the 1990s, where attempts by ICSTIS (and BT) to enforce the then Code against a service accessible through an international call was challenged (with some success) before the courts: Anthony Sylvester and John Edwards, 'A law by any other name – ICSTIS' (1997) 3 *Computer and Telecommunications Law Review* 157.

parties (such as content providers) was therefore indirect, such as directing regulated parties to bar access to non-compliant content service providers, and stipulating that contracts with others required compliance with the Code. In 2011, this distinction was removed.[8]

Ofcom describes the purpose of PRS regulation as targeting and preventing consumer harm relating to services which 'based on their characteristics, could give rise to a particular type of risk and which may not otherwise be effectively covered by existing means of consumer protection'.[9] As such, the general requirements of the code relate to legality, consumer protection (transparency and pricing, fairness, maximum charges) and privacy. The content requirements are principally avoiding the causing of harm or 'unreasonable offence' to consumers or the general public and a prohibition on incitement to hatred. This is a narrower intervention than in respect of broadcasting, but still, as with the regulation of VOD in Chapter 6, goes beyond the general law and the minimalist requirements on online services under the Electronic Commerce Directive.[10] There are some specific provisions in respect of children which also go beyond general consumer law on children, e.g. a prohibition on PRS aimed at or likely to be particularly attractive to children containing 'anything which a reasonable parent would not wish their child to see or hear in this way' (rule 2.5.8). Until recently, the Code also required provision of pricing information in a specific way, when PRS were advertised on television or other audio/visual formats; this led to a debate between Ofcom (highlighting the possible need for a television-specific rule if moving images would have more of an impact on the appreciation of price) and the industry (who argued that it made short advertising difficult to design and singled out television advertising without proper justification).[11] A similar issue was discussed with reference to radio advertising in Chapter 5, although on this occasion it is even more interesting through being a medium-specific rule regarding the promotion of another medium.

The most recent editions of the Code represented a new approach to regulation. The Code is now framed as 'outcomes-based'. Due to controversy and a proposed application for judicial review by some companies in the sector, Ofcom and the PSA deferred the procedural changes (e.g. for investigating alleged breaches), which were eventually brought about in the 14th edition, but proceeded with the other changes in the 13th edition.

8 Ofcom, 'Modifying who is subject to the premium rate services condition' (2011) www.ofcom.org.uk/__data/assets/pdf_file/0019/42085/statement.pdf

9 Ofcom, 'Review of premium rate services: an application of the analytical framework' (2011) www.ofcom.org.uk/__data/assets/pdf_file/0014/42053/condoc.pdf [2.4].

10 For instance, the provision of contact details for the service provider (art 5): Directive 2000/31/EC of 8 June 2000 on certain legal aspects of information society services, in particular electronic commerce, in the Internal Market [2000] OJ L178/1.

11 Ofcom, 'Approval of the PhonepayPlus Code of Practice (13th edition)' (2015) www.ofcom.org.uk/__data/assets/pdf_file/0030/49692/final_statement.pdf [3.22–29]. The rule, which applied to services costing above £3.83 excluding VAT, was removed from the 13th edition of the Code, pending a further review.

Prior permission and special conditions

Some controlled PRS are considered to present a higher risk. Until recently, they required prior permission (section 3.10 of previous Codes). Further requirements applied to particular types of prior-permission services, e.g. posting a bond and recording of calls for live entertainment services (e.g. chat or psychic), requiring formal qualifications, professional body membership and supervision for all operators on a counselling service, and a maximum duration of 20 minutes (one-off) or one hour (ongoing service).

The category was defined by the PSA through separate publications (i.e. neither the Communications Act or the Code) and consisted of services such as pay-per-page, gambling, professional advice, live chat, PRS promoted within television programmes (discussed below), and services costing over £1.28 + VAT per minute.[12] In turn, some services that would have been subject to the prior permission rules were exempted (i.e. returned to the 'normal' PRS regulatory regime), such as live customer support or live non-professional advice, subject to cost caps.[13]

The prior permission system was frequently updated, normally in respect of one of the sub-categories rather than across the board. For instance, the PSA applied an enhanced regulatory regime to consumer credit PRS, which were typically services offering access to credit to customers with poor credit records, where the service provider funded their operation in part through higher-tariff phone calls for customer requests. However, it recently withdrew some aspects of this oversight,[14] arguing that the role of the Financial Conduct Authority offered more appropriate protection. Again, this illustrates the regulatory consequences of the choice of platform, as well as the ongoing discussion on what to do when more than one regulator is active (with different goals or mandates); this issue is considered at the end of this chapter.

By 2015, there were 17 different prior permission regimes in force. The PSA identified that a majority simply restated existing Code obligations, albeit still requiring a greater degree of contact or advanced notice on the part of service providers. Because a minority did apply context-specific rules, however, a complete withdrawal of the prior permission requirements could have caused difficulties. Of course, as with many regulators, Ofcom and the PSA are encountering the reality of regulation, where a broad-brush approach is compelling in theory but potentially harmful in practice. As such, the new approach is that there are 24 conditions

12 PhonepayPlus, 'Check if you need permission to set up a premium rate service' (2012) https://web.archive.org/web/20150206073101/ www.phonepayplus.org.uk/For-Business/Prior-permission.aspx

13 PhonepayPlus, 'Live services list of current exemptions from prior permission' (2011) https://web.archive.org/web/20150206073101/ www.phonepayplus.org.uk/For-Business/~/media/Files/PhonepayPlus/Prior_permission/Prior_permission_Live_services_exemptions.pdf

14 PhonepayPlus, 'Review of prior permission conditions for consumer credit services operating on premium rate' (2014) http://psauthority.org.uk/News-And-Events/News/2014/12/~/media/Files/PhonepayPlus/News%202014/Final%20statement%20on%20consumer%20credit%20services_Nov_2014.pdf

for special situations; there is no longer a requirement to seek authorisation, but notification is required, as is compliance with the special conditions.[15]

New areas for PRS

Apps

PSA guidance on PRS regulation and app payments applies familiar PRS issues (e.g. making the charge and future charges clear, disclosing exchange rates and expiry dates concerning virtual currency) in the app environment, where payment is by means of PRS.[16] A specific warning is issued that 'informing consumers of the price of extra items at the start of a video game or virtual world, and then charging them without further consent as soon as their avatar makes contact with extra items within the service' needs positive, auditable advance consent (including the likely charges), if a finding of breach is to be avoided.

The PSA Tribunal has issued fines against a number of PRS providers using apps. The first significant case concerned 'Battery Booster UK', an Android app which after (free) download generated SMS messages to a premium rate shortcode (i.e. sent by the user's phone). The terms and conditions of the app included the ability to send and receive SMS messages, but the document contained no reference to the premium rate service 'subscribed' to (for video clips). Multiple Code violations were found, and the provider was fined £135,000.[17] In another case, agreeing to download an app (through two pages, the first being the correct Android page and the second designed by the provider) triggered a chargeable text message with little notice to the consumer that any charge would apply.[18] Code provisions breached in these cases included rules on pricing (e.g. failure to provide clear information before a purchase is made, applying a charge without proof of consent, omitting the required reminders for subscription services), and the general rule against misleading the consumer.

ICSS

The PSA has handled a body of work relating to what are termed 'information, connection and/or signposting services' (ICSS). These services became controversial because many of them are advertised through search engines, and offered

15 Ofcom, 'Approval of the PhonepayPlus Code of Practice (13th edition)' (n 11) 28–9.

16 Phone-paid Services Authority, 'Application-based payments' (2016) http://psauthority.org.uk/-/media/Files/PSA/For-Businesses/Guidance-and-compliance/Explore-our-guidance/Guidance-files/01_App-based-payments.ashx?la=en. Limited exemptions were available on a trial basis: http://psauthority.org.uk/-/media/Files/PhonepayPlus/News-Items/2015Aug/Notification-of-exemption-for-app-developers-and-app-stores.ashx?la=en.

17 Case 852607 *mBlox* (9 June 2011). A similar service was the subject of a later case: Case 01921 *Echovox* (1 September 2011). All decisions of the Tribunal referred to in this chapter can be accessed at www.psauthority.org.uk/

18 Case 06161 *Connect Ltd t/a SMSBill* (16 August 2012); fine of £50,000.

access to services that were already available at free or low cost, or provided information easily accessible through other means. Examples include services connecting a user to an official application service or helpline, or providing contact details for public bodies and major private companies. One body (the Driving Standards Agency as it was then known) highlighted how in December 2012, a majority of calls made to it by the general public came through gateways of this or similar types.[19] Press coverage highlighted the complaints of consumers who had searched for a term via Google, seen the prominent advertisement placed by the PRS provider, and called the PRS number, thereby incurring unnecessary additional costs;[20] this formed part of a wider set of practices, which also included websites charging higher fees for the submission of online applications to public authorities (i.e. beyond the scope of PRS regulation).

As with apps, where this business model made use of PRS, a particularly strong form of regulation became possible. For instance, the PSA was able to note the increase in complaints, and that standard methods of enforcement were proving ineffective. Its Tribunal sanctioned a number of service providers.[21] Then, after two consultations[22] and further research, it reclassified most ICSS as requiring prior permission.[23]

PRS as a payment mechanism

Some forms of premium rate service have been the subject of significant market change in recent years. While some consumers identify that PRS have value (including anonymity and discretion), and continue to use landlines rather than mobile in order to avoid higher charges for accessing PRS by mobile, the broader shift to mobile and to the accessibility of Internet content via smartphone started to

19 PhonepayPlus, 'Further assessment of information, connection and/or signposting services: final statement' (2013) http://psauthority.org.uk/~/media/Files/PhonepayPlus/Consultation-PDFs/ICSS/ICSS-statement–31-July-2013.pdf [2.5].

20 Miles Brignall, 'Google Adword: beware copycat websites in paid-for search results' *Guardian* (London, 1 June 2013) www.theguardian.com/money/2013/jun/01/google-adword-copycat-websites-search-results

21 See for example case 10748 *ITS Technical* (22 November 2012); case 18936 *Book Your Theory Test Ltd* (16 May 2013).

22 PhonepayPlus, 'Review of information, connection and/or signposting services: consultation' (2012) http://psauthority.org.uk/-/media/Files/PhonepayPlus/Consultation-PDFs/ICSS/ICSS-Consultation-Document.pdf; PhonepayPlus, 'Further assessment of information, connection and/or signposting services: a public consultation' (2013) http://psauthority.org.uk/-/media/Files/PhonepayPlus/Consultation-PDFs/CD_ICSS_24_April_2013.pdf

23 PhonepayPlus (as it then was) did face the possibility of judicial review of its ICSS provisions, but the case was settled in April 2014, with a number of changes to the draft provisions being made by the organisation. See PhonepayPlus, 'Further assessment of ICSS' (6 December 2013) http://psauthority.org.uk/for-business/public-consultations/past-consultations/further-assessment-of-icss (suspension of implementation); PhonepayPlus, 'ICSS update' (24 April 2014) http://psauthority.org.uk/-/media/Files/PhonepayPlus/Consultation-PDFs/ICSS/ICSS_Update_April_2014.pdf (amendments and end of suspension).

have a major impact around five years ago.[24] After that initial shift to mobile and smartphone, there has also been a general decline in the use of SMS,[25] influenced by the availability of alternatives that are free to the user, such as WhatsApp and social networking sites.

There is, however, an emerging role for PRS as a more general payment mechanism,[26] as compared with its conventional function as linked to specific, phone-delivered content, whether that be the earlier model of information and chat or the later emergence of voting, ringtones[27] and the like. By 2011 it was clear that the micropayments market was fragmenting, although the growth in popularity of apps presented new opportunities for payments – whether for the app itself or for in-app content.[28] In that year, the PSA and a number of trade associations wrote to the Government arguing that the PRS model could be useful for other forms of micropayment, and that there were risks associated with having a range of systems (framed in terms of weaker consumer protection and barriers to innovation).[29] The development of the 'Payforit' service, an initiative of the UK mobile phone companies which allowed for the charging of goods and services to a mobile phone bill, offered some potential; it fell squarely within the statutory definition of a PRS, and Ofcom exercised its discretion (in the face of sustained criticism from industry) in 2012 to regulate it as controlled PRS.[30] However, to date it has seen very low consumer awareness.[31]

24 BDRC Continental, 'Consumer engagement with PRS, 2012–3' (2013) http://psauthority.org.uk/For-Business/Research/~/media/Files/PhonepayPlus/Research/Consumer%20Research/2013_Consumer_Engagement_with_PRS_2012_2013.pdf

25 Deloitte, 'The future for phone-paid digital goods and services' (2014) http://psauthority.org.uk/For-Business/~/media/Files/PhonepayPlus/Research/Nov2014_Deloitte_research.pdf 4

26 PhonepayPlus, 'Business Plan and Budget 2014/15' (2013) http://psauthority.org.uk/~/media/Files/PhonepayPlus/Consultation-PDFs/STATEMENT-ON-BUSINESS-PLAN-201415-PUBLISHED.pdf 12

27 In the first decade of the twenty-first century, this was both a successful business model and an area where violations of the Code were found. See Simon Burlinson, 'Crazy for trying? Service providers beware – ICSTIS and the nature of premium rate service providers' (2006) 17(4) *Entertainment Law Review* 125; Sumanth S. Gopinath, *The ringtone dialectic: economy and cultural form* (MIT Press 2013) 134ff. Now, however, the market only amounts to 1% of what it was a decade ago: Deloitte (n 25) 4.

28 Analysys Mason, *The marketplace for and regulation of micropayment services in the UK* (2010) 31.

29 Alistair Graham, 'Letter to the Secretary of State for Culture, Media and Sport' (30 June 2011) http://old.culture.gov.uk/images/consultation_responses/CR2011-Phonepay_Plus.pdf

30 Ofcom, 'Review of premium rate services: decision on an application of the analytical framework' (2012) www.ofcom.org.uk/__data/assets/pdf_file/0019/46513/statement.pdf 40–60. Note however that Ofcom determined at the same time that it would not regulate 'portal content', a once-popular service provided by mobile phone companies for consumer access to audiovisual content through a platform operated by that company. It even noted, as a reason not to regulate, that video-on-demand (which was available on such portals) was separately regulated (the system discussed in Chapter 6).

31 PhonepayPlus, 'Annual market review 2015–16' (2016) http://psauthority.org.uk//media/Files/PhonepayPlus/Research/2016/AMR_PPP_Report2016.ashx?la=en

Across the board, though, it was possible by 2016 to attribute the 'mini-recovery' in the declining PRS market to PRS as a payment mechanism.[32] Research commissioned by the PSA identified digital content in the form of gaming apps (especially in-app purchases) and quasi-physical goods (such as travel tickets and parking fees) as particularly plausible, but was more sceptical regarding some digital content (ebooks and music), perhaps because of the existence of popular (and non-PRS) payment mechanisms in this sector already.[33] Charitable donations, however, have emerged as the largest single category of PRS.[34]

Abuse and enforcement

The PRS environment has proven to be susceptible to some quite specific forms of abuse. This demonstrates particular risks associated with the choice made by a consumer to engage with this format rather than another. It is also not without significance that PRS consumers are, compared to the population at large, twice as likely to be classed as vulnerable consumers.[35] The mutation of PRS into micropayments has also highlighted the role of the PSA as a regulator of services used by young people, including the risks associated with in-app purchases, banner ads, and the like.[36]

However, an assessment of abuse in the sector also demonstrates the significance of the existence of a regulatory regime, as the options for redress are much more extensive than they are for comparable Internet or smartphone-related exploitation. For instance, a provider of an Android VOD app was the subject of a small fine and reprimand in respect of errors,[37] and then in subsequent decisions on subscription policies, required to go through a preapproval process in order to ensure that the Code was being complied with.[38] This was only possible because the payment was by SMS; had the app been on a different platform (e.g. Apple) where payments are processed by the store operator with credit card details, the PRS enforcement system would not have had any relevance.

A 2012 report reviewed the range of technological and social abuses of PRS, including missed calls, deceptive links, and the installation of malicious software (e.g. which sends premium SMS).[39] One recent court decision, regarding the

32 Ibid.

33 Deloitte (n 25) 11–12.

34 PhonepayPlus, 'Annual market review 2015–16' (n 31).

35 PhonepayPlus, 'Vulnerability: a PhonepayPlus discussion document' (2015) http://psauthority.org.uk/-/media/Files/PhonepayPlus/Research/Vulnerability-discussion-document-2015.ashx?la=en 3

36 Ibid. 11.

37 Case 02896 *txtNation* (19 January 2012).

38 Case 06717 *Mobegen* (2 August 2012); Case 08458 *txtNation* (16 August 2012).

39 Nico Flores, Helen Karapandzic and Jyotin Chhatwal Roy, 'International-scale issues of non-compliance with premium-rate services: a report for PhonepayPlus' (2012) http://psauthority.org.uk//media/Files/PhonepayPlus/Research/International-Scale-issues-of-non-compliance-with-premium-rate-services.pdf

proportionality of sanctions, highlighted the use of ransomware by affiliate marketing companies (i.e. inducing users to download software which was said to assist with wifi hacking, but actually locked their browser and directing them to use a PRS in order to unlock it; in this case, doing so did not even result in unlocking).[40] The growth in popularity of in-app purchases, especially in apps directed at children, has also given rise to problems. For instance, one scheme involved fake versions of games (e.g. Angry Birds) supplied via Android app stores, where opening the app generated premium SMS (i.e. a subscription by SMS to a service where messages were received at high cost); the software also disabled notifications so the user was not aware that the messages were being sent or received.[41] More recent abuses have included the misleading presentation of buttons (e.g. the last in a series of yes/no quiz buttons being presented in a visually identical fashion but with the text and function of confirming a subscription) and the deceptive use of hyperlinks.[42] In general, the risks of mobile payments (whether PRS or otherwise) include non-delivery of content (or poor instructions on how to download), susceptibility to unauthorised purchases, poor disclosure of terms and conditions or data charges, and cancellation problems.[43]

In recent times, the PSA has identified the relationship between declines in the market and the attractiveness of scams to service providers,[44] while trust has proven to be a key factor in consumer decisions to stop using PRS, especially in the adult content sector.[45] Some consumers are expressing a preference for non-PRS micropayments.[46] Ofcom has also pointed to pressure within the market as a justification for the increase in permitted charges.[47]

Complaints can be made to the PSA or it can instigate its own investigations. Two investigation procedures are available, as set out in section 4.3 of the Code. The track 1 procedure is typically used when there is little or no consumer harm or where the provider has no history of breaches, and requires the provider to follow an action plan determined by the PSA. Under track 2 (which includes cases where the use of track 1 is disputed), the service provider has an opportunity to respond to the PSA's initial findings, and the matter is referred to a

40 *R (Ordanduu and Optimus Mobile)* v. *PhonepayPlus* [2015] EWHC 50 (Admin).

41 PhonepayPlus, 'Children as connected consumers' (2013) http://psauthority.org.uk/-/media/Files/PhonepayPlus/Research/Children-as-connected-consumers.ashx?la=en 11

42 Craft Strategy, 'A study of consumer journeys relating to online competition and adult PRS' (2016) http://psauthority.org.uk/-/media/Files/PhonepayPlus/Research/2016/Summary-report-on-A-study-of-consumer-journeys-relating-to-online-competition-and-adult-PRS.ashx?la=en

43 Analysys Mason (n 28) 76.

44 PhonepayPlus, 'Business plan and budget 2014/15' (n 26).

45 Mobile Squared, 'The PRS consumer report: a report for PhonepayPlus' (2016) www.mobilesquared.co.uk/media/97469/15_5841_MobileSquared_Report_pages_v5–1-.pdf; Phonepay Plus, 'Annual market review 2015–16' (n 31).

46 Jigsaw Research, 'Understanding consumer journeys: premium rate service and micropayment markets' (2014) http://psauthority.org.uk/-/media/Files/PhonepayPlus/Research/Consumer-Research/PhonepayPlus-Consumer-Journey-February-2014.pdf

47 Ofcom, 'Approval of the PhonepayPlus Code of Practice (13th edition)' (n 11) [1.11].

Tribunal. Tribunal membership is drawn from a panel of up to 17 members, who do not have a commercial interest in PRS;[48] the panel must include a number of legally qualified members, as each tribunal must have one legally qualified member and two lay members.

The maximum penalty for a breach of section 120 is currently £250,000;[49] directions can also be issued to communications providers including that the provision of PRS be suspended.[50] The Consumer Rights Act 2015 amended these provisions, so as to clarify that in the event of multiple breaches (i.e. of various Code provisions), the maximum penalty can be applied to each breach.[51] A Tribunal also has a wide range of sanctions at its disposal, including formal warnings, fines, mandatory refunds for consumers, barring of services, and prohibitions on individuals.

Court decisions regarding the PSA confirm its own powers; for instance, it can take action to recover a debt (e.g. unpaid fines).[52] In *Andronikou*, it was held that the then Code allowed the PSA to recover revenue withheld from a service provider – but not revenue which had been directed to be withheld but was not in fact withheld. As such, the Code now provides that failure to withhold (either for the standard 30-day period applying to all network providers, or in accordance with a direction by the PSA for a longer period) can itself be the basis of a direction for payment (section 3.5.2).

A fast 'interim' procedure is available in appropriate cases including temporary remedies such as suspension;[53] at the other end of the process, Tribunal decisions can be reviewed (through application to the panel chair or their substitute and review by a differently constituted tribunal along the lines of judicial review e.g. irrationality).[54] The PSA and Tribunal are also subject to judicial review as public authorities.[55]

48 Under previous versions of the Code, some members of the Board of what was then PhonepayPlus would be members of the panel; this is no longer possible.

49 Communications Act 2003, s 123.

50 Communications Act 2003, s 124.

51 Consumer Rights Act 2015, s 80.

52 *ICSTIS* v. *Andronikou (liquidators of Allied Communications Ltd)* [2007] EWHC 2307 (Admin); *PhonepayPlus* v. *Ashraf* [2014] EWHC 4303 (Ch). See now Communications Act 2003, s 120(3) (za) (inserted by Consumer Rights Act, s 80) which confirms the powers of PhonepayPlus, on Ofcom's behalf, to enforce Code compliance; this clause was considered in *Ashraf* while it was before Parliament, but the High Court ultimately concluded that the enforcement of the decision and fine in Ashraf's case was justified by the existing provisions, although the new language was commended as clearer.

53 The then-applicable 'emergency procedure' under the Code was considered in *Ordanduu* (n 40), where the High Court found that the PSA's use of this procedure in a particular case was not in accordance with EU law, primarily on proportionality grounds (EU law was engaged because the service providers were established in Germany). A revised procedure now appears in section 4.6 of the Code (on 'interim measures').

54 In the 14th Code, this replaced a former procedure involving an Independent Appeals Body (IAB).

55 *Andronikou* (n 52); *R* v. *ICSTIS ex parte Firstcode* [1993] COD 325.

Overlapping regulation

So far, our focus has been on the characteristics of the PRS regulatory system and, to some extent, on the way in which questions of scope are dealt with (e.g. whether a particular service or business model meets the definition of PRS, or indeed whether it falls within a subcategory and must therefore follow particular rules). In this section, a different question is addressed. That is the extent to which the detailed, essentially self-contained approach discussed above might, in fact, be challenged or affected by other regulatory systems. Some of the examples here relate to a specific medium, while others are more general in nature. Even the general examples, though, may arise because of the fact that the technology used in PRS meets more than one definition. Attention to these issues of boundaries and demarcation can illustrate whether a medium-focused system can exist alongside other regulatory approaches.

The first example is the Electronic Commerce Directive, a broad piece of legislation on approaches to Internet regulation, dating from 2000. A second set of examples deals with content regulation, including the controversial link between PRS and television. A final section looks at broader consumer issues, in relation to privacy and payments.

PRS and the Electronic Commerce Directive

The E-Commerce Directive[56] provides a basic level of regulation for information society services. This includes some requirements to provide information, but also restricts the ability of member states to apply national rules to service providers within the scope of the Directive who are established in another member state.

This has the potential to affect the work of the PSA. In order to prevent infringement of the Directive, the application of the Code is restricted in the case that a controlled PRS is also an information society service. Such a situation arises where a service is accessed through the Internet, and is dealt with by section 5 of the Code. There are two restrictions of note. The first is that an additional threshold for regulation is applicable; services established in other member states are only covered if they are or may be accessed within the UK or if conditions for derogation are satisfied. The other is a general provision that gives priority to the Directive in case of conflict; the Code specifically mentions the Directive's prohibition on requiring certain service providers (intermediaries) to monitor content.[57]

The matter of derogation requires a little more attention. Derogation (i.e. applying national rules to service providers established in other member states) is permitted under the Directive if a member state finds it necessary to do so for reasons of public policy (e.g. the prevention of crime), security or protecting

56 Directive 2000/31/EC (n 10).
57 Ibid., art 15.

public health.[58] Normally, states must ask the other state concerned to act and only proceed if this did not resolve the problem, and also notify the European Commission. In urgent cases, the derogating state can act first and communicate with the other state and the Commission afterwards.[59]

This option has only been exercised on isolated occasions and not by all member states. Nonetheless, the UK has notified the European authorities of its derogation in relation to two separate providers of dialler software, which had both violated rules on payment information and made reference to unlawful sexual activity in advertising. Although the service providers were established in other member states, they were fined and prevented from operating in the UK.[60] A more difficult situation arose in *Ordanduu*,[61] where although the PSA subsequently argued that it was covered by the provisions on urgent derogation, no specific reference had been made to the Directive or its provisions in the initial process. Moreover, the court found that it could not be justified in the case in question because too many discrete issues were taken together, and necessity could not be demonstrated.

PRS and broadcasting law

In 2006–2007, various broadcasters came under criticism for their use of PRS in various programmes.[62] This included competitions, voting, and the like, and in some cases challenges or lengthy programmes entirely dedicated to PRS-driven quizzes. (Some of these services may feel like interactive games, although the interaction is indirect as it typically involved two platforms – the broadcast and the associated communication via telephone or SMS.) A report to Ofcom and an inquiry by a committee of the House of Commons both criticised a range of practices, including deceiving consumers as to their chances of winning a competition or influencing a vote.[63] Some broadcasters were the subject of Ofcom fines (for breach of the Broadcasting Code), and the PSA also issued fines for breaches under its jurisdiction.

The current Broadcasting Code requires that competitions and voting be conducted fairly, with the cost of services made clear; broadcasters must ensure that the PSA Code is complied with.[64] Licences to operate television services, in

58 Ibid., art 3(4).

59 Ibid., art 3(5).

60 Julia Hörnle, 'Country of origin regulation in cross border media: one step beyond the freedom to provide services?' (2005) 54 *International and Comparative Law Quarterly* 89, 106–7; Alex Kirkhope, 'I just called to say … a review of the regulation of premium rate phone services in the UK' (2003) 9 *Computer and Telecommunications Law Review* 93, 94.

61 See n 40.

62 Marsden (n 3) 137–8.

63 House of Commons Culture, Media and Sport Committee, *Call TV quiz shows* (HC 72, 2006–2007); Richard Ayre, 'Report of an inquiry into television broadcasters' use of premium rate telephone services in programmes' (2007) www.ofcom.org.uk/__data/assets/pdf_file/0020/42914/report.pdf

64 See also Ofcom, 'The use of non-geographic numbers in broadcasting' (2014) www.ofcom.org.uk/__data/assets/pdf_file/0021/55452/statement.pdf

addition, specifically provide that the broadcaster is responsible for audience interaction and for PSA compliance – and third party verification is also mandatory where PRS is used. PRS must not be used other than as a subsidiary purpose; if the PRS is the primary purpose (as discussed below) it is classified as a type of advertising. Ofcom has also acted to allow the use of apps as payment mechanisms as a substitute for PRS; the Broadcasting Code does generally stipulate that payment for interaction (with television services) must be via PRS or by 'other telephony services for which the revenue is shared' between the broadcaster and others, so specific action was required in respect of an new non-PRS model.[65] In some cases where PRS use was extensive for some years, the use of apps and free voting has been favoured by broadcasters as a way to promote engagement.[66]

Programmes that primarily promote a PRS (or other paid interaction with viewers), as compared with programmes that merely make use of PRS, are classified as a type of commercial communication under the Audiovisual Media Services Directive,[67] and are labelled by Ofcom as 'participation TV' (PTV).[68] This means that the rules on acceptable content are found in the code of practice of the Broadcast Committee of Advertising Practice (albeit enforced by Ofcom rather than the Advertising Standards Authority, which normally polices BCAP compliance in the first instance), and the scheduling requirements of the code on the scheduling of television advertising (also handled by Ofcom). PTV services operate in sectors such as 'adult chat', gambling, and quizzes, often obtaining a significant proportion of their income from PRS revenue.[69]

This change required an amendment to be made to the BCAP Code. Otherwise, a general rule on television advertising would have made PTV in two fields (adult chat and 'psychic' services) unlawful. As such, the BCAP Code now contains specific content provisions for 'telecommunications-based sexual entertainment services', including restrictions on timing (after midnight or 9 pm on digital terrestrial (Freeview) and other platforms respectively), and carriage (encryption and/or the organisation of an electronic programme guide); specific rules for psychic services also apply.

Questions also arise regarding the regulation of PRS content. As discussed throughout this book, the matter of regulating sexually explicit material is typically where specific action may be thought desirable – especially when platforms are compared. This is a particularly tricky issue in PRS, given the long association between PRS and access to material not readily available through other means. Successive PRS codes have however offered some form of content

65 Broadcast Bulletin 186 (18 July 2011).

66 Deloitte (n 25) 4.

67 Case C-195/06 *Kommunikationsbehörde* v. *ORF* [2007] ECR I-8817.

68 Ofcom, 'Participation TV: regulatory statement, rules on the promotion of premium rate services' (2010) www.ofcom.org.uk/__data/assets/pdf_file/0025/55708/statement.pdf

69 Damian Tambini, Danilo Leonardi and Christopher Marsden, *Codifying cyberspace: communications self-regulation in the age of Internet convergence* (Routledge 2008) 219.

regulation, through general requirements such as that services not cause harm or reasonable offence, and specific requirements for sexual entertainment services[70] in terms of age verification and promotion.[71] Over the course of a few months in late 2016, for instance, large fines were imposed on a number of providers of 'glamour' video services, including one maximum fine of £500,000 for supplying false logs to the PSA and a failure to ensure that consumers had consented to PRS charges.[72] Indeed, recent work by the PSA highlights the challenges here. Its current work on special conditions, for instance, notes an upcoming review of whether material that the BBFC would rate at 18 is being offered to younger audiences by PRS proviers.[73] Again, the availability of PRS as a payment mechanism is a factor; if an online streaming or download service is paid for through PRS rather than a credit card, the PRS regulatory system (and indeed the special conditions applicable to online adult services) applies, above and beyond the voluntary systems discussed in other chapters, e.g. BBFC Online.

Other provisions

Privacy and financial services law are also engaged by the PRS business model – both in terms of consumer protection. First, there is the potential for conflict between the specific rules on PRS and the broader regulation of commercial messaging under the Privacy and Electronic Communications Directive.[74] This Directive governs the conditions under which emails and (of relevance here) SMS messages can be sent to consumers, with certain prohibitions of unsolicited messages. The PSA Code, on the other hand, requires confirmation by SMS of (for instance) pricing and subscription information where a transaction begins with the inputting of a telephone number on a website (whether by the consumer or by someone else). This issue required discussions between the PSA and the Information Commissioner (the public authority charged with enforcing the Directive in the UK), clarifying that the ICO would treat certain information provided in pursuit of PSA Code compliance as a service message rather than an

70 This is a PRS-specific definition adopted by Ofcom: 'entertainment service of a clearly sexual nature, or any service for which the associated promotional material is of a clearly sexual nature, or indicates directly, or implies, that the service is of a sexual nature'.

71 These provisions are found in the Code (e.g. s 2.3.7 on taking 'all reasonable steps to … prevent use by those under 18') and also in special conditions for online adult services and live entertainment and chat services.

72 Case 72142 *Tijamobile* (22 December 2016). See also, for instance, case 77718 *Skybytes* (9 November 2016) (consent to charge); case 72416 *Marketbybrand* (15 December 2016) (consent to charge and requirement to remind subscribers of spend monthly and when caps are exceeded).

73 Phone-paid Services Authority, 'Statement on introducing special conditions for online competition services and online adult premium rate services' (2016) http://psauthority.org.uk/-/media/Files/PSA/News-and-Events/News/2016/November/Statement-on-introducing-Special-conditions-for-online-competition-services–online-adult-premium-rate-services-FINAL-30–11–2016.ashx?la=en [3.5].

74 Directive 2002/58/EC of 12 July 2002 concerning the processing of personal data and the protection of privacy in the electronic communications sector [2002] OJ L201/37.

unlawful commercial communication.[75] Although the issue was resolved, it highlighted the potential for inconsistency between the specific rules of the PRS regulatory system and the broader scope (albeit still medium-based in that it related to SMS) of the law on privacy.

Second, the Payment Services Directive (recently reviewed, with the new version due to be implemented by January 2018)[76] includes a definition of payment institutions and sets thresholds for regulation. Of note to the PRS sector is the exclusion for the 'purchase of digital content and voice-based services, regardless of the device used for the purchase or consumption of the digital content and charged to the related bill' and 'performed from or via an electronic device and charged to the related bill within the framework of a charitable activity or for the purchase of tickets'. These exclusions only apply to transactions of up to €50 (or €300 per month), but they are expected to lead to an increase in the charging of low-value items to phone bills through various means. This law means a number of different things for PRS. On the one hand, it serves to promote the use of PRS (and therefore bringing more service providers into the PSA's remit) through offering regulatory forbearance for a business model that is primarily but not exclusively within the definition of PRS. On the other, it uses a different set of definitions and caps, which may, in time, require the PSA and Ofcom to adopt similar approaches (although the UK's planned exit from the European Union may be a factor).

Conclusion

Despite its beginnings as a response to a distant set of circumstances relating to telephone call charges in the 1980s, the potential for overlap with a range of other and sometimes better-known regulatory mechanisms, and a threatened collapse in the business more than once, the system for regulating PRS has survived to the present day. Not only that, but it has proven a convenient response to potentially harmful situations in emerging markets. The problem is, of course, that in today's marketplace, it is almost accidental whether a problem is governed by the elaborate mechanism for PRS or is left to the general law and to the willingness of (often) an intermediary to assist a disappointed user. It is not as unreasonable as it first sounds to suggest that a system akin to that of the PSA could be created for other areas, such as apps.[77] If this would draw an arbitrary

75 Phone-paid Services Authority, 'Clarity of information to be provided to consumers via text messages following mobile number entry into online promotions' (2017) http://psauthority.org.uk/-/media/Files/PSA/For-Businesses/Guidance-and-compliance/Compliance-updates/Clarity-of-information-to-be-provided-to-consumers-via-text-messages-following-mobile-number-entry-into-online-promotions-16–01–2017.ashx?la=en

76 Directive 2015/2366 of 25 November 2015 on payment services in the internal market [2015] OJ L337/35.

77 I made this suggestion in work focused on the problems of regulating the app market: Daithí Mac Síthigh, 'App law within: rights and regulation in the smartphone age' (2013) 21 *International Journal of Law and Information Technology* 154, 178.

line between regulated and unregulated, this would be the moving of a line rather than it being conjured out of thin air. The PRS system also demonstrates that regulating within a particular medium (or a particular use of more than one medium) can be feasible, because it is calibrated to work within the particular conditions of that medium.

8 That's entertainment?

Introduction

Licensing legislation across the UK provides for a whole serious of inclusions and exclusions that depend on concepts (often undefined in the legislation) such as plays, music and even Morris dancing. In England and Wales, the Licensing Act 2003 (LA2003) consolidated close to a century's worth of legislation on alcohol, entertainment and various activities; throughout the twentieth century, the control of entertainment saw a range of statutes adopted to respond to particular problems or control certain aspects of entertainment and of the related question of the consumption of alcohol. Arguably based on assumptions about disorder and danger in urban life (especially working-class life),[1] these provisions had, by the twentieth century, become a series of overlapping provisions, pursuing diverse goals, open to circumvention or having unexpected effects. As such, a landmark project of licensing and entertainment law reform[2] culminated in the 2003 Act.

LA2003 was already discussed in brief in Chapter 3, as the successor to the Cinematograph Acts on the regulation of cinemas and the ultimate legal basis for the enforceability of BBFC classification. It is at the heart of this chapter, however, because it demonstrates how socially and commercially significant decisions such as whether advance permission is required to run a particular activity depend so much (even after reform and 'deregulation') on the medium of communication. It also highlights the link between a medium and the effects and meanings attributed to it – by users and by regulators.

The Licensing Act

General approach

LA2003 deals with 'regulated entertainment' in England and Wales, where one needs a licence to put on that entertainment (indoors or outdoors) if it takes place

1 Paul Chatterton and Robert Hollands, *Urban nightscapes: youth cultures, pleasure spaces and corporate power* (Routledge 2003) 47–8.

2 Home Office, *Time for reform: proposals for the modernisation of our licensing laws* (Cm 4696, 2000).

in the presence of an audience, for the public or (where there is a charge with a view to profit) in private.[3] The main form of regulated entertainment specified in premises licences has been music.[4] Entertainment is, in turn, one of four broad classes of licensable activity; the others relate to the sale or supply of alcohol and the late-night provision of food and drink. Essentially the statutory requirement (across all classes) is for the licensing of premises; a licence may refer to more than one activity (e.g. selling alcohol and putting on dance performances). Licences are issued by licensing authorities (in essence, local authorities) and last, subject to continued payment of an annual fee, until they are revoked or given up. Licences can also be varied. Temporary event notices (TENs) can be used instead of premises licences for occasional events. Decisions regarding licences and their conditions are made in pursuit of four licensing objectives: preventing crime and disorder, preventing public nuisance, promoting public safety, protecting children from harm.[5] There is an effective presumption in favour of granting licences – e.g. refusal is only possible if there is a valid objection relating to at least one of the objectives.

Exceptions

Conscious of the need to avoid classing too many activities as regulated and therefore only capable of being done in duly licensed premises, the drafters of LA2003 included a wide range of exceptions. For instance, the 'exhibition of a film' is regulated, but not where it 'consists of or forms part of an exhibit put on show for any purposes of a museum or art gallery'.[6] As, for instance, an art gallery is not itself within the scope of LA2003, including a film within an exhibition in a gallery would not mean that the said gallery would require a premises licence.

Some exceptions single out a whole genre or category. For instance, 'a performance of morris dancing or any dancing of a similar nature',[7] or the playing of music (live or recorded) as part of that performance, was exempted from the 2003 Act. Acts of worship, and activities in places of public religious worship, also fall outside of the licensing regime;[8] this is an example of an exclusion that relates to the motive or purpose, the location, and also the content.

LA2003 has also been amended, with the explicit aim of removing certain activities from the ambit of the legislation. This has been done by standalone primary legislation and as part of broader legislative reform (ultimately by statutory instrument). The Department for Culture, Media and Sport summarises these changes as removing 'unnecessary burdens for lower risk entertainment

3 Licensing Act 2003, s 1; sch 1, para 1.

4 Home Office, *Post-legislative scrutiny of the Licensing Act 2003* (Cm 9278, 2016) [211].

5 Licensing Act 2003, s 4(2).

6 Licensing Act 2003, sch 1, para 6.

7 Licensing Act 2003, sch 1, para 11.

8 Licensing Act 2003, sch 1, para 9; see also, to similar effect in Northern Ireland, Local Government (Miscellaneous Provisions) (Northern Ireland) Order 1985, SI 1985/1208, sch 1, para 1(3)(a).

activities which might otherwise hamper cultural and community creativity' and facilitating diversification by providers.[9] In order to understand the impact of these changes, we will now consider a number of forms of entertainment, setting out the degree to which various activities are now exempted from the licensing requirements.

Theatre

The 2003 Act incorporated theatre-specific provisions that had already become law through the Theatres Act 1968, thereby abolishing the concept of the theatre licence. Through the 1968 Act, the focus of regulation shifted from the regulation of content on the stage to aspects of the physical venue. Until then, the infamous role of the Lord Chamberlain as approver of scripts (with a particular concern to prevent the portrayal of the living or recently dead[10]), originally set out in the Licensing Act 1737 and Theatres Act 1843, had remained in place, albeit circumvented at times through the use of 'club' performances which were not considered to be public performances.[11]

While LA2003 preserved these principles, the regulation of the medium has (in common with a number of other forms of communication discussed in this chapter) been revisited in later years. In 2013, the performance of a play or of dance to an audience of up to 500 people between 8 am and 11 pm became exempt.[12] In Scotland, theatre licensing was not brought into the broader public entertainment licensing system until 2015. This means that (as discussed in more detail below) individual local authorities in Scotland can now determine the extent to which the performance of plays will require a licence.

Definitions of theatre and of dance have been at issue in entertainment law for many years. In the eighteenth century, courts had to establish whether the then-popular performance of 'tumbling' constituted 'other entertainment of the stage', for the purposes of the 1737 legislation on theatres.[13] It took a narrow approach and found that the answer was no, because the legislation was penal in nature and should therefore not extend to performances not contemplated by Parliament, and unenforceable because a script could not be sent for approval. In doing so, the court rejecting an early version of a convergence argument made by counsel – that a goal of the legislation was to 'prevent the assembling together of a large number of the lower orders of the people in place of public entertainment, without regard to the particular thing to be represented'. Multimedia entertainment did however face some challenges. Under the Disorderly Houses Act 1751, it was found that a venue

9 Home Office, *Post-legislative scrutiny of the Licensing Act 2003* (n 4) [188].
10 Chris Megson, 'The Theatres Act (1968), documentary theatre and the actor's "overwhelming reality"' (2011) 31 *Studies in Theatre and Performance* 137.
11 David Thomas, David Carlton and Anne Etienne, *Theatre censorship: from Walpole to Wilson* (Oxford University Press 2007) 186 (club performances), 206ff. (introduction of Theatres Bill).
12 Licensing Act 2003 (Descriptions of Entertainment) (Amendment) Order, SI 2013/1578.
13 *R* v. *Handy* (1795) 101 ER 556.

licensed only for music could not put on a divertissement ballet where two dancers performed on stage.[14] The court noted that 'a house kept for public music … is totally different in its effect from a house kept for public dancing', highlighting that 'mischief does sometimes arise' in the latter case. The 1968 Act stipulated that a play is a 'dramatic piece' (which could include improvisation, and meant the 'playing of a role' by the performer(s), through speech, song, or action) or a ballet.

Specific forms of theatre, or more precisely how to categorise specific forms of entertainment as theatre or otherwise, continue to provoke debate. For instance, questions have arisen as to the status of stand-up comedy. Recent consultations in England and Wales noted that performances by comedians are already beyond the scope of LA2003[15] (although often regulated in practice by being in venues licensed to serve alcohol), while the recent review of entertainment law in Northern Ireland included a recommendation that 'comedy events such as stand up comedians' be confirmed as within the regulation of 'theatrical performances'.[16] Another specific issue relates to hypnotism, because it is the subject of specific legislation adopted in response to allegations that hypnotism can cause harm to participants. The Hypnotism Act 1952 vests local authorities with the responsibility of regulating performances, although an exception exists for science, research, and treatment. Again, the Northern Ireland review group proposed that hypnotism should be regulated as a form of theatre.

Music

An example of the primary legislative route for new exceptions is the Live Music Act 2012, which started life as a Private Member's Bill in the House of Lords (based on two previous, unsuccessful PMBs, but this time with Government support). Music had been a contentious area during the passage of LA2003,[17] and a major review of the Act concluded that it had proven to have a

14 *Brown* v. *Nugent* (1871–1872) LR 7 QB 588.

15 Department for Culture, Media and Sport, 'Regulated entertainment: a consultation proposal to examine the deregulation of Schedule One of the Licensing Act 2003' (2011) www.gov.uk/government/uploads/system/uploads/attachment_data/file/72904/consultation_deregulation-scheduleone_2011_vs2.pdf [3.23]; House of Commons Regulatory Reform Committee, *Draft Legislative Reform (Entertainment Licensing) Order 2014* (HC 742, 2014–5) 14.

16 Entertainment Licensing Review Group (Northern Ireland), 'Entertainment licensing review' (2015) www.communities-ni.gov.uk/sites/default/files/consultations/doe/council-consultation-entertainment-licensing-review-2015.pdf [47].

17 'The newspaper coverage from this period suggests that the most contentious part of the Act at the time was not the prospect of "twenty-four hour drinking" but the changes made to the rules regarding the provision of live music' (Henry Yeomans, 'Spirited measures and Victorian hangovers: public attitudes to alcohol, the law and moral regulation' (PhD, University of Plymouth 2012) 240). But see also Phil Hadfield, *Bar wars: contesting the night in contemporary British cities* (Oxford University Press 2006) 3 (on the significance of Labour's manifesto promises and text message campaigning re licensing hours); Phil Hubbard, *Cities and sexualities* (Routledge 2012) 138 (on the conflict between the declared aims to promote a more relaxed atmosphere through licensing reform, and the corporate, high-volume dimension aspects of licensed premises after deregulation).

negative impact on the availability of music in small venues.[18] The Act as amended now provides that live music is exempt from regulation in a venue licensed to serve alcohol.[19] This arises more often than one might imagine, as it is up to the applicant whether to specific various forms of entertainment when they apply. So, it is perfectly plausible that a pub owner would have applied for a premises licence without specifying music as one of the activities proposed,[20] or would have avoided doing so or been required to do so in light of possible or actual neighbour objections.[21] Nonetheless the exemption is conditional, in that it only applies at certain times of the day (8 am–11 pm) and to smaller venues in the case of amplified music (originally with a capacity of 200, subsequently raised to 500). Moreover, it is possible for a licence to be required, and conditions imposed, in respect of music after the premises licence is reviewed. The Act also provided a new exemption for unamplified music outside alcohol licensed venues, again between 8 am and 11 pm.[22]

It is easy to see how the legislation is justified by its proponents by reference to concepts of medium and of cultural significance. The Bill's proposer, Lord Clement-Jones, asked his colleagues to compare 'the freedom to show large-screen broadcasts of football matches in pubs without a licence' with the then-position of live music. Showing television broadcasts is indeed exempted, as discussed in more detail in Chapter 3 in the context of livecasts[23] (although the underlying content is regulated under broadcasting legislation).

An example of the alternative route is the Legislative Reform (Entertainment Licensing) Order 2014 (see also Chapter 3, where this Order was discussed in the context of cinema licensing). This Order utilised a broad power granted by the Legislative and Regulatory Reform Act 2006 for statutory instruments to amend primary legislation, where doing so would remove or reduce a legislative burden.

This even revisited what had just been changed by the Live Music Act two years previously. In particular, the original facilitation of 'live' music was

18 House of Commons Culture, Media and Sport Committee, *The Licensing Act 2003* (HC 492, 2008–9) [86–9].

19 Licensing Act 2003, s 177A; Licensing Act 2003, sch 1, para 12A; both as inserted by Live Music Act 2012.

20 There was, in theory, the protection of Licensing Act 2003, s 177, which provided for the disapplication of conditions regarding on music in small venues, although this was of limited value as it was only operative where music had been included in the activities listed in the licence application.

21 A common objection not to the licence per se but to the inclusion of music as a potential noise nuisance is noted in Steven Cammiss and Colin Manchester, 'Application process and decision-making under the Licensing Act 2003' [2011] 4 *Web Journal of Current Legal Issues* 4, http://webjcli.ncl.ac.uk/2011/issue4/cammiss4.html

22 Licensing Act 2003, sch 1, para 12C, as inserted by Live Music Act 2012. In terms of amplified music (live or recorded), an exemption for certain premises (e.g. community premises, local authority premises), for up to 500 people and between 8 am–11 pm, is now also available by way of Licensing Act 2003, sch 1, para 12ZB, as inserted by Legislative Reform (Entertainment Licensing) Order 2014, SI 2014/3253.

23 Licensing Act 2003, sch 1, para 8.

amended to 'live or recorded', broadening the exemption even further. It is now possible for venues not licensed for music to host, for instance, a broader range of DJ sets.[24]

On one hand, this goes well beyond the arguments for the LMA, which was framed in terms of restoring something in the spirit of the pre-LA2003 system (the 'two in a bar' rule, whereby no licence was required for 'music and singing' by 'not more than two performers',[25] whether amplified or not) and promoting the 'starters' in the music industry; as argued during the Parliamentary consideration of the LMA, many young artists got their foot on the music industry ladder through pub performances.[26]

The consultation on the 2014 changes also disclosed concerns that extending the exemption to recorded music would mean that venues would be more likely to put on activities that would disturb neighbours. The target of this approach is easily identified from the explanatory document prepared by the sponsoring department – because 'recorded music events have in the past been more prone to noise and public order problems from unscrupulous operators (e.g. pop-up parties/raves in unoccupied property)',[27] it is only recorded music events in licensed premises that are exempted. On the other hand, the change can be seen as belated recognition that 'liveness' is a poor proxy for that which deserves support within 'music' – challenging the medium-led assumptions that underpinned the LMA.

Circuses

The 2014 package of changes also created a new exception in respect of circuses.[28] This had already emerged as a consequence of the 2003 Act, where circuses and travelling theatres had complained that the new approach to licensing premises made it difficult for performances in this form to happen (because of,

24 Current guidance holds that 'The performance of a DJ who is merely playing tracks would not be classified as live music, but it might if he or she was performing a set which largely consisted of mixing recorded music in a live performance to create new sounds; this would include "scratching"': Home Office, *Revised Guidance issued under section 182 of the Licensing Act 2003* (2015) [15.30].

25 Licensing Act 1964, s 182.

26 The proposer, Lord Clement-Jones, quoted the same statement of John Whittingdale (as chair of the Commons Culture, Media and Sport Committee) on each of the three occasions he introduced the Bill: 'Young musicians often get their first break through performing live at small venues' (e.g. HL Deb 15 January 2010, vol. 716, col. 749). Others made similar arguments in both Houses, e.g. 'Many of our biggest selling British artists started out by playing gigs in pubs' (Lord Colywn): HL Deb 4 March 2011, vol. 725, col. 1321; 'The old saying is that rock stars have to start in the pubs before doing the stadiums' (David Morris MP): Live Music Bill Deb 14 December 2011, col. 11.

27 Department for Culture, Media and Sport, 'Legislative Reform (Entertainment Licensing) Order 2014: explanatory document' (2014) www.gov.uk/government/uploads/system/uploads/attachment_data/file/328492/Entertainment_Licensing_Legislative_Reform_Order_Explanatory_Document.pdf [3.13].

28 Licensing Act 2003, sch 1, para 12D.

for instance, last-minute site changes, and stipulations as to the length of temporary events).[29] A combination of encouraging local authorities to seek broad premises licences for public spaces, and an extension to the permitted length of temporary events, was considered to have addressed these problems.[30] However, the question was revisited in the 2014 changes (in light of what was said to be different approaches by different authorities as to whether circus performances constituted licensable activities, e.g. as plays, sport, etc.). The result was to put 'travelling circuses' beyond the legislation entirely. Entertainment (other than exhibiting films or putting on wrestling or boxing) 'that consists of or forms part of a performance by a travelling circus' now falls outside of LA2003, subject to a number of conditions. Some conditions are familiar from earlier reforms (e.g. between 8 am and 11 pm), while others relate specifically to the circus context (the entertainment takes place and the audience is accommodated within a moveable structure) and to the temporary nature (not on the same site for more than 28 consecutive days).

Note, in particular, that circus is defined by reference to its medium rather than its content – that it is in a moveable structure and does not stay on one site. The only content-focused dimension, to some extent, is the anti-avoidance measure that provides that a film or a boxing match does not become a circus simply because it meets the technical criteria. Of course, one can identify the cultural value of the circus by implication and from the DCMS supporting material. However, on the face of the statute, the circus is deserving of greater freedom from regulation because it is in a moveable structure.

A different road is taken in Northern Ireland, where a circus performance is treated as a form of indoor entertainment, by means of circuses being included in the definition of such.[31] In current discussions of modernising the entertainment licensing system, it is now being proposed that some of the scrutiny mechanisms be rationalised (e.g. a single set of checks on the tent itself, rather than repeat testing by each local authority, as the circus moves between areas), but that others remain within the purview of each authority (e.g. issues specific to a given site).[32] A related proposal was made by the Commons Culture, Media and Sport Committee in 2008 (i.e. before the broader exempting of circuses), when it suggested adapting the licensing model for cruise ships (licensing by a 'home' authority) to the position of circuses and other travelling entertainment.

An alternative approach: defining entertainment at the local level

In Scotland, entertainment is regulated under the Civic Government (Scotland) Act 1982, as amended. Under this statute, local authorities must opt in to requiring a licence for various classes of activity. One of those classes is found in s 41,

29 House of Commons Culture, Media and Sport Committee (n 18) [107–112].

30 Home Office, *Post-legislative scrutiny of the Licensing Act 2003* (n 4) [127].

31 Local Government (Miscellaneous Provisions) (Northern Ireland) Order 1985, sch 1, para 1(2)(c).

32 Entertainment Licensing Review Group (Northern Ireland) (n 16) 21–2.

on 'public entertainment', potentially requiring a licence for the use of a premises where 'members of the public are admitted or may use any facilities for the purposes of entertainment or recreation'. Until 2010, this was further qualified by a requirement of admission for money or money's worth. The initial exclusions are a mixture of the general (premises belonging to or occupied by any religious body while being used wholly or mainly for purposes connected with that body) and those to avoid double regulation (e.g. Theatres Act 1968, Cinemas Act 1985, and premises licensed for alcohol under the Licensing (Scotland) Act 2005 where the entertainment is specified in the operating plan[33]). Licences under the 1982 Act are valid for three years, or for a shorter period if so issued by the local authority.

Public entertainment is not further defined,[34] but when a local authority opts in to s 41, it will set out in a Public Entertainment Resolution what it means by public entertainment. As such, local authorities can and do set out, in more detail, the activities that requires its permission. These Resolutions are masterpieces of medium-specific law. The current resolution in the City of Edinburgh, for instance, mentions 'laser displays and games' and 'performing animals' as requiring a licence, but excludes exhibitions of art work (as an exception to the general requirement to get a licence for an exhibition).[35] A former version of Edinburgh's Resolution included 'Premises used for oral recitals including poetry reading and story telling' but this was deleted in recent years on the grounds that it was a low risk activity.[36] The localised system has also allowed some local authorities (but certainly not all) to license massage parlours/saunas, as part of a tacit acknowledgement of prostitution and sexual activities, taking an approach that licensing allows for inspection and some measure of control.[37]

Deregulation, reregulation and sexual entertainment

All of these reforms are happening while there is interest in greater regulation in certain sectors, most notably sexually explicit performances such as lap dancing. This led to a new category of licensing for England and Wales outside the 2003 Act, introduced in 2009 and in force from April 2010, for 'sexual entertainment

33 Although, the Air Weapons and Licensing (Scotland) Act 2015, s 75, amends this so that the exemption from entertainment licensing only applies to full premises licences, not occasional licences.

34 It is however still subject to limits, such as the finding that providing meals is not in itself entertainment: *Loosefoot Entertainment* v. *City of Glasgow District Licensing Board* 1991 SLT 843.

35 Edinburgh City Council, 'Public Entertainment Resolution' (2014) www.edinburgh.gov.uk/download/downloads/id/4189/public_entertainment_resolution.pdf

36 Edinburgh City Council Regulatory Committee, 'Public entertainment licensing: reommendations of member-officer working group' (2012) www.edinburgh.gov.uk/download/meetings/id/37139/item_6_1-public_entertainment_licensing-recommendations_of_the_member_officer_working_group

37 Phil Hubbard and others, 'Prostitution, gentrification, and the limits of neighbourhood space' in Rowland Atkinson and Gesa Helms (eds), *Securing an urban renaissance* (Policy Press 2007); see also *Scanlan* 1995 SLT Sh Ct 89.

venues' – although in practice venues now require both a LA2003 licence and a SEV licence.[38] Such had already been debated on an number of previous occasions, such as an unsuccessful amendment[39] proposed in the House of Lords in 2003 by Baroness O'Cathain, that would have added 'adult cabaret clubs' to the 1982 Act.[40] The 1982 Act as amended regulated 'sex encounter establishments' in London,[41] which did not normally cover lap dancing (under the 2003 Act, a premises licence meant that the premises could not be regulated as a sex encounter establishment); outside London, the 1982 Act only regulated sex shops and cinemas. Now, sexual entertainment venues sit alongside sex shops and sex cinemas as types of 'sex establishment'.

This now includes 'any live performance or any live display of nudity[42] which it must reasonably be assumed to be provided solely or principally for the purpose of sexually stimulating any member of the audience (whether by verbal or other means)'. Licensing authorities have greater powers over SEVs (for instance, they can refuse on the grounds that the activity would be inappropriate in light of the character of the locality, or can rule out licences in a particular area entirely) and licences must be renewed annually. Moreover, this change takes on greater significance if one notes how some of the types of entertainment that would have been how lap dancing was classified prior to the 2009 changes[43] have subsequently been removed from the ambit of LA2003.

Indeed, the history of the regulation of entertainment in the twentieth century saw an association between deregulation and freedom (e.g. Roy Jenkins' comment, regarding the Theatres Act 1968, that legislation on sexuality and abortion 'created a momentum which carried through into theatre censorship'[44]), although changes were also influenced by emergent disparities between media; in the case of the Theatres Act, this included the lack of any role for the Lord Chamberlain in respect of television[45] and an aborted plan to assign a role in respect of plays to the BBFC.[46]

This recalls the classic dilemma faced by Governments wishing to deregulate while also respond to pressure (internal or external) to 'do something' about controversial activities. In the 1980s, for instance, the regulatory system for cable television was designed to be a light touch one, but there were clear anxieties around the need to continue enforcing, for instance, broadcast-style standards of taste and

38 Policing and Crime Act 2009, s 27, amending Local Government (Miscellaneous Provisions) Act 1982.

39 See further Baptiste Coulmont and Phil Hubbard, 'Consuming sex: socio-legal shifts in the space and place of sex shops' (2010) 37 *Journal of Law and Society* 189.

40 HL Deb 17 July 2003, vol. 651, col. 996.

41 Greater London Council (General Powers) Act 1986.

42 Nudity is further defined as the exposure of the anus, genitals, pubic area or (female) nipples.

43 See for instance the discussion of the pre-2009 licensing of premises in Oxford for lap dancing: *R (Thompson)* v. *Oxford City Council* [2013] EWHC 1819 (Admin) [5]; *R (Thompson)* v. *Oxford City Council* [2014] EWCA Civ 94 [9].

44 Thomas, Carlton and Etienne (n 11) 182.

45 Ibid. 190.

46 Ibid. 196–7.

decency.[47] Similarly, the broad theme of deregulation in relation to telecommunications law comes into conflict with policy goals regarding high-speed broadband or consumer protection – not to mention the desire to co-opt intermediaries as enforcers of copyright or anti-terror laws.[48]

The specific difficulties of the 1982 Act can also be noted. As Hubbard argues, the regulatory tool is spatial rather than social, in that local authorities take a black box approach; 'whether the sexual entertainment is for a male/female, straight/gay audience is not considered relevant, and often not even explored'.[49] A second point made by Hubbard, that the 'nature of the performance' is disregarded (he notes that burlesque performances and "bump and grind" striptease are treated as equivalent'[50]), highlights a problem that has continued to cause difficulties for entertainment in some areas. For instance, Camden's adoption of a sex establishment policy drew criticism on the grounds of the impact it would have on burlesque venues by bringing them within the scope of the policy. (This pre-dated the 2009 Act; as noted above, 'sex encounter venues' were already the subject of regulation in London, where the venue was not separately regulated under LA2003.) Camden's current position is to explain that its policy could apply to burlesque, as the application of the 2009 Act 'shall depend on the content of the entertainment and not the name it is given', with decisions being made on a 'case by case basis'.[51] (There is a power for the Secretary of State to create exclusions from relevant entertainment, which has not yet been exercised.)

This debate also highlights something quite paradoxical in the 2009 Act, in that it creates a new and potentially judgmental regulatory category. This would mean (as the Equity union pointed out) that performers would be classed as working in sex establishments, with consequences for their safety and reputation;[52] a House of Commons Committee similarly expressed concerns that classifying lap dancing clubs as such could erroneously suggest that sex was for sale at such venues.[53] Moreover, the legislation could have the unintended consequence of encouraging the provision of the whole range of SEV entertainment

47 Timothy Hollins, *Beyond broadcasting: into the cable age* (British Film Institute 1984).

48 Daithí Mac Síthigh, 'The fragmentation of intermediary liability in the UK' (2013) 8 *Journal of Intellectual Property Law and Practice* 521.

49 Phil Hubbard, 'Law, sex and the city: regulating sexual entertainment venues in England and Wales' (2015) 7 *International Journal of Law in the Built Environment* 5, 14.

50 Ibid.

51 London Borough of Camden, 'Sex establishments policy' (2011) www.camden.gov.uk/ccm/cms-service/download/asset?asset_id=3189646 [91]. This language is identical to that found in a paragraph (in a more general context which does not specifically identify burlesque) in Home Office guidance on sexual entertainment venues, which has been incorporated into numerous local authority documents: Home Office, 'Sexual entertainment venues: guidance for England and Wales' (2010) http://webarchive.nationalarchives.gov.uk/20100413151441/http:/crimereduction.homeoffice.gov.uk/crimereduction057a.pdf [2.4].

52 Lalayn Baluch, 'Equity warns that "sex encounter establishment" branding will put dancers at risk' *The Stage* (London, 18 August 2009) www.thestage.co.uk/news/2009/equity-warns-that-sex-encounter-establishment-branding-will-put-dancers-at-risk/

53 House of Commons Culture, Media and Sport Committee (n 18) [122].

– as if a burlesque venue required a SEV licence, it would then be authorised to put on not just that, but also lap-dancing, peep shows and the like.[54] Indeed, this could also highlight a further dimension of Equity's argument, that if a broad approach to the new category were taken, it would bring in those who would contest that classification, and potentially be affected by that potential misclassification.

Beyond the Licensing Act

Busking is normally understood to fall outside of LA2003. As current Home Office guidance to local authorities sets out, the premises is not made available for the purposes of providing entertainment, and the entertainment is usually incidental (rather cruelly, this is explained by saying that 'there are few circumstances in which anyone would go out specifically to watch buskers').[55] Moreover, unamplified live music is no longer regulated entertainment, as discussed above.

The regulation of 'street music' exercised Parliament in the mid-nineteenth century[56] and has also been affected by the law on highways and on nuisance.[57] In present times, local authorities in Greater London have an optional power, under the London Local Authorities Act 2000, s 33, to require that busking ('the provision of entertainment in a street') be licensed, within the whole area of an authority or a particular part of that area. For the latter, it is clear that the adoption of the power needs to be justified by reference to the presence or likelihood of undue interference, inconvenience, or risk to street users, or nuisance to property occupiers. It is not clear whether the same justification is necessary in respect of an authority-wide exercise of the power.[58]

Camden's introduction of the licensing of busking (with an annual licence fee of £19, normally on standard conditions) was unsuccessfully challenged by the campaign group Keep Streets Live. The court countered a claim that the regulated class was unacceptably vague by reference to a dictionary definition of entertainment ('a form of activity that holds the attention and interest of an audience, or gives pleasure and delight'[59]). It also dismissed an argument that the policy violated Article 10 ECHR.

Unsurprisingly, the decision also indicates that similar issues as under LA2003 arise. For instance, a wide range of exceptions are included. One group relates to activities without music or amplification, including mime (including living statutes), some forms of juggling, clowning, 'theatrical and poetic recital', puppet shows, and magic. Others are excluded entirely, including Morris dancing, carols and protest marches. For those licensed, there is not just a time restriction (10 am–9 pm), but also specific restrictions on permitted instruments

54 I am grateful to Gavin Sutter (QMUL) for this point.

55 Home Office, *Revised Guidance issued under section 182 of the Licensing Act 2003* (n 24) [15.63].

56 E.g. Street Music (Metropolis) Act 1864.

57 *H & K* v. *United Kingdom* (1984) 6 EHRR CD362 (app no 10317/83).

58 *Keep Streets Live Campaign* v. *London Borough of Camden* [2014] EWHC 607 (Admin)

59 Ibid. [44].

(no drums, drum kits, or 'wind instruments, including brass instruments and woodwind instruments, but not including flutes or recorders'[60]); these restrictions can be lifted or varied under a 'special licence'.

This controversial policy also highlighted the creativity of those regulated. As the statute itself excluded 'music performed as part of a religious meeting, procession or service' from the local authority's busking licensing powers,[61] the campaigners who had applied for judicial review formed the Church of the Holy Kazoo,[62] in order to benefit from this exception (and, presumably, keep in the public eye their criticism of the policy). This also formed two of the '100 acts of minor dissent' highlighted in a book and show by comedian Mark Thomas.[63] Indeed, the policy has continued to provoke criticism, such as after the first prosecution (of Fredy Beats and ABH Beatbox, convicted for beatboxing in March 2016); the performers offered particular criticism of the Council's requirement that amplifiers (under special licences) be limited to 5W, which they considered inappropriate for beatboxing.[64] This is a useful example of a medium restriction that has a particular impact in one cultural field over others.

The regulation of busking is also carried out through new public space protection orders (PSPOs). These orders are promulgated by local authorities, under the authority of the Anti-social Behaviour, Crime and Policing Act 2014,[65] and can regulate activities that would have 'a detrimental effect on the quality of life of those in the locality'. Breach of a PSPO can be a criminal offence. Although the PSPO system replaced a patchwork of similar local orders on issues such as dog fouling and drinking alcohol (which, unlike PSPOs, had required Government confirmation of each local order), it is framed in general terms. That is, the power is about activities with detrimental effects, rather than specific activities identified by Parliament perhaps because of that assumed effect. This means that it can be used to regulate a sphere of activity such as busking, subject to the various statutory tests being met. Despite a broad caution against over-application to entertainment in Government guidance,[66] recent examples include an abandoned proposal in Birmingham to proscribe all

60 London Borough of Camden, 'Street entertainment policy' (2013) www.camden.gov.uk/ccm/cms-service/stream/asset/?asset_id=3181229& 15.

61 London Local Authorities Act 2000, s 32.

62 Madeline Davies, 'Buskers get holy to avoid ban' *Church Times* (4 April 2014) 2.

63 Mark Thomas, *100 acts of minor dissent* (September Publishing 2015) 122–5.

64 Serina Sandhu, 'Fredy Beats and ABH Beatbox: Camden Council prosecutes champion beatboxers for busking without licence' *The Independent* (5 March 2016) www.independent.co.uk/news/uk/home-news/fredy-beats-and-abh-beatbox-camden-council-prosecutes-champion-beatboxers-for-busking-without-a6914481.html

65 Anti-social Behaviour, Crime and Policing Act 2014, ss 59–61.

66 Home Office, 'Reform of anti-social behaviour powers' (2014) www.gov.uk/government/uploads/system/uploads/attachment_data/file/364851/Public_and_open_spaces_information_note.pdf 4:

> Busking and other forms of street entertainment can enrich a community's quality of life, play an important role in community life and can generate a positive atmosphere that is enjoyed by all. The police or local councils should not use the anti-social behaviour powers to stop or prevent appropriate busking or other street entertainment where it is not causing anti-social behaviour.

amplification (by protestors, buskers and others) in the city centre,[67] and a similarly abandoned proposal in Chester to require buskers and street entertainers to obtain permission, in order to avoid prohibition under a PSPO.[68] A London local authority made use of its PSPO power to prohibit busking in the area around Shepherd's Bush tube station after 6 pm, which also required buskers, street entertainers etc. to be at least 50 m from each other and to perform for no more than an hour in any 24 hour period.[69] Northampton's proposed PSPO would prohibit any busking 'that may cause a nuisance to nearby premises or members of the public'[70] in parts of the city centre – an interesting redefinition of the statutory test as a nuisance test.

Making sense of the legislation – and its exceptions

Many of the exemptions discussed in this chapter come as a result of lobbying or special pleading, or in order to maintain the credibility and efficient working of the law through avoiding absurdity. This proved to be important in the parliamentary process; Light notes, with a judiciously used exclamation mark, that the exemption of Morris dancing secured the passage of what is now LA2003.[71] But the subsequent chopping away (for deregulatory purposes) has reemphasised the relationship between regulation and the choice of medium. New exceptions, however well-founded in their own terms, have also served to highlight how the remaining forms of communication are singled out for special legal control. In any event, the one-stop-shop idea was unquestionably undermined (whatever one thinks about the underlying policy, for better or for worse), through the 2009 changes regarding sex entertainment venues.

Moreover, even where regulatory oversight is reduced in one area, it can continue in another. In a pre-LMA discussion of the position of live music, Cloonan highlights LA2003 as only one of five regulatory issues that those in the sector must face. Other challenges noted in his study, including controls on flyposting and the police use of an infamous risk assessment form (Form 696), were not affected by the LMA.[72] A high-profile instance of control under other legislation,

67 Liberty, 'Liberty welcomes Birmingham City Council's decision to scrap shameful PSPO plans' (16 September 2015) www.liberty-human-rights.org.uk/news/press-releases-and-statements/liberty-welcomes-birmingham-city-council's-decision-scrap

68 David Holmes, 'Chester council drops rough sleeping and busker element of PSPO' *Chester Chronicle* (Chester, 18 November 2015) www.chesterchronicle.co.uk/news/chester-cheshire-news/chester-council-drops-rough-sleeping-10462772

69 London Borough of Hammersfield and Fulham, 'Public Spaces Protection Order for Shepherds Bush Station' (2016) www.lbhf.gov.uk/environment/noise-and-nuisance/public-spaces-protection-order-shepherds-bush-station

70 Northampton Borough Council, 'Draft Public Spaces Protection Order' (2016) www.northampton.gov.uk/downloads/file/9044/draft-public-spaces-protection-order

71 Roy Light, 'The Licensing Act 2003: liberal constraint?' (2005) 68 *Modern Law Review* 268, 272.

72 Martin Cloonan, 'Researching live music: some thoughts on policy implications' (2011) 17 *International Journal of Cultural Policy* 405, 407–9. See also House of Commons, Culture Media and Sport Committee (n 18) [96–7] (recommending that the use of form 696 be discontinued, in order to promote a wide range of live music).

in Scotland, was the end of the 'Sound House' project in Edinburgh, on the grounds that the venue ('a makeshift stage in an Abbeyhill living room', according to the local newspaper[73]) was the subject of an unauthorised material change of use.[74]

It is often argued that the regulation of entertainment is content neutral or somewhat disinterested in the rights and wrongs of the substantive content (in the way discussed in Chapter 2). The Theatres Act 1968 sets a tone here, through an express prohibition on the regulation of on-stage content by local authorities.[75] Camden's regulation of busking included a clause stipulating that 'there is no restriction on the content of any busking'.[76] Even older approaches to sexual entertainment saw it argued, with success, that the question was not one of moral approval or disapproval;[77] the Home Office states that the current principle is that 'objections should not be based on moral grounds/values',[78] and as much was confirmed in an early case under the 2009 Act.[79]

But this does not tell the full story, by any means. The existence of a separate scheme for sexual entertainment and, crucially, different grounds for objection and the making of decisions (addressing perceived 'disenfranchisement' under LA2003[80]), means that this medium in particular is regulated by reference to 'form and content'.[81] This is not unique to the arguably special case of sexually explicit performances, either; it was held (obiter due to other failings) by a Scottish court that the refusal of a local authority to license a circus on the grounds of disapproval of animals being required to perform for an audience was an irrational exercise of its licensing powers.[82] Camden might disavow reviewing the content of busking, but other local authorities are less cautious.[83] More generally, Black's expanded definition of the effect of censorship and licensing ('not simply means of restriction, but also of legitimation, marking the boundary of what was respectable'[84]) rings true, although in some cases it now seems that *deregulation* is also part of the way in which legitimacy is conferred.

73 'City to pull the plug on concerts at party flat' (*Edinburgh Evening News*, 30 November 2012) www.edinburghnews.scotsman.com/news/city-to-pull-the-plug-on-concerts-at-party-flat-1–2669299
74 For a broader discussion of the interaction between licensing law and planning law, see *R (Blackwood)* v. *Birmingham Magistrates* [2006] EWHC 1800 (Admin).
75 Section 1(2), in particular that 'the licensing authority shall not have power to impose any term, condition or restriction as to the nature of the plays which may be performed under the licence or as to the manner of performing plays thereunder'.
76 London Borough of Camden, 'Street entertainment policy' (n 60) 3.
77 *R* v. *Newcastle City Council ex parte Christian Institute* [2001] BLGR 165 [19–21].
78 Home Office, 'Sexual entertainment venues: guidance for England and Wales' (n 51) [3.23].
79 *R (Thompson)* v. *Oxford City Council* (n 43) [50].
80 House of Commons Culture, Media and Sport Committee (n 18) [118].
81 Hubbard, *Cities and sexualities* (n 17) 166.
82 *Gerry Cottle's Circus Ltd* v. *City of Edinburgh District Council* 1990 SLT 235.
83 Laura Hill, 'Intermission in plan to audition city's buskers' *Evening Chronicle* (Newcastle, 18 August 2016) 53.
84 Jeremy Black, *The power of knowledge: how information and technology made the modern world* (Yale University Press 2015) 95.

Conclusion

In this chapter, I have summarised the complex structure of exceptions to the general principle of entertainment licensing under the 2003 Act, whether contained within the Act or operating from outside it. While the goal of consolidating alcohol and entertainment law into a single statute has been achieved in some respects (especially as regards local authority procedures), the result cannot be described as anything other than a differently constituted set of medium-specific rules, some of which favour or disfavour particular forms of communication for one reason or another (precisely echoing the criticism of content neutral laws noted in Chapter 2). Doing so falls within a long-established practice in the regulation of entertainment. The advocacy that underpinned the Street Music Act 1864 had one fundamental principle: 'working-class tastes for organ-ground music played in the streets were intruding into the more refined sensibilities and spaces of the middle-classes'.[85] Licensing laws in New York affected the composition of instrumental groups,[86] in an even more obvious fashion than the 'two in a bar' rules discussed in this chapter. The Criminal Justice and Public Order Act 1994 singled out 'raves' (amplified music in the open air, including 'sounds wholly or predominantly characterised by the emission of a succession of repetitive beats' within music, in case a court were to find otherwise) for special control.[87] Even after purported convergence, neither Parliament nor Government can resist the temptation to regulate, especially when it comes to the special circumstances (good or bad) of a particular form of communication.

85 Paul Simpson, 'The history of street performance: "music by handle" and the silencing of street musicians in the metropolis' (Gresham College Public Lecture, London, 9 July 2015) 7.

86 John Street, *Music and politics* (Polity 2012) 20–1; Paul Chevigny, *Gigs: jazz and the cabaret laws in New York* (Routledge 1991) 75ff.

87 Criminal Justice and Public Order Act 1994, ss 63–6; see also Hadfield (n 17) 52 (attributing blame to the 'alcohol lobby' in particular, as raves were not held in licensed venues and did not attract a conventional alcohol-drinking crowd), Chatterton and Hollands (n 1) 219–21 (emphasising the class dimension).

9 The message about the medium

Introduction

In Chapter 2, I argued that the study of the role of the medium in media law could bring about a better understanding of the body of media law, and in particular why it consists of a number of medium-specific provisions, even in the face of apparent convergence and consolidation. Perhaps appropriately, though, the juxtaposition of the various medium-specific investigations in Chapters 3 through 8 does highlight a number of cross-cutting themes regarding the relationship between the medium and the law. Four such themes – human rights law, technology, regulatory 'borrowing', and transparency regarding assumptions – are discussed in this concluding chapter.

Human rights law

The changing technological shape of the media industries can reopen debates regarding the regulation of content within a human rights framework. For instance, even if the statutory regulation of films exhibited in a cinema can be justified by reference to a combination of Articles 10(1) and 10(2) ECHR, the same work could be the subject of different regulatory requirements across a number of statutes. Examples of this phenomenon identified in the present study include the emerging genre or field of livecasts (Chapter 3), the relationship between the laws on broadcasting, video-on-demand, video recordings and the Internet (Chapter 6), and the continued role for the regulator of premium rate services (Chapter 7). One initial difficulty may be sustaining the concepts of necessity and proportionality under the ECHR, especially as the general laws of copyright, defamation, obscenity and privacy also apply in most cases. A further question is whether the specific requirements for a given medium can be justified. Barendt questions this with respect to the distinction between the prior scrutiny applicable in the UK for film (whether exhibited in cinema or distributed on video) and the lack of such in the cases of television and indeed live theatre.[1] Other examples which are potentially problematic in human rights terms have been identified in the present study, including the broad thrust of video game regulation on physical platforms (without

1 Eric Barendt, *Freedom of speech* (2nd edn, Oxford University Press 2005) 131.

any binding equivalent in downloadable games), and certain aspects of entertainment licensing as applied to different art forms.

Identifying an appropriate response to difficult questions such as the above requires a certain level of proper scrutiny and debate. Unfortunately, many of the legislative changes discussed in this book could hardly be described as having been debated to their full extent. Examples include the extensive rolling back of the Licensing Act and the creation of new dividing lines between regulated and unregulated through multiple provisions of secondary legislation adopted over a short period (Chapter 8), the delegation of power to define the scope of exemptions regarding video works and video games to Ministers (where the delegation itself was the subject of cursory parliamentary debate) (Chapter 4), and the continued significance of guidance and regulatory codes across the range of media discussed in this book (e.g. the BBFC's classification criteria, the PSA Code, and the Home Office Licensing Guidance).

Technology

On the other hand, technological developments have also, at times, been a driver of legislative change, or at least of reflection upon the effectiveness of existing legislation. The 'unregulated' competition for commercial radio from online music services and the like (Chapter 5) is clearly a factor in the willingness of Ofcom and of Government to revisit, in the near future, the approach to radio regulation. (Indeed, this was also part of the case for the initial adoption of the Audiovisual Media Services Directive a decade ago, as noted in Chapter 6.) But this is not just about deregulation. The gradual application of strict rules regarding sexually explicit content distributed as VOD and on the Internet, too, is justified by reference to the availability of new means of distribution. This is, however, inconsistent, as can be seen in Chapters 3 and 4 through noting the position of games (where, despite a significant extension of the scope of statutory regulation in terms of the range of games subject to classification, the legislation continues only to capture games distributed on disc or similar) and of film (where the distinction between cinema exhibition, video distribution and other means remains salient, even including the fiscal power of the state in terms of the payment of tax).

One point shared by those who disregard the medium with some of its defenders is an assumption of the linear development of technologies. The convergence camp, in particular, affects disdain for the complex and medium-specific laws of the past, and look forward to the replacement of these provisions with a single clear set of rules. But even assuming, for the sake of argument, that technological innovations always represent an advance, this does not necessarily mean that the implications and uses will be similarly linear. It is noted, for instance, that there are similarities between the impact on cultural life of early cinema and of emergent forms of online cinema.[2] An accurate understanding of the regulation of a medium

2 Paul Grainge, 'Introduction' in Paul Grainge (ed.), *Ephemeral media: transitory screen culture from television to YouTube* (British Film Institute 2011) 5.

may therefore require something more nuanced than comparing it with its immediate 'predecessor'. The selection of the comparator may also have consequences. Is video-on-demand the next iteration of video recordings, or of television, or something else? What is on-demand 'radio'? In a changing market, are premium rate services sui generis, or do they share features with other forms of communication?

Borrowing

The answer to the question above is that in the event that legislative drafting does not start with a blank page (that is, nearly all of the time), the laws applying to one medium (or to more than one) are typically a starting point. Numerous examples were discussed in this book, including the popular reporting of new aspects of regulation as 'film-like', the copying across (and then amendment once the consequences were realised) of creative industry tax relief schemes from one medium to another,[3] and the re-use of language between the various new exceptions to the Licensing Act. Indeed, this ever-present question of how to define medium-based categories and delimit the scope of regulation even arose in the report of the Leveson Inquiry, the major public inquiry set up in the aftermath of controversy surrounding the practices and ethics of the media (primarily the press). The report touched on the scope of a future regulatory system and how it would differentiate between platforms, although left the detail to those who would implement it.[4] Indeed, in the legislative implementation of the recommendations through the (subsequently stalled) system for the recognition of press regulatory bodies, definitional questions remained in play.[5]

The use of a medium-related term in statute does not necessarily provide clarity, though. In discussing judicial review in Chapter 1, I mentioned a decision regarding the definition of a newspaper. Returning to that case, having reviewed a range of definitions across the chapters that followed, illustrates the problem. The High Court was asked to determine whether a lanyard with football and gig dates constituted a newspaper for the purposes of legislation on

3 Indeed, even as this book was being completed, the Treasury was grappling with entirely predictable questions of scope and definition in yet another new tax credit – this time for museums and galleries: HM Treasury, *Museums and galleries tax relief: response to the consultation* (2016).

4 Leveson Inquiry, *An inquiry into the culture, practices and ethics of the press* (HC 2012, 780-I) 166; (HC 2012, 780-II) 736; (HC 2012, 780-IV) 1791–3.

5 For instance, Crime and Courts Act 2013, sch 15, para 1 specifies the BBC, S4C, and 'the holder of a licence under the Broadcasting Act 1990 or 1996 who publishes news-related material in connection with the broadcasting activities authorised under the licence' (in practice, radio and television services) as falling outside of the proposed system. This would mean, for one, that on-demand audiovisual services would fall within it, unless otherwise exempted on the basis of being a micro-business. For discussion, see Paul Wragg, 'Leveson's vision for press reform: one year on' (2014) 19 *Communications Law* 6, 7; Expert Group on the Leveson Report in Scotland, *Advice and recommendations* (2013) [39–40] (a similar discussion in respect of Scotland).

street trading.[6] Street trading requires a licence, but not where a newsvendor is selling 'current newspapers or periodicals' and complies with other conditions. As no definition of newspaper or periodical was included in the statute, a seller contended that he had registered his lanyards under the Newspaper Libel and Registration Act 1881 (where newspaper is defined as 'any paper containing public news, intelligence, or occurrences, or any remarks or observations therein printed for sale', published periodically). The High Court, however, found neither the registration nor the 1881 definition determinative, and instead considered the point anew. It did find (in the applicant's favour) that the term newspaper did not exclude publications on the grounds of their shape and size (such as the applicant's use of a lanyard rather than, say, paper in tabloid size), but ultimately found against him because the publication did not contain any news. So we see here a contest as to what Parliament meant by newspaper: did it mean the existing statutory concept? Or the size? Or, as the High Court found, something else? Even if the court can find a workable legal answer where challenges arise, there are still a number of areas where a medium is mentioned, without proper attention to the policy goal that is being pursued. Examples from the chapters above include the systems for tax relief discussed in Chapters 3 and 4, the 'comparability' test in the law on video-on-demand critiqued in Chapter 6, and a number of the exceptions from entertainment licensing law presented in Chapter 8 (e.g. circuses).

Unpacking assumptions

Questions also need to be asked about the role of qualitative research in the process of making and enforcing the law. Barker offers a sceptical assessment of the use of such by the BBFC in updating its classification guidelines, arguing that the research in question made use of poorly-defined terms, an incomplete and effects-led model, and contained insufficient information in order to be robust enough for criticism and further debate.[7] In Chapter 6, I expressed similar doubts about the use of focus group research on video-on-demand services in the application of rules on whether a service is sufficiently 'TV-like' to meet the statutory requirements for regulation. Courts can suffer from similar disadvantages, in assessing how to approach a relatively unfamiliar medium such as a video game, even on determining whether the game should be played, or discussed, or presented through screenshots, and so on, as noted in Chapter 4. Legislative and judicial assumptions about the significance of a particular medium (e.g. as discussed in Chapter 2 regarding advertising and processions) do not always make use of useful evidence.

6 *Davis* v. *Westminster City Council* [2012] EHWC 2303 (Admin), considering City of Westminster Act 1999, ss 3 and 27(1).

7 Martin Barker, '"Knowledge-U-Like": The British Board of Film Classification and its research' (2016) 13 *Journal of British Cinema and Television* 121, 133.

There is of course a place for qualitative research in the assessment of the fitness for purpose of media law, as demonstrated in the ongoing consideration of changes in the markets for micropayments and phone-paid services carried out by the PSA and discussed in Chapter 7. But where it is necessary to turn to research in order to work out what the law should be (or in the case of VOD, what it already is), placing undue weight on one type of research has its weaknesses. For instance, if it is right that Ofcom give detailed consideration to what is TV-like in one genre versus another, then there are forms of textual and aesthetic analysis that would add value to that conversation. If the BBFC's research is going to inform what ends up as a statute-backed system of criminal penalties which is, at least, a prima facie interference with freedom of expression, its robustness must be beyond question. At the parliamentary level, the decision to allow one form of entertainment to proceed without authorisation, but to require another to be the subject of an advance application and requirement to pay a fee, is surely strengthened by an overt acknowledgement of the material differences between the forms and why differential treatment is in the public interest.

The acknowledgement of the active choice of medium made by one who wishes to communicate is nowhere near as unusual as it often seems in the convergence-focused twenty-first century. It has of course been with us for a long time; every time a church chose to commission an artist to depict a point of theological significance alongside or in place of distributing a written text or having a cleric speak from a pulpit, assumptions were being made about the alignment between medium and message (as the ritualism controversies set out in Chapter 2 demonstrated). Innis, McLuhan, and others identified countless examples of the impact of a change in medium. Many pieces of twentieth-century media legislation were similarly based on assumptions (however well founded) about the affordances, audiences, and risks of a medium; the regulation of conduct, clothing, and the like, beyond the core of media law, is similarly attractive because of these considerations.

So when the well-meaning drafter, regulator or judge tries to put all of this behind them and focus upon the message, how do they fare? Quickly, it seems, the implications become clear, and the medium comes back into view. Even after the broad project of liberalising and consolidating entertainment licensing law, for example, the question of 'do I need permission to perform this song' is still only a starting point. The much more pertinent questions include whether you sing it during an act of worship, what type of instruments you use, how big the audience is, whether other forms such as video or theatre are used, and so on. Radio and television may share many features and all be dealt with by a super-regulator, but the broad principle of wishing to protect children is put into operation through two different concepts of the watershed, informed not least by the knowledge that cars are (for now, at least) much more likely to contain a radio than a television.

Even where a deliberate attempt is made to transcend the medium (the imagined legislative blank page referred to above), this tends to be incomplete. The abolition of the distinction between television services delivered over-the-air, by satellite or by cable on one hand and streamed on the Internet on the other[8] might seem to make the medium less significant, but it still represents just one part of the audiovisual ecosystem. Having a single statutory basis for the regulation of video and games may have seemed logical, but the difficulties of treating two different things according to the same rules put the system under so much strain and criticism (especially that the assumptions and practices of the regulator were inseparable from its long-standing focus on film) that the result was the creation of two separate regulatory bodies (during a period when the Government of the day was abolishing and merging public bodies at a record pace). Not only that, but even when it was agreed that there ought to be a video body and a games body, elaborate provisions to deal with overlapping jurisdiction needed to be added.

A final word

Innis's arguments on time and space, McLuhan's analysis of the medium and its properties, and all the aphorisms and explanations, point to a common principle – a need to take a more holistic approach to media-related research. What I take from this work, in writing on the regulation of the media through law, is that the medium is far from irrelevant. It is therefore right to wonder, for instance, whether the differences in the legal treatment of a cinema exhibition as compared with an online video are warranted. But it is just as important to consider whether applying the same rules to a game and to a film could have differential consequences, despite the ostensibly common legal regime. It is also crucial that the use of medium-led regulation as a proxy for unspoken assumptions about value, culture and desirable or undesirable behaviour be exposed. I have done so here through a discussion of the engagement between law and media studies, although there is certainly scope for further work encompassing, for instance, anthropology or economics.

We need the Toronto School's advice on how to approach the medium. Otherwise, we focus too tightly on what makes sense from a legal point of view – what is elegant drafting or a workable set of categories, or is driven by a seemingly convenient set of changes in technology and the market. The later, post-Innis and post-McLuhan work by the Toronto School adds material evidence as to the characteristics of a medium. But Innis himself identifies the need to talk about what makes a medium distinctive; even in his earlier work, he knows that you cannot tell a story of trade in Canada without knowing something of its geography and geology. I have in this book tried to show that media law benefits from a greater focus on the characteristics of each medium and of the way in which a medium is defined and used in the law. The medium is not necessarily always the message, but an account of media law that focuses on the regulation of the message will only ever be an incomplete and unsatisfying one.

8 Directive 2010/13/EU of 10 March 2010 on the coordination of certain provisions laid down by law, regulation or administrative action in Member States concerning the provision of audiovisual media services [2010] OJ L263/15, art 1(1)(a)(i).

Bibliography

All URLs last accessed 1 March 2017.

Acland, Charles. (2006). Harold Innis, cultural policy and residual media. *International Journal of Cultural Policy*, 12(2), 171–85.

Albanesius, Chloe. (2011). Apple bans DUI checkpoint apps in App Store. *PC Magazine*. 9 June 2011. www.pcmag.com/article2/0,2817,2386693,00.asp

Allen, Robert, and Hill, Annette. (2004). Modes of television. In Robert Allen and Annette Hill (eds), *The television studies reader* (pp. 163–9). Routledge.

Analysys Mason. (2010). *The marketplace for and regulation of micropayment services in the UK.*

Anderson, John Nathan. (2012). Radio broadcasting's digital dilemma. *Convergence: The International Journal of Research into New Media Technologies*, 19(2), 177–99.

Applebome, Peter. (2013). Veterans group, flying a flag with a message, ruffles a city. *New York Times*, p. A13. 7 August 2013.

Arsenault, Dominic. (2008). The Nintendo Entertainment System. In Mark Wolf (ed.), *The video game explosion: a history from PONG to PlayStation and beyond* (pp. 109–12). Greenwood.

Atkinson, Benedict. (2007). *The true history of copyright.* Sydney University Press.

Atton, Chris. (2004). *An alternative Internet.* Edinburgh University Press.

Attwood, Feona, Barker, Meg, Bragg, Sara, Egan, Danielle, Evans, Adrienne, Harvey, Laura, … van Zoonen, Liesbet. (2012). Engaging with the Bailey Review: blogging, academia and authenticity. *Psychology and Sexuality*, 3(1), 69–94.

Australian Law Reform Commission. (2012). *Classification – content regulation and convergent media*

Ayre, Richard. (2007). Report of an inquiry into television broadcasters' use of premium rate telephone services in programmes. www.ofcom.org.uk/__data/assets/pdf_file/0020/42914/report.pdf

Babe, Robert. (2000). *Canadian communication thought: ten foundational writers.* University of Toronto Press.

Babe, Robert. (2004). McLuhan and Canadian communication thought. In John George Moss and Linda M. Morra (eds), *At the speed of light there is only illumination: a reappraisal of Marshall McLuhan* (pp. 37–62). University of Ottawa Press.

Babe, Robert. (2006). Innis and the news. *Javnost – The Public*, 13(3), 43–55.

Babe, Robert. (2008). Innis and the emergence of Canadian communication/media studies. *Global Media Journal – Canadian Edition*, 1(1), 9–23.

Babe, Robert. (2009). *Cultural studies and political economy: toward a new integration.* Lexington.

Babe, Robert. (2015). Innis' great transformation: staples thesis/medium theory. *Canadian Journal of Communication*, 40(3), 489–501.

Baluch, Lalayn. (2009). Equity warns that 'sex encounter establishment' branding will put dancers at risk. *The Stage*. 18 August 2009. www.thestage.co.uk/news/2009/equity-warns-that-sex-encounter-establishment-branding-will-put-dancers-at-risk/

Barber, Sian. (2016). Exploiting local controversy: regional British censorship of Last Tango in Paris (1972). *Historical Journal of Film, Radio and Television*, 36(4), 587–603.

Barendt, Eric. (2005). *Freedom of speech* (2nd edn). Oxford University Press.

Barker, Martin. (2013). *Live to your local cinema: the remarkable rise of livecasting*. Palgrave Macmillan.

Barker, Martin. (2016). 'Knowledge-U-Like': The British Board of Film Classification and its research. *Journal of British Cinema and Television*, 13(1), 121–40.

Barlow, Aaron. (2005). *The DVD revolution: movies, culture, and technology*. Praeger.

Barnes, Susan. (2005). The global village versus tribal man: the paradox of the medium and the message. In Lance Strate and Edward Wachtel (eds), *The legacy of McLuhan* (pp. 247–60). Hampton.

Barraclogh, Leo. (2010). Arthouses hedge bets. *Variety*, p. 15. 29 November 2010.

Barrett, Brian. (2015). Internet radio is fixing to make a comeback. *Wired*. September 2015.

Barron, Anne. (2004). The legal properties of film. *Modern Law Review*, 67(2), 177–208.

BDRC Continental. (2013). Consumer engagement with PRS, 2012–2013. http://psauthority.org.uk/For-Business/Research/~/media/Files/PhonepayPlus/Research/Consumer%20Research/2013_Consumer_Engagement_with_PRS_2012_2013.pdf

Bélanger, Pierre C., and Manchester, Geoffrey. (2013). 'Beyond the clouds': insider perceptions on the transmutation of terrestrial radio in Canada. *Journal of Radio & Audio Media*, 20(2), 358–77.

Belavusau, Uladzislau. (2010). Sex in the union: EU law, taxation and the adult industry. *European Law Reporter*, (4), 144–50.

Belton, John. (2014). If film is dead, what is cinema? *Screen*, 55(4), 460–70.

Bennett, Catherine. (2011). Teenagers won't be shocked by a naked man on the stage. *Observer*. 27 February 2011. www.theguardian.com/commentisfree/2011/feb/27/catherine-bennett-frankenstein-children

Bennett, James. (2011). Architectures of participation: fame, television and web 2.0. In James Bennett and Niki Strange (eds), *Television as digital media* (pp. 332–57). Duke University Press.

Benson-Allott, Caetlin. (2013). *Killer tapes and shattered screens: video spectatorship from VHS to file sharing*. University of California Press.

Bentley, James. (1978). *Ritualism and politics in Victorian Britain: the attempt to legislate for belief*. Oxford University Press.

Berens, Kate, and Howard, Geoff. (2002). *The rough guide to videogaming* (2nd edn). Rough Guides.

Berry, Richard. (2006). Will the iPod kill the radio star? Profiling podcasting as radio. *Convergence: The International Journal of Research into New Media Technologies*, 12(2), 143–62.

Bielby, Denise, and Harrington, C. Lee. (2008). *Global TV: exporting television and culture in the world market*. New York University Press.

Bignell, Jonathan. (2013). *An introduction to television studies* (3rd edn). Routledge.
Bishop, Chris. (2011). Canaries fan from King's Lynn threatened with £2,500 fine for flying a Norwich City flag in his back garden. *Norwich Evening News*. 5 November 2011.
Black, David. (2001). Internet radio: a case study in medium specificity. *Media, Culture and Society*, 23(3), 397–408.
Black, Jeremy. (2015). *The power of knowledge: how information and technology made the modern world*. Yale University Press.
Blondheim, Menahem, and Watson, Rita. (2007). Innis, McLuhan, and the Toronto School. In Menahem Blondheim and Rita Watson (eds), *The Toronto School of Communication Theory: interpretations, extensions, applications* (pp. 7–26). Hebrew University Magnes Press.
Bogost, Ian. (2007). *Persuasive games: the expressive power of videogames*. MIT Press.
Bonnett, John. (2013). *Emergence and empire: Innis, complexity, and the trajectory of history*. McGill-Queen's University Press.
Booton, David, and MacCulloch, Angus. (2012). Liability for the circumvention of technological protection measures applied to videogames: lessons from the United Kingdom's experience. *Journal of Business Law* (3), 165–89.
BOP Consulting. (2014). Review of the film sector in Scotland. www.creativescotland.com/__data/assets/pdf_file/0018/25245/Review_of_the_Film_Sector_in_Scotland_-_Jan_2014.pdf
Bottomley, Andrew J. (2015). Podcasting: a decade in the life of a 'new' audio medium. *Journal of Radio and Audio Media*, 22(2), 164–9.
Bowker, Geoffrey C., and Star, Susan Leigh. (1999). *Sorting things out: classification and its consequences*. MIT Press.
Boyden, Bruce. (2011). Games and other uncopyrightable systems. *George Mason Law Review*, 18(2), 439–77.
Brereton, Pat. (2012). *Smart cinema: DVD add-ons and new audience pleasures*. Palgrave Macmillan.
Briden, Timothy. (2013). *Moore's introduction to English canon law* (4th edn). Bloomsbury.
Brignall, Miles. (2013). Google Adword: beware copycat websites in paid-for search results. *Guardian*. 1 June 2013. www.theguardian.com/money/2013/jun/01/google-adword-copycat-websites-search-results
British Board of Film Classification. (1994). *Annual report 1993*.
British Board of Film Classification. (1996). *Annual report for 1995/96*.
British Board of Film Classification. (1997). *Annual report for 1996/97*.
British Board of Film Classification. (1998). *Annual report for 1997/98*.
British Board of Film Classification. (1999). *Annual report 1998*.
British Board of Film Classification. (2002). *Annual report 2001*.
British Board of Film Classification. (2006). *Annual report 2005*.
British Board of Film Classification. (2008). *Annual report 2007*.
British Board of Film Classification. (2009). *Classification guidelines 2009*.
British Board of Film Classification. (2010). As live. www.bbfc.co.uk/industry-services/theatrical-ratings/as-live
British Board of Film Classification. (2010). Guidance for distributors: submitting a work for as live classification. www.bbfc.co.uk/sites/default/files/attachments/As%20Live%20-%20Guidance%20for%20Distributors.pdf
British Board of Film Classification. (2014). Classification guidelines 2014. www.bbfc.co.uk/sites/default/files/attachments/BBFC%20Classification%20Guidelines%202014_5.pdf

British Board of Film Classification. (2016). *Annual report and accounts 2015.*

British Film Institute. (2016). *Statistical yearbook 2016.* BFI.

British Film Institute. (2016). Video games cultural test guidance notes. www.bfi.org.uk/sites/bfi.org.uk/files/downloads/bfi-british-film-certification-cultural-test-for-video-games-guidance-notes-2016-03.pdf

Brown, Ian, and Marsden, Christopher T. (2013). *Regulating code: good governance and better regulation in the information age*. MIT Press.

Brown, Simon. (2012). Censorship under siege: the BBFC in the silent era. In Edward Lamberti (ed.), *Behind the scenes at the BBFC: film classification from the silver screen to the digital age* (pp. 3–15). British Film Institute.

Bull, Michael. (2007). *Sound moves: iPod culture and urban experience*. Routledge.

Burlinson, Simon. (2006). Crazy for trying? Service providers beware – ICSTIS and the nature of premium rate service providers. *Entertainment Law Review*, 17(4), 125–7.

Burnham, Van, and Anuff, Joey. (2001). *Supercade: a visual history of the videogame age, 1971–1984*. MIT Press.

Butler, Jeremy. (2010). *Television style*. Routledge.

Butler, Jeremy. (2012). *Television: critical methods and applications* (4th edn). Routledge.

Buxton, William. (2004). Harold Innis' 'French inflection': origins, themes, and implications of his 1951 address at le Collège de France. *Canadian Journal of Communication*, 29(2), 171–86.

Buxton, William. (2015). The rise of McLuhanism, the loss of Innis-sense: rethinking the origins of the Toronto School of Communication. *Canadian Journal of Communication*, 37(4), 577–93.

Caldwell, John. (2004). Convergence television: aggregating form and repurposing content in the culture of conglomeration. In Lynn Spigel and Jan Olsson (eds), *Television after TV: essays on a medium in transition* (pp. 41–74). Duke University Press.

Cammiss, Steven, and Manchester, Colin. (2011). Application process and decision-making under the Licensing Act 2003. *Web Journal of Current Legal Issues*, (4). http://webjcli.ncl.ac.uk/2011/issue4/cammiss4.html

Cardwell, Sarah. (2006). Television aesthetics. *Critical Studies in Television*, 1(1), 72–80.

Carey, James. (1967). Harold Adams Innis and Marshall McLuhan. *Antioch Review*, 27(1), 5–39.

Carey, James. (1989). *Communication as culture: essays on media and society*. Unwin Hyman.

Chadwick, Owen. (1972). *The Victorian church* (2nd edn). A & C Black.

Chandler, Michael. (1995). *The life and work of John Mason Neale, 1818–1866*. Gracewing.

Chapman, James. (2007). EU flag is given national status. *Daily Mail*, p. 36. 16 March 2007.

Chatfield, Tom. (2010). *Fun Inc.: why gaming will dominate the twenty-first century*. Pegasus Books.

Chatterton, Paul, and Hollands, Robert. (2003). *Urban nightscapes: youth cultures, pleasure spaces and corporate power*. Routledge.

Chen, Chi-Ying. (2013). Is the video game a cultural vehicle? *Games and Culture*, 8(6), 408–27.

Chevigny, Paul. (1991). *Gigs: jazz and the cabaret laws in New York*. Routledge.

Christian, Aymar Jean. (2011). Joe Swanberg, intimacy, and the digital aesthetic. *Cinema Journal*, 50(4), 117–35.

Cloonan, Martin. (1996). *Banned!: Censorship of popular music in Britain, 1967–92*. Arena.

Cloonan, Martin. (2011). Researching live music: some thoughts on policy implications. *International Journal of Cultural Policy*, 17(4), 405–20.

Cohen, Julie. (2012). *Configuring the networked self: law, code, and the play of everyday practice*. Yale University Press.

Compton, Sara, and Connor, Edward. (2007). The integrated news spectacle, Live 8, and the annihilation of time. *Canadian Journal of Communication*, 32(1), 29–53.

Cookson, Robert. (2013). Alternative content draws in the masses. *Financial Times*, p. 18. 15 June 2013.

Corcoran, Michael. (2007). *For which it stands: an anecdotal biography of the American flag*. Simon & Schuster.

Corliss, Jonathan. (2011). The social science study of video games. *Games and Culture*, 6(1), 3–16.

Coulmont, Baptiste, and Hubbard, Phil. (2010). Consuming sex: socio-legal shifts in the space and place of sex shops. *Journal of Law and Society*, 37(1), 189–209.

Cox, Robert. (1995). Civilizations: encounters and transformations. *Studies in Political Economy*, 47, 7–31.

Craft Strategy. (2016). A study of consumer journeys relating to online competition and adult PRS. http://psauthority.org.uk/-/media/Files/PhonepayPlus/Research/2016/Summary-report-on-A-study-of-consumer-journeys-relating-to-online-competition-and-adult-PRS.ashx?la=en

Craufurd Smith, Rachael. (2007). Media convergence and the regulation of audiovisual content. *Current Legal Problems*, 70, 238–77.

Creeber, Glen. (2013). *Small screen aesthetics: from TV to the Internet*. Palgrave Macmillan.

Crofts, Charlotte. (2011). Cinema distribution in the age of digital projection. *Post Script*, (30)2, 82–98.

Cwynar, Christopher. (2015). More than a 'VCR for Radio': the CBC, the Radio 3 podcast, and the uses of an emerging medium. *Journal of Radio and Audio Media*, 22(2), 190–9.

Czitrom, Daniel. (1982). *Media and the American mind: from Morse to McLuhan*. University of North Carolina Press.

Daly, Angela. (2016). *Private power, online information flows and EU law: mind the gap*. Hart.

Darnley, Aredhel. (2013). Creative sector tax reliefs – Treasury proposals elicit detailed responses as DCMS consults on cultural tests. *Entertainment Law Review*, 24(1), 6–9.

Dauncey, Hugh. (2012). French videogaming: what kind of culture and what support? *Convergence: The International Journal of Research into New Media Technologies*, 18(4), 385–402.

Davies, Madeline. (2014). Buskers get holy to avoid ban. *Church Times*, p. 2. 4 April 2014.

Davies, Rosamund. (2011). Digital intimacies: aesthetic and affective strategies in the production and use of online video. In Paul Grainge (ed.), *Ephemeral media: transitory screen culture from television to YouTube* (pp. 214–27). BFI.

Davis, Andrew. (2002). A kick in the fiscals. *Financial Times*, p. 16. 30 April 2002.

Davison, Annette. (2014). The end is nigh. *Music, Sound, and the Moving Image*, 8(2), 195–215.

Dawson, Max. (2011). Television's aesthetic of efficiency: convergence television and the digital short. In James Bennett and Niki Strange (eds), *Television as digital media* (pp. 204–29). Duke University Press.

Dawtrey, Adam. (2010). An Alice in Wonderland nightmare as Disney battles the cinemas. *Guardian*, p. 22. 24 February 2010.

Day Good, Katie. (2016). Radio's forgotten visuals. *Journal of Radio and Audio Media*, 23(2), 364–8.

Day, Terri, and Hall, Ryan. (2010). Déjà vu: from comic books to video games: legislative reliance on 'soft science' to protect against uncertain societal harm linked to violence v. the First Amendment. *Oregon Law Review*, 89(2), 415–52.

de Grazia, Edward. (1992). *Girls lean back everywhere: the law of obscenity and the assault on genius*. Random House.

de Jongh, Nicholas. (2000). *Politics, prudery and perversions: censorship of the English stage, 1901–1968*. Methuen.

de Kerckhove, Derrick. (1989). McLuhan and the 'Toronto School of Communication'. *Canadian Journal of Communication*, 14(4), 76–9.

Deegan, Matt. (2016). YouTubers doing podcasts and the iTunes chart. 15 December 2016. www.mattdeegan.com/2016/12/15/youtubers-podcasts-itunes-chart/

Deibert, Ronald. (1997). *Parchment, printing, and hypermedia: communication in world order transformation*. Columbia University Press.

Delafons, John. (1993). Planning and censorship. *Journal of Planning and Environment Law*, 527–33.

Deloitte. (2014). The future for phone-paid digital goods and services. http://psauthority.org.uk/For-Business/~/media/Files/PhonepayPlus/Research/Nov2014_Deloitte_research.pdf

Department for Children, Schools and Families. (2008). Safer children in a digital world: the report of the Byron Review. http://data.parliament.uk/DepositedPapers/Files/DEP2008-0831/DEP2008-0831.pdf

Department for Communities and Local Government. (2012). Spirit of the summer realised with relaxation of flag flying rules. 20 September 2012. www.gov.uk/government/news/spirit-of-the-summer-realised-with-relaxation-of-flag-flying-rules

Department for Culture, Media and Sport. (2008). Video games classification: a consultation. http://dera.ioe.ac.uk/8338/5/VideoGames2008.pdf

Department for Culture, Media and Sport. (2011). Regulated entertainment: a consultation proposal to examine the deregulation of Schedule One of the Licensing Act 2003. www.gov.uk/government/uploads/system/uploads/attachment_data/file/72904/consultation_deregulation-scheduleone_2011_vs2.pdf

Department for Culture, Media and Sport. (2012). Consultation on exemptions to the Video Recordings Act and on advertising in cinemas. www.gov.uk/government/uploads/system/uploads/attachment_data/file/73028/VRACinemaads_consultation_May2012.pdf

Department for Culture, Media and Sport. (2013). Consultation on exemptions to the Video Recordings Act and on advertising in cinemas: Government response. www.gov.uk/government/uploads/system/uploads/attachment_data/file/202904/Government_response_VRA_and_Cinema_Ads__FINAL_approved_version.docx

Department for Culture, Media and Sport. (2013). Community film exhibition: a consultation. www.gov.uk/government/uploads/system/uploads/attachment_data/file/210729/Community_film_consultation.pdf

Department for Culture, Media and Sport. (2014). Legislative Reform (Entertainment Licensing) Order 2014: explanatory document. www.gov.uk/government/uploads/system/uploads/attachment_data/file/328492/Entertainment_Licensing_Legislative_Reform_Order_Explanatory_Document.pdf

Department for Culture, Media and Sport. (2014). Impact assessment: R18 content access controls. www.gov.uk/government/uploads/system/uploads/attachment_data/file/225877/R18_content_access_controls.pdf

Department for Culture, Media and Sport. (2015). Action to protect children from viewing age-inappropriate music videos online. www.gov.uk/government/news/actiontoprotect childrenfromviewingageinappropriatemusicvideosonline

Department for Culture, Media and Sport. (2016). Child safety online: age verification for pornography. www.gov.uk/government/uploads/system/uploads/attachment_data/file/541366/AV_ConsultationDCMS_20160216_Final__4_.pdf

Department for Education. (2011). *Letting children be children: report of an independent review of the commercialisation and sexualisation of childhood*

di Norcia, Vincent. (1986). Of stone, books and freedom. *Visible Language*, 12(3), 344–55.

di Norcia, Vincent. (1990). Communications, time and power: an Innisian view. *Canadian Journal of Political Science/Revue canadienne de science politique*, 23(2), 335–57.

Dickinson, Margaret, and Street, Sarah. (1985). *Cinema and state: the film industry and the government 1927–84*. British Film Institute.

Dickson, Gareth. (2014). Game over for excessive TPM? *Computers and Law*, 24(4), 5–7.

Dovey, Jon. (2004). Camcorder cults. In Robert Allen and Annette Hill (eds), *The television studies reader* (pp. 557–68). Routledge.

Dovey, Jon. (2011). Time slice: web drama and the attention economy. In Paul Grainge (ed.), *Ephemeral media: transitory screen culture from television to YouTube* (pp. 138–55). British Film Institute.

Doyle, Gillian, Schlesinger, Philip, Boyle, Raymond, and Kelly, Lisa W. (2015). *The rise and fall of the UK Film Council*. Edinburgh University Press.

Drache, Daniel. (1995). *Staples, markets, and cultural change*. McGill-Queen's University Press.

Dredge, Stuart. (2011). Apple bans satirical iPhone game Phone Story from its App Store. 14 September 2011. www.guardian.co.uk/technology/appsblog/2011/sep/14/apple-phone-story-rejection

Dredge, Stuart. (2014). Disney's YouTube deal is a real game changer. *The Observer*, p. 21. 30 March 2014.

Druick, Zoë. (2007). *Projecting Canada: government policy and documentary film at the National Film Board of Canada*. McGill-Queen's University Press.

Dymek, Mikolaj. (2012). Video games: a subcultural industry. In Peter Zackariasson and Timothy Wilson (eds), *The video game industry: formation, present state, and future* (pp. 34–56). Routledge.

Eastman, Susan Tyler, and Neal-Lunsford, Jeffrey. (1995). Coping with grazing: prime-time strategies for accelerated program transitions. *Journal of Broadcasting and Electronic Media*, 39(1), 91–109.

Edery, David, and Mollick, Ethan. (2009). *Changing the game: how video games are transforming the future of business*. FT Press.

Edinburgh City Council. (2014). Public Entertainment Resolution. www.edinburgh.gov.uk/download/downloads/id/1189/public_entertainment_resolution.pdf

Edinburgh City Council Regulatory Committee. (2012). Public entertainment licensing: recommendations of member-officer working group. www.edinburgh.gov.uk/download/meetings/id/37139/item_6_1-public_entertainment_licensing-recommendations_of_the_member_officer_working_group

Edmond, Maura. (2014). Here we go again: music videos after YouTube. *Television and New Media*, 15(4), 305–20.

Egan, Kate. (2007). *Trash or treasure?: Censorship and the changing meanings of the video nasties*. Manchester University Press.

Elberse, Anita. (2014). *Blockbusters: why big hits – and big risks – are the future of the entertainment business*. Faber & Faber.

Ellis, John. (2004). Television production. In Robert Allen and Annette Hill (eds), *The television studies reader* (pp. 275–92). Routledge.

Ellis, John. (2006). Defining the medium: TV form and aesthetics. In Glen Creeber (ed.), *Tele-visions: an introduction to studying television* (pp. 12–19). BFI.

Ellis, John. (2011). Interstitials: how the 'bits in between' define the programmes. In Paul Grainge (ed.), *Ephemeral media: transitory screen culture from television to YouTube* (pp. 59–69). British Film Institute.

Ellis-Petersen, Hannah. (2016). Music streaming hailed as industry's saviour as labels enjoy profit surge. Guardian. 30 December 2016. www.theguardian.com/technology/2016/dec/29/music-streaming-industry-saviour-labels-spotify-apple-music

Entertainment and Leisure Software Publishers' Association. (1998). *Playing for success*.

Entertainment Licensing Review Group (Northern Ireland). (2015). Entertainment licensing review. www.communities-ni.gov.uk/sites/default/files/consultations/doe/council-consultation-entertainment-licensing-review-2015.pdf

Erwin, Alan. (2015). Loyalist Famine Song bandsmen convicted 'outrageous' sectarian behaviour outside Catholic church. *Belfast Telegraph*. 30 April 2015. www.belfasttelegraph.co.uk/news/northern-ireland/loyalist-famine-song-bandsmen-convicted-outrageous-sectarian-behaviour-outside-catholic-church-31183254.html

Escobedo Shepherd, Julianne. (2015). Tyler, the Creator, on being banned from the UK: 'I'm being treated like a terrorist'. *Guardian*. 1 September 2015. www.theguardian.com/music/musicblog/2015/sep/01/tyler-the-creator-comments-banned-uk-freedom-of-speech

Essential Research. (2009). The regulation of video-on-demand: consumer views on what makes audiovisual services 'TV-like'. www.ofcom.org.uk/__data/assets/pdf_file/0018/16218/vod.pdf

Essential Research. (2012). On-demand services: understanding consumer choices. www.ofcom.org.uk/__data/assets/pdf_file/0025/28906/research_report.pdf

Evans, Elizabeth Jane, and McDonald, Paul. (2014). Online distribution of film and television in the UK: behavior, taste, and value. In Jennifer Holt and Kevin Sanson (eds), *Connected viewing: selling, streaming, and sharing media in the digital era* (pp. 158–79). Taylor & Francis.

Expert Group on the Leveson Report in Scotland. (2013). *Advice and recommendations*

Farman, Jason. (2012). Historicizing mobile media: locating the transformations of embodied space. In Noah Arceneaux and Anandau Kavoori (eds), *The mobile media reader* (pp. 9–22). Peter Lang.

Fausset, Richard. (2015). Era ends as South Carolina lowers Confederate flag. *New York Times*, p. A9. 11 July 2015.

Fausset, Richard, and Blinder, Alan. (2015). South Carolina settles its decades-old dispute over a Confederate flag. *New York Times*, p. A16. 10 July 2015.

Favale, Marcella. (2015). A Wii too stretched? The ECJ extends to game consoles the protection of DRM – on tough conditions. *European Intellectual Property Review*, 37(2), 101–6.

Feasey, Rebecca. (2003). Sex, controversy, box-office: from blockbuster to bonkbuster. In Julian Stringer (ed.), *Movie blockbusters* (pp. 167–77). Routledge.

Feijoó, Claudio. (2012). An exploration of the mobile gaming ecosystem from developers' perspective. In Peter Zackariasson and Timothy Wilson (eds), *The video game industry: formation, present state, and future* (pp. 76–98). Routledge.

Feldman, David. (1998). Content neutrality. In Ian Loveland (ed.), *Importing the First Amendment: freedom of speech and expression in Britain, Europe and the USA* (pp. 139–71). Hart.

Felini, Damiano. (2014). Beyond today's video game rating systems: a critical approach to PEGI and ESRB, and proposed improvements. *Games and Culture*, 10(1), 106–22.

Ferguson, Amanda. (2013). No Blurred Lines at all as Queen's University students ban Robin Thicke's hit song. *Belfast Telegraph*, p. 3. 21 November 2013.

Film Policy Review Panel. (2012). A future for British film. www.gov.uk/government/uploads/system/uploads/attachment_data/file/78460/DCMS_film_policy_review_report-2012_update.pdf

Film Policy Review Panel. (2014). It's still about the audience: two years on from the Film Policy Review. www.gov.uk/government/uploads/system/uploads/attachment_data/file/274265/1316-A_Film_Policy_Doc_ACCESSIBLE.pdf

Fisher, Marc. (2007). *Something in the air: radio, rock, and the revolution that shaped a generation*. Random House.

Flayhan, Donna. (2005). Early medium theory, or, roots of technological determinism in North American communications theory. In Lance Strate and Edward Wachtel (eds), *The legacy of McLuhan* (pp. 247–60). Hampton.

Flores, Nico, Karapandzic, Helen, and Roy, Jyotin Chhatwal. (2012). International-scale issues of non-compliance with premium-rate services: a report for PhonepayPlus. http://psauthority.org.uk/-/media/Files/PhonepayPlus/Research/International-Scale-issues-of-non-compliance-with-premium-rate-services.pdf

Fried, Carrie. (1996). Bad rap for rap: bias in reactions to music lyrics. *Journal of Applied Social Psychology*, 26(23), 2135–40.

Fried, Carrie. (1999). Who's afraid of rap: demographics and differential reactions to music lyrics. *Journal of Applied Social Psychology*, 29(4), 705–21.

Fry, Robin. (2015). Reselling software licences. *Computers and Law*, 26(4), 19–23.

Fussfeld Cohen, Orit. (2014). The new language of the digital film. *Journal of Popular Film and Television*, 42(1), 47–58.

Gannagé-Stewart, Hannah. (2016). BBC plans 'Netflix of spoken word'. *Broadcast*. 23 November 2016. www.broadcastnow.co.uk/news/bbc-plans-netflix-of-spoken-word/5111585.article

Gant, Andrew. (2015). *O sing unto the Lord: a history of English church music*. Profile.

Gant, Charles. (2012). Video on demand: kill or cure for arthouse cinemas. *Guardian*, p. 14. 5 April 2012.

Gentleman, Amelia. (2014). Sex doesn't sell: the decline of British porn. *Guardian*. 6 October 2014. www.theguardian.com/culture/2014/oct/05/sex-sell-decline-british-porn-xbiz-regulations-children

Gilbey, Ryan. (2012). Banish the truffle oil! *New Statesman*. 17 April 2012. www.newstatesman.com/blogs/film/2012/04/banish-truffle-oil

Gillan, Jennifer. (2010). *Television and new media*. Routledge.

Gillan, Jennifer. (2014). *Television brandcasting: the return of the content-promotion hybrid*. Routledge.

Gillen, Martina. (2014). DRM and modchips: time for the Court of Justice to do the 'right' thing. *SCRIPTed*, 11(3), 229–44.

Glantz, Mark. (2016). Internet radio adopts a human touch: a study of 12 streaming music services. *Journal of Radio and Audio Media*, 23(1), 36–49.

Gomery, Douglas. (1985). Theatre television: the missing link of technological change in the US motion picture industry. *Velvet Light Trap*, 21, 54–61.

Good, Natasha, and Goldberg, Stuart. (2006). European reaction to the proposed new Audiovisual Services Directive. *Communications Law*, 11(6), 183–6.

Gopinath, Sumanth S. (2013). *The ringtone dialectic: economy and cultural form*. MIT Press.

Gopnik, Alison. (2016). *The gardener and the carpenter: what the new science of child development tells us about the relationship between parents and children*. Random House.

Gottlich, Paul. (2007). Online games from the standpoint of media and copyright law. *IRIS Plus* (10), 8–10.

Graber, Christoph Beat. (2010). State aid for digital games and cultural diversity: a critical reflection in the light of EU and WTO law. In Christoph Beat Graber and Miri Burri-Nenova (eds), *Governance of digital game environments and cultural diversity* (pp. 170–201). Edward Elgar.

Graeber, David. (2015). *The utopia of rules: on technology, stupidity, and the secret joys of bureaucracy*. Melville House.

Graham, Alistair. (2011). Letter to the Secretary of State for Culture, Media and Sport. 30 June 2011. http://old.culture.gov.uk/images/consultation_responses/CR2011-Phonepay_Plus.pdf

Grainge, Paul. (2011). Introduction. In Paul Grainge (ed.), *Ephemeral media: transitory screen culture from television to YouTube* (pp. 1–19). British Film Institute.

Grandoni, Dino. (2012). YouTube's original channels are a risky bet, but Google doubles down. 12 November 2012. www.huffingtonpost.com/2012/11/12/youtube-original-channels_n_2117717.html

Gray, Jonathan. (2010). *Show sold separately: promos, spoilers, and other media paratexts*. New York University Press.

Greenberg, Joshua M. (2008). *From BetaMax to Blockbuster: video stores and the invention of movies on video*. MIT Press.

Groening, Stephen. (2016). 'No one likes to be a captive audience': headphones and in-flight cinema. *Film History*, 28(3), 114–138.

Guider, Elizabeth, and Mohr, Ian. (2007). Pop goes the opera. *Variety*, p. 5. 2 April 2007.

Gunter, Barrie. (2010). *Television versus the internet: will TV prosper or perish as the world moves online?* Chandos.

Hadfield, Phil. (2006). *Bar wars: contesting the night in contemporary British cities*. Oxford University Press.

Hamilton, Michael. (2015). Processions, protests and other meetings. In Brice Dickson (ed.), *Human Rights in Northern Ireland* (pp. 179–206). Hart.

Hancock, Matt. (2016). Speech at Radio Festival 2016. 26 September 2016. www.gov.uk/government/speeches/minister-for-digital-and-culture-speech-the-radio-festival-2016

Hanley, Brian, and Millar, Scott. (2010). *The lost revolution: the story of the Official IRA and the Workers' Party*. Penguin.

Hanson, Stuart. (2007). *From silent screen to multi-screen: a history of cinema exhibition in Britain since 1896*. Manchester University Press.

Hargrave, Andrea Millwood, and Livingstone, Sonia. (2009). *Harm and offence in media content: a review of the evidence* (2nd edn). Intellect.

Harris Interactive. (2011). Portrayal v. betrayal: an investigation of diverse and mainstream UK film audiences. www.bfi.org.uk/sites/bfi.org.uk/files/downloads/uk-film-council-portrayal-vs-betrayal-case-study.pdf

Hassoun, Dan. (2016). Engaging distractions: regulating second-screen use in the theater. *Cinema Journal*, 55(2), 89–111.

Häusermann, Jüerg. (2009). Radio broadcasting: from secret to public to private. In Charley Rowe and Eva Lia Wyss (eds), *Language and new media: linguistic, cultural, and technological evolutions* (pp. 185–211). Hampton Press.

Hayles, N. Katherine. (2004). Print is flat, code is deep: the importance of media-specific analysis. *Poetics Today*, 25(1), 67–90.

Herrman, John. (2016). Podcasts surge, but producers fear Apple isn't listening. *New York Times*, p. BU1. 8 May 2016.

Heyer, Paul. (2003). *Harold Innis*. Rowman and Littlefield.

Higson, Andrew. (2011). *Film England: culturally English filmmaking since the 1990s*. IB Tauris.

Hill, John. (2016). Living with Hollywood: British film policy and the definition of 'nationality'. *International Journal of Cultural Policy*, 22(5), 706–23.

Hill, Laura. (2016). Intermission in plan to audition city's buskers. *Evening Chronicle*, p. 53. 18 August 2016.

Hilmes, Michele. (1990). *Hollywood and broadcasting: from radio to cable*. University of Illinois Press.

Hilmes, Michele. (2013). The new materiality of radio: sound on screens. In Jason Loviglio and Michele Hilmes (eds), *Radio's new wave: global sound in the digital era* (pp. 43–61). Routledge.

HM Treasury. (2012). *Creative sector tax reliefs: response to consultation.*

HM Treasury. (2012). *Consultation on creative sector tax reliefs.*

HM Treasury. (2014). Video games tax relief passes final hurdle. 27 March 2014. www.gov.uk/government/news/video-games-tax-relief-passes-final-hurdle

HM Treasury. (2015). *Orchestra tax relief: response to the consultation.*

HM Treasury. (2016). *Museums and galleries tax relief: response to the consultation.*

Hollins, Timothy. (1984). *Beyond broadcasting: into the cable age*. British Film Institute.

Holmes, David. (2015). Chester council drops rough sleeping and busker element of PSPO. *Chester Chronicle*. 18 November 2015. www.chesterchronicle.co.uk/news/chester-cheshire-news/chester-council-drops-rough-sleeping-10462772

Home Office. (2000). *Time for reform: proposals for the modernisation of our licensing laws*. Cm 4696.

Home Office. (2010). Sexual entertainment venues: guidance for England and Wales. http://webarchive.nationalarchives.gov.uk/20100413151441/http:/crimereduction.homeoffice.gov.uk/crimereduction057a.pdf

Home Office. (2014). Reform of anti-social behaviour powers. www.gov.uk/government/uploads/system/uploads/attachment_data/file/364851/Public_and_open_spaces_information_note.pdf

Home Office. (2015). *Revised Guidance issued under section 182 of the Licensing Act 2003.*

Home Office. (2016). *Post-legislative scrutiny of the Licensing Act 2003*. Cm 9278.

Hörnle, Julia. (2005). Country of origin regulation in cross border media: one step beyond the freedom to provide services? *International and Comparative Law Quarterly*, 54(1), 89–126.

Houlder, Vanessa. (2016). Film investors face 'life-changing' bills for tax avoidance. *Financial Times*, p. 1. 19 November 2016.

House of Commons Culture, Media and Sport Committee. (2007). *Call TV quiz shows*. HC 72, 2006–2007.

House of Commons Culture, Media and Sport Committee. (2008). *Harmful content on the Internet and in video games*. HC 353, 2007–2008.

House of Commons Culture, Media and Sport Committee. (2009). *The Licensing Act 2003*. HC 492, 2008–2009.

House of Commons Regulatory Reform Committee. (2014). *Draft Legislative Reform (Entertainment Licensing) Order 2014*. HC 742, 2014–2015.

House of Commons Scottish Affairs Committee. (2011). *Video games industry in Scotland*. HC500, 2010–2011.

House of Lords Delegated Powers and Regulatory Reform Committee. (2009). *2nd report of session 2009–10*. HL 24, 2009–2010.

House of Lords Select Committee on Communications. (2013). *Media convergence*. HL 154, 2012–2013.

Howells, Sacha. (2002). Watching a game, playing a movie: when media collide. In Geoff King and Tanya Krzywinska (eds), *Screenplay: cinema/videogames/interfaces* (pp. 110–21). Wallflower.

Hubbard, Phil. (2012). *Cities and sexualities*. Routledge.

Hubbard, Phil. (2015). Law, sex and the city: regulating sexual entertainment venues in England and Wales. *International Journal of Law in the Built Environment*, 7(1), 5–20.

Hubbard, Phil, Campbell, Rosie, O'Neill, Maggie, Pitcher, Jane, and Scoular, Jane. (2007). Prostitution, gentrification, and the limits of neighbourhood space. In Rowland Atkinson and Gesa Helms (eds), *Securing an urban renaissance* (pp. 203–17). Policy Press.

Hunnings, Thomas. (1967). *Film censors and the law*. George Allen & Unwin.

Hunt, Jeremy. (2011). Boldness be my friend. 14 September 2011. www.gov.uk/government/speeches/royal-television-society-2

Hunter, I. Q. (2014). Naughty realism: the Britishness of British hardcore R18s. *Journal of British Cinema and Television*, 11(2), 152–71.

Innis, Harold. (1930). *The fur trade in Canada*. Yale University Press.

Innis, Harold. (1950). *Empire and communications*. Clarendon Press.

Innis, Harold. (1951). *The bias of communication*. University of Toronto Press.

Innis, Harold. (1952). *Changing concepts of time*. University of Toronto Press.

Inoue, Osamu. (2009). *Nintendo magic: winning the videogame wars*. Vertical.

Jacobs, Jason. (2001). Issues of judgement and value in television studies. *International Journal of Cultural Studies*, 4(4), 427–47.

Jancovich, Mark, and Faire, Lucy. (2003). The best place to see a film: the blockbuster, the multiplex, and the contexts of consumption. In Julian Stringer (ed.), *Movie blockbusters* (pp. 190–200). Routledge.

Janssen, Mike. (2016). NPR Board approves donations from overseas NPR One listeners. 29 November 2016. http://current.org/2016/11/npr-board-approves-donations-from-overseas-npr-one-listeners/

Janssens, Marie-Christine. (2014). The Software Directive. In Irini A. Stamatoudi and Paul Torremans (eds), *EU copyright law: a commentary* (pp. 89–148). Edward Elgar.

Jay, Elisabeth. (1986). *Faith and doubt in Victorian Britain*. Macmillan.

Jenkins, Henry. (2006). *Convergence culture: where old and new media collide*. New York University Press.

Jigsaw Research. (2014). Understanding consumer journeys: premium rate service and micropayment markets. http://psauthority.org.uk/-/media/Files/PhonepayPlus/Research/Consumer-Research/PhonepayPlus-Consumer-Journey-February-2014.pdf

Johnson, Aredhel, and Revington, Harriet. (2014). Creative sector tax reliefs: HMRC publishes guidance on animation and high-end TV reliefs. *Entertainment Law Review*, 25(7), 246–8.

Johnson, Catherine. (2012). *Branding television*. Routledge.

Jones, Jonathan. (2013). Look and learn: live art screenings, a new global phenomenon. *Guardian*. 19 June 2013. www.theguardian.com/artanddesign/jonathanjonesblog/2013/jun/18/live-art-screenings-cinema-pompeii

Judge, Igor (Lord). (2016). Ceding power to the executive: the resurrection of Henry VIII. 12 April 2016. www.kcl.ac.uk/law/newsevents/newsrecords/2015-16/Ceding-Power-to-the-Executive--Lord-Judge--130416.pdf

Juul, Jesper. (2005). *Half-real: video games between real rules and fictional worlds*. MIT Press.

Juul, Jesper. (2010). *A casual revolution: reinventing video games and their players*. MIT Press.

Katsirea, Irini. (2015). Electronic press: 'press-like' or 'television-like'? *International Journal of Law and Information Technology*, 23(2), 134–56.

Katz, Elihu. (2007). The Toronto School and communication research. In Menahem Blondheim and Rita Watson (eds), *The Toronto School of Communication Theory: interpretations, extensions, applications* (pp. 1–5). Hebrew University Magnes Press.

Kay, Jeremy. (2013). Crossover traffic. *Screen International*. November 2013.

Kermode, Mark. (2009). Should we avoid violent video games? *Guardian*, p. 15. 11 December 2009.

Kerr, Aphra. (2012). The UK and Irish game industries. In Peter Zackariasson and Timothy Wilson (eds), *The video game industry: formation, present state, and future* (pp. 116–33). Routledge.

King, Geoff, and Krzywinska, Tanya. (2002). *Screenplay: cinema/videogames/interfaces*. Wallflower.

Kirkhope, Alex. (2003). I just called to say … a review of the regulation of premium rate phone services in the UK. *Computer and Telecommunications Law Review*, 9(4), 93–4.

Kirkup, James. (2008). Film-style age classifications for online computer games. *Daily Telegraph*, p. 12. 1 August 2008.

Kittler, Friedrich. (1999). *Gramophone, film, typewriter* (Geoffrey Winthrop-Young and Michael Wutz, trans.). Stanford University Press.

Kline, Stephen, Dyer-Witheford, Nick, and De Peuter, Greig. (2003). *Digital play: the interaction of technology, culture and marketing*. McGill-Queen's University Press.

Klinenberg, Eric. (2007). *Fighting for air: the battle to control America's media*. Metropolitan Books.

Klinger, Barbara. (2006). *Beyond the multiplex: cinema, new technologies, and the home*. University of California Press.

Klinger, Barbara. (2007). Cinema's shadow: reconsidering non-theatrical exhibition. In Richard Maltby, Melbyn Stokes, and Robert Allen (eds), *Going to the movies: Hollywood and the social experience of cinema* (pp. 273–90). University of Exeter Press.

Kociemba, David. (2006). 'Actually, it explains a *lot*': reading the opening title sequences of 'Buffy the Vampire Slayer'. *Slayage: The Journal of the Whedon Studies Association*, 6(2).

Kompare, Derek. (2006). Publishing flow: DVD box sets and the reconception of television. *Television and New Media*, 7(4), 335–60.

Kramer, Peter. (1994). The lure of the big picture: film, television and Hollywood. In John Hill and Martin McLoore (eds), *Big picture, small screen: the relations between film and television* (pp. 9–46). University of London Press.

Krause, Amanda, North, Adrian, and Hewitt, Lauren. (2014). Music selection behaviors in everyday listening. *Journal of Broadcasting and Electronic Media*, 58(2), 306–23.

Kroker, Arthur. (1984). *Technology and the Canadian mind: Innis, McLuhan, Grant*. New World Perspectives.

Krzywinska, Tanya. (2012). The strange case of the misappearance of sex in video games. In Johannes Fromme and Alexander Unger (eds), *Computer games and new media cultures* (pp. 143–60). Springer.

Lacey, Kate. (2013). Listening in the digital age. In Jason Loviglio and Michele Hilmes (eds), *Radio's new wave: global sound in the digital era* (pp. 9–23). Routledge.

Lai, Stanley. (2000). *The copyright protection of computer software in the United Kingdom*. Hart.

Larson, Sarah. (2014). 'Serial': the podcast we've been waiting for. *New Yorker*. 9 October. www.newyorker.com/culture/sarah-larson/serial-podcast-weve-waiting

Lauder, Adam. (2012). Bertram Brooker and the Toronto School of Communication. *Topia: Canadian Journal of Cultural Studies*, 27, 67–110.

Lax, Stephen, Ala-Fossi, Marko, Jauert, Per, and Shaw, Helen. (2008). DAB: the future of radio? The development of digital radio in four European countries. *Media, Culture and Society*, 30(2), 151–66.

Lehu, Jean-Marc. (2009). *Branded entertainment: product placement and brand strategy in the entertainment business*. Kogan Page.

Lessig, Lawrence. (1999). *Code and other laws of cyberspace*. Basic Books.

Leverette, Marc. (2008). 'Cocksucker, Motherfucker, Tits'. In Marc Leverette, Brian L. Ott, and Cara Louise Buckley (eds), *It's not TV: watching HBO in the post-television era* (pp. 123–51). Routledge.

Levine, Robert. (2011). *Free ride: how the internet is destroying the culture business and how the culture business can fight back*. Bodley Head.

Levinson, Paul. (1999). *Digital McLuhan: a guide to the information millennium*. Routledge.

Liberty. (2015). Liberty welcomes Birmingham City Council's decision to scrap shameful PSPO plans. 16 September 2015. www.liberty-human-rights.org.uk/news/press-releases-and-statements/liberty-welcomes-birmingham-city-council's-decision-scrap

Lievens, Eva. (2006). Harmful new media content: the latest regulatory trends. *Communications Law*, 11(4), 113–23.

Light, Roy. (2005). The Licensing Act 2003: liberal constraint? *Modern Law Review*, 68(2), 268–85.

Lodderhose, Diana. (2011). Live feeds fatten exhibs. *Variety*, p. 5. 8 August 2011.

Loguidice, Bill, and Barton, Matt. (2009). *Vintage games: an insider look at the history of Grand Theft Auto, Super Mario and the most influential games of all time*. Focal.

London Borough of Camden. (2011). Sex establishments policy. www.camden.gov.uk/ccm/cms-service/download/asset?asset_id=3189646

London Borough of Camden. (2013). Street entertainment policy. www.camden.gov.uk/ccm/cms-service/stream/asset/?asset_id=3181229&

London Borough of Hammersfield and Fulham. (2016). Public Spaces Protection Order for Shepherds Bush Station. www.lbhf.gov.uk/environment/noise-and-nuisance/public-spaces-protection-order-shepherds-bush-station

Lovell, Nicholas. (2014). *The curve: turning followers into superfans* (revised edn). Penguin.

Lury, Karen. (2005). *Interpreting television*. Hodder Arnold.

Mac Síthigh, Daithí. (2010). More than words: the introduction of internationalised domain names and the reform of generic top-level domains at ICANN. *International Journal of Law and Information Technology*, 18(3), 274–300.

Mac Síthigh, Daithí. (2010). The regulation of video games: past, present and future. *Entertainment Law Review*, 21(8), 298–303.

Mac Síthigh, Daithí. (2013). App law within: rights and regulation in the smartphone age. *International Journal of Law and Information Technology*, 21(2), 154–86.

Mac Síthigh, Daithí. (2013). From freedom of speech to the right to communicate. In Monroe Price, Stefaan Verhulst and Libby Morgan (eds), *Routledge Handbook of Media Law* (pp. 175–92). Routledge.

Mac Síthigh, Daithí. (2013). The fragmentation of intermediary liability in the UK. *Journal of Intellectual Property Law and Practice*, 8(7), 521–31.

Mac Síthigh, Daithí. (2014). Multiplayer games: tax, copyright, consumers and the video game industries. *European Journal of Law and Technology*, 5(3).

Mac Síthigh, Daithí. (2014). Principles for a second century of film legislation. *Legal Studies*, 34(4), 609.

Mac Síthigh, Daithí. (2017). The game's the thing: property, priorities and perceptions in the video games industries. In Megan Richardson and Sam Ricketson (eds), *Research handbook on intellectual property in media and entertainment* (pp. 344–66). Edward Elgar.

Mac Síthigh, Daithí. (2017). 'TV-like': aesthetics, quality and genre in the regulation of video-on-demand services. *Journal of British Cinema and Television*, 14(3).

MacNab, Geoffrey. (2009). The big switch. *Sight and Sound*, p. 46. September 2009.

Manchester, Colin. (1995). Criminal Justice and Public Order Act 1994. *Criminal Law Review*, 123–31.

Markman, Kris M., and Sawyer, Caroline E. (2014). Why Pod? Further explorations of the motivations for independent podcasting. *Journal of Radio and Audio Media*, 21(1), 20–35.

Marsden, Christopher. (2010). *Net neutrality: towards a co-regulatory solution*. Bloomsbury Academic.

Marsden, Christopher. (2011). *Internet co-regulation: European law, regulatory governance and legitimacy in cyberspace*. Cambridge University Press.

Marsh, Peter. (1969). *The Victorian church in decline: Archbishop Tait and the Church of England, 1868–1882*. Routledge.

Mathews, Tom. (1994). *Censored: the story of film censorship in Britain*. Chatto and Windus.

Mayer, Vicki. (2008). Guys gone wild? Soft-core video professionalism and new realities in television production. *Cinema Journal*, 47(2), 97–116.

McDonald, Paul. (2007). *Video and DVD industries*. British Film Institute.

McGurran, Aidan. (2008). Barmy flag ban: Council tells Dave to take down troop tribute. *Daily Mirror*, p. 23. 17 September 2008.

McKeown, Lesley-Anne. (2012). Protesters attempt to storm Belfast city hall after flag vote. *Irish Independent*. 4 December 2012.

McKerrell, Simon. (2012). Hearing sectarianism: understanding Scottish sectarianism as song. *Critical Discourse Studies*, 9(4), 1–12.

McKibben, Bill. (2007). Radio free everywhere. *Atlantic Monthly*. December 2007. www.theatlantic.com/magazine/archive/2007/12/radio-free-everywhere/306433/

McKibben, Bill. (2010). All programs considered. *New York Review of Books*, pp. 44–6. 11 November 2010.

McLuhan, Marshall. (1953). The later Innis. *Queen's Quarterly*, 60, 385–94.

McLuhan, Marshall. (1962). *The Gutenberg galaxy*. University of Toronto Press.

McLuhan, Marshall. (1964). *Understanding media: the extensions of man*. McGraw-Hill.

McLuhan, Marshall. (1995). Letter to Harold Adams Innis (1951). In Eric McLuhan and Frank Zingrone (eds), *Essential McLuhan* (pp. 72–5). House of Anansi.

Mead, David. (2010). *The new law of peaceful protest*. Hart.

Megson, Chris. (2011). The Theatres Act (1968), documentary theatre and the actor's 'overwhelming reality'. *Studies in Theatre and Performance*, 31(2), 137–51.

Meyrowitz, Joshua. (1985). *No sense of place: the impact of electronic media on social behavior*. Oxford University Press.

Meyrowitz, Joshua. (2005). From tribal to global: a brief history of civilization from a McLuhanesque perspective. In Lance Strate and Edward Wachtel (eds), *The legacy of McLuhan* (pp. 35–42). Hampton.

Miller, Toby. (2000). Apparatus theory. In Robert Stam and Toby Miller (eds), *Film and theory* (pp. 403–7). Blackwell.

Mobile Squared. (2016). The PRS consumer report: a report for PhonepayPlus. www.mobilesquared.co.uk/media/97469/15_5841_MobileSquared_Report_pages_v5-1-.pdf

Montfort, Nick, and Bogost, Ian. (2009). *Racing the beam: the Atari Video computer system*. MIT Press.

Moon, Ken. (2015). Another nail in the coffin for non-literal software copyright infringement? *Journal of Intellectual Property Law and Practice*, 10(12), 921–30.

Moore, Martin. (2015). Plurality and local media. In Steven Barnett and Judith Townend (eds), *Media power and plurality: from hyperlocal to high-level policy* (pp. 65–82). Palgrave Macmillan.

Morris, Ewan. (2005). *Our own devices: national symbols and political conflict in twentieth-century Ireland*. Irish Academic Press.

Morris, Jeremy Wade, and Patterson, Eleanor. (2015). Podcasting and its apps: software, sound, and the interfaces of digital audio. *Journal of Radio and Audio Media*, 22(2), 220–30.

Mullen, Megan. (2008). Space bias/time bias: Harold Innis, empire and communications. *Technology and Culture*, 50(1), 175–86.

Mundell, Ian. (2009). Digital starts to make good on promises of riches. *Variety*, p. 1. 15 June 2009.

Murray, Andrew. (2007). *The regulation of cyberspace*. Routledge.

Napoli, Philip. (2011). *Audience evolution: new technologies and the transformation of media audiences*. Columbia University Press.

Naughton, John. (2010). Buck naked on your iPad? No way.... *Observer*. 20 June 2010. www.theguardian.com/technology/2010/jun/20/james-joyce-ulysses-seen-app

Nelson, Elissa. (2014). Windows into the digital world: distributor strategies and consumer choice in an era of connected viewing. In Jennifer Holt and Kevin Sanson (eds), *Connected viewing: selling, streaming, and sharing media in the digital era* (pp. 62–77). Taylor & Francis.

Newman, James. (2007). *100 videogames*. British Film Institute.

Newman, James. (2013). *Videogames* (2nd edn). Routledge.

Nichols, Randy. (2014). *The video game business*. British Film Institute.

Nicholson, Andrew. (2013). Old habits die hard?: UsedSoft v. Oracle. *SCRIPTed*, 10(3), 389–408.

Nicholson, Judith. (2010). The third screen as cultural form in North America. In Barbara Crow, Michael Longford, and Kim Sawchuk (eds), *The wireless spectrum: the politics, practices, and poetics of mobile media* (pp. 77–94). University of Toronto Press.

Northampton Borough Council. (2016). Draft Public Spaces Protection Order. www.northampton.gov.uk/downloads/file/9044/draft-public-spaces-protection-order

Northern Ireland Executive. (2016). Foster and McGuinness announce membership of the Commission on Flags, Identity, Culture and Tradition. 20 June 2016. www.northernireland.gov.uk/news/foster-and-mcguinness-announce-membership-commission-flags-identity-culture-and-tradition

Norton, James. (1995). Digital media works. *International Media Law*, 13, 59.

Ofcom. (2009). Radio in digital Britain. http://webarchive.nationalarchives.gov.uk/20100304014526/ http://ofcom.org.uk/radio/ifi/radio_digitalbritain/digitalbrit.pdf

Ofcom. (2009). The regulation of video-on-demand services. www.ofcom.org.uk/__data/assets/pdf_file/0020/36407/vodstatement.pdf

Ofcom. (2010). Participation TV: regulatory statement, rules on the promotion of premium rate services. www.ofcom.org.uk/__data/assets/pdf_file/0025/55708/statement.pdf

Ofcom. (2011). Offensive language on radio. www.ofcom.org.uk/__data/assets/pdf_file/0014/40541/offensive-language.pdf

Ofcom. (2011). Sexually explicit material and video-on-demand services. www.ofcom.org.uk/__data/assets/pdf_file/0023/23738/explicit-material-vod.pdf

Ofcom. (2011). Observing the watershed on television and music videos. www.ofcom.org.uk/__data/assets/pdf_file/0030/86781/watershed-on-tv.pdf

Ofcom. (2011). Modifying who is subject to the premium rate services condition. www.ofcom.org.uk/__data/assets/pdf_file/0019/42085/statement.pdf

Ofcom. (2011). Review of premium rate services: an application of the analytical framework. www.ofcom.org.uk/__data/assets/pdf_file/0014/42053/condoc.pdf

Ofcom. (2012). Service charge caps for 09 and 118 services. www.ofcom.org.uk/__data/assets/pdf_file/0031/47767/condoc.pdf

Ofcom. (2012). Review of premium rate services: decision on an application of the analytical framework. www.ofcom.org.uk/__data/assets/pdf_file/0019/46513/statement.pdf

Ofcom. (2014). The use of non-geographic numbers in broadcasting. www.ofcom.org.uk/__data/assets/pdf_file/0021/55452/statement.pdf

Ofcom. (2015). Review of music in radio Formats: statement. www.ofcom.org.uk/__data/assets/pdf_file/0025/51667/statement.pdf

Ofcom. (2015). Approval of the PhonepayPlus Code of Practice (13th edition). www.ofcom.org.uk/__data/assets/pdf_file/0030/49692/final_statement.pdf

Ofcom. (2016). Radio deregulation: letter to Ed Vaizey MP. 23 February 2016. www.ofcom.org.uk/__data/assets/pdf_file/0030/76908/letter_to_ed_vaizey_mp_230216.pdf

Ofcom. (2016). The communications market: digital radio report. www.ofcom.org.uk/__data/assets/pdf_file/0032/94838/The-Communications-Market-Digital-Radio-Report-2016.pdf

Ofcom. (u.d.). The regulation of Format changes. www.ofcom.org.uk/__data/assets/pdf_file/0024/87405/The-regulation-of-Format-changes.pdf

Oxford Economics. (2011). More than a support act: the true value of video entertainment in the UK. www.bva.org.uk/files/u1/Oxford-Economics-Value-of-video.pdf

Palmer, Bernard. (1993). *Reverend rebels: five Victorian clerics and their fight against authority*. Darton, Longman & Todd.

Parker, Ian. (1993). Innis and the geography of communications and empire. *Canadian Geographer*, 37(4), 353–5.

Parry, Roger. (2011). *The ascent of media: from Gilgamesh to Google via Gutenberg*. Nicholas Brealey.

Pasquale, Frank. (2015). *The black box society: the secret algorithms that control money and information.* Harvard University Press.

Pauewls, Caroline, and Donders, Karen. (2011). From Television Without Frontiers to the digital Big Bang: the EU's continuous efforts to create a future-proof internal media market. In Robin Mansell and Marc Raboy (eds), *Handbook of global media and communication policy* (pp. 525–42). Blackwell.

Paz, DG. (1992). *Popular anti-Catholicism in mid-Victorian England.* Stanford University Press.

Perera, Shyama. (1989). Phone watchdog warns porn lines. *Guardian*, p. 2. 22 March 1989.

Perkins, Sean. (2012). Film in the UK, 2001–2010: a statistical overview. *Journal of British Cinema and Television*, 9(3), 310–32.

Petersen, Jennifer. (2014). Behind the screen: visuality, law, and new media. *Popular Communication*, 12(3), 166–77.

Petley, Julian. (2012). Head-on collisions: the BBFC in the 1990s. In Edward Lamberti (ed.), *Behind the scenes at the BBFC: film classification from the silver screen to the digital age* (pp. 127–45). BFI.

Petley, Julian. (2014). The regulation of pornography on video-on-demand in the United Kingdom. *Porn Studies*, 1(3), 260–84.

Pett, Emma. (2014). A new media landscape? The BBFC, extreme cinema as cult, and technological change. *New Review of Film and Television Studies*, 13(1), 83–99.

Phillips, Tom. (2015). 'Don't clone my indie game, bro': informal cultures of videogame regulation in the independent sector. *Cultural Trends*, 24(2), 143–53.

Phone-paid Services Authority. (2016). Application-based payments. http://psauthority.org.uk/-/media/Files/PSA/For-Businesses/Guidance-and-compliance/Explore-our-guidance/Guidance-files/01_App-based-payments.ashx?la=en

Phone-paid Services Authority. (2017). Clarity of information to be provided to consumers via text messages following mobile number entry into online promotions. http://psauthority.org.uk/-/media/Files/PSA/For-Businesses/Guidance-and-compliance/Compliance-updates/Clarity-of-information-to-be-provided-to-consumers-via-text-messages-following-mobile-number-entry-into-online-promotions-16-01-2017.ashx?la=en

PhonepayPlus. (2011). Live services – list of current exemptions from prior permission. https://web.archive.org/web/20150206073101/ www.phonepayplus.org.uk/For-Business/~/media/Files/PhonepayPlus/Prior_permission/Prior_permission_Live_services_exemptions.pdf

PhonepayPlus. (2012). Review of information, connection and/or signposting services: consultation. http://psauthority.org.uk/-/media/Files/PhonepayPlus/Consultation-PDFs/ICSS/ICSS-Consultation-Document.pdf

PhonepayPlus. (2012). Check if you need permission to set up a premium rate service. https://web.archive.org/web/20150206073101/www.phonepayplus.org.uk/For-Business/Prior-permission.aspx

PhonepayPlus. (2013). Further assessment of information, connection and/or signposting services: final statement. http://psauthority.org.uk/~/media/Files/PhonepayPlus/Consultation-PDFs/ICSS/ICSS-statement-31-July-2013.pdf

PhonepayPlus. (2013). Children as connected consumers. http://psauthority.org.uk/-/media/Files/PhonepayPlus/Research/Children-as-connected-consumers.ashx?la=en

PhonepayPlus. (2013). Business plan and budget 2014/15. http://psauthority.org.uk/~/media/Files/PhonepayPlus/Consultation-PDFs/STATEMENT-ON-BUSINESS-PLAN-201415-PUBLISHED.pdf

PhonepayPlus. (2013). Further assessment of information, connection and/or signposting services: a public consultation. http://psauthority.org.uk/-/media/Files/PhonepayPlus/Consultation-PDFs/CD_ICSS_24_April_2013.pdf

PhonepayPlus. (2013). Further assessment of ICSS. 6 December 2013. http://psauthority.org.uk/for-business/public-consultations/past-consultations/further-assessment-of-icss

PhonepayPlus. (2014). ICSS Update. 24 April 2014. http://psauthority.org.uk/-/media/Files/PhonepayPlus/Consultation-PDFs/ICSS/ICSS_Update_April_2014.pdf

PhonepayPlus. (2014). Review of prior permission conditions for consumer credit services operating on premium rate. http://psauthority.org.uk/News-And-Events/News/2014/12/~/media/Files/PhonepayPlus/News%202014/Final%20statement%20on%20consumer%20credit%20services_Nov_2014.pdf

PhonepayPlus. (2015). Vulnerability: a PhonepayPlus discussion document. http://psauthority.org.uk/-/media/Files/PhonepayPlus/Research/Vulnerability-discussion-document-2015.ashx?la=en

PhonepayPlus. (2016). Annual market review 2015–2016. http://psauthority.org.uk/-/media/Files/PhonepayPlus/Research/2016/AMR_PPP_Report2016.ashx?la=en

Picarelli, Enrica. (2013). Aspirational paratexts: the case of 'quality openers' in TV promotion. *Frames Cinema Journal*, 3.

Plunkett, John. (2009). Apple's new iPod Nano is great news for radio – but not for DAB. *Guardian*. 10 September 2009. www.theguardian.com/media/organgrinder/2009/sep/10/ipod-nano-digital-radio

Pluskota, Jonathan P. (2015). The perfect technology: radio and mobility. *Journal of Radio and Audio Media*, 22(2), 325–36.

Pool, Ithiel de Sola. (1983). *Technologies of freedom*. Harvard University Press.

Poole, Steven. (2000). *Trigger happy: the inner life of videogames*. Fourth Estate.

Poole, Steven. (2013). Why does Apple hate video games so much? *Edge*, p. 32. June 2013.

Poulter, Seán. (2009). Call for cinema-style age ratings on games. *Daily Mail*, p. 12. 27 February 2009.

Prime Minister's Office. (2015). Curbing access to pornographic websites for under 18s. 30 July 2015. www.gov.uk/government/news/curbingaccesstopornographicwebsites-forunder18s

Reed, Chris. (2012). *Making laws for cyberspace*. Oxford University Press.

Richards, Ed. (2012). Speech to the Oxford Media Convention. 25 January 2012. www.theguardian.com/oxfordmediaconvention/ed-richards-speech

Richards, Jeffrey, and Robertson, James. (2009). British film censorship. In Robert Murphy (ed.), *The British cinema book* (3rd edn) (pp. 67–77). Palgrave Macmillan.

Robertson, Geoffrey, and Nicol, Andrew. (2008). *Media law* (5th revised edn). Penguin.

Robertson, James. (1993). *The hidden cinema: British film censorship in action, 1913–1975*. Routledge.

Robinson, Paul. (2013). Can radio outsmart the smartphones? *Broadcast*. 19 March 2013. www.broadcastnow.co.uk/opinion/can-radio-outsmart-the-smartphones/5053094.article

Rombes, Nicholas. (2009). *Cinema in the digital age*. Wallflower.

Rosenbaum, Jonathan. (2000). *Movie wars: how Hollywood and the media conspire to limit what films we can see*. A Capella.

Rudd, Matt. (2012). There's no escape. *Sunday Times*, pp. 20–5. 12 February 2012.

Rudin, Richard. (2006). The development of DAB digital radio in the UK: the battle for control of a new technology in an old medium. *Convergence: The International Journal of Research into New Media Technologies*, 12(2), 163–78.

Sandhu, Serina. (2016). Fredy Beats and ABH Beatbox: Camden Council prosecutes champion beatboxers for busking without licence. *The Independent.* 5 March 2016. www.independent.co.uk/news/uk/home-news/fredy-beats-and-abh-beatbox-camden-council-prosecutes-champion-beatboxers-for-busking-without-a6914481.html

Santo, Avi. (2008). Para-television and discourses of distinction: the culture of production at HBO. In Marc Leverette, Brian L. Ott, and Cara Louise Buckley (eds), *It's not TV: watching HBO in the post-television era* (pp. 19–45). Routledge.

Savič, Maša. (2015). The legality of resale of digital content after UsedSoft in subsequent German and CJEU case law. *European Intellectual Property Review*, 37(7), 414–29.

Schafer, Liz. (2015). Alice in Cameraland. *Times Higher Education.* 18 January 2015. www.timeshighereducation.com/features/culture/the-royal-ballet-alices-adventures-in-wonderland/2017857.article

Schneider, Marc. (2016). Facebook debuts live audio broadcasts. *Billboard.* 21 December 2016. www.billboard.com/articles/business/7632362/facebook-debuts-live-audio

Segrave, Kerry. (1999). *Movies at home: how Hollywood came to television.* McFarland.

Shipwright, Adrian. (2006). Finance Act notes: films and sound recordings. *British Tax Review*, (5), 517–30.

Simpson, Paul. (2015). *The history of street performance: 'music by handle' and the silencing of street musicians in the metropolis.* Paper presented at the Gresham College Public Lecture, London, 9 July 2015. www.gresham.ac.uk/lecture/transcript/download/the-history-of-street-performance/

Skinner, SA. (2014). *Tractarians and the 'Condition of England': the social and political thought of the Oxford Movement.* Oxford University Press.

Slesenger Research. (2008). Classifying games: qualitative research findings. www.bbfc.co.uk/sites/default/files/attachments/Classifying%20Games%20-%20Qualitative%20Research%20Findings%20(January%202008)_0.pdf

Starkey, Guy. (2007). *Balance and bias in journalism: representation, regulation and democracy.* Palgrave Macmillan.

Starkey, Guy. (2011). *Local radio, going global.* Palgrave Macmillan.

Starkey, Guy. (2014). *Radio in context* (2nd edn). Palgrave Macmillan.

Starkey, Guy. (2015). Cultural policy in the coalition years: laissez-faire regulation, the public spending squeeze and the drive to digital. *Cultural Trends*, 24(1), 80–4.

Stevenson, Nick. (2010). Marshall McLuhan and media and cultural studies. In Paul Grosswiler (ed.), *Transforming McLuhan: cultural, critical, and postmodern perspectives* (pp. 17–36). Peter Lang.

Stokes, Simon. (2012). *Art and copyright* (2nd edn). Hart.

Stoller, Tony. (2010). *Sounds of your life: the rise and fall of independent radio in the UK.* John Libbey.

Strangelove, Michael. (2010). *Watching YouTube: extraordinary videos by ordinary people.* University of Toronto Press.

Straw, Will. (2007). Embedded memories. In Charles Acland (ed.), *Residual media* (pp. 3–15). University of Minnesota Press.

Street, John. (2012). *Music and politics.* Polity.

Stuart, Keith. (2010). Tiga, tax breaks and the future of the UK games industry. 10 October 2010. www.theguardian.com/technology/gamesblog/2011/oct/10/tiga-richard-wilson-interview

Stuart, Keith. (2010). Budget 2010: video games tax relief disappears. *Guardian.* 23 June 2010. www.theguardian.com/uk/2010/jun/22/budget-2010-video-games-tax-relief-disappears

Swedish Radio and TV Authority. (2008). *The future of radio*

Sweney, Mark. (2013). Netflix bets $100m on digital appetite for remakes. *Guardian*, p. 14. 2 February 2013.

Sweney, Mark. (2016). Cut the 'small print' from ends of radio ads, stations to ask Brussels. *Guardian*. 14 October 2016. www.theguardian.com/media/2016/mar/14/cut-small-print-from-end-radio-ads-stations-ask-eu

Sylvester, Anthony, and Edwards, John. (1997). A law by any other name – ICSTIS. *Computer and Telecommunications Law Review*, 3(4), 157–60.

Tambini, Damian, Leonardi, Danilo, and Marsden, Christopher (2008). *Codifying cyberspace: communications self-regulation in the age of Internet convergence*. Routledge.

Taub, Eric. (2009). When the Web is in reach, so is a radio universe. *New York Times*, p. B7. 31 December 2009.

Teo, Mark. (2015). CBC Radio 3's new format replaces hosts with musicians. 9 March 2015. www.aux.tv/2015/03/cbc-radio-3s-new-format-replaces-hosts-with-musicians/

Terdiman, Daniel. (2010). Will Apple offer ratings for iPhone games? 10 June 2010. http://news.cnet.com/8301-10797_3-10262087-235.html

Thomas, David, Carlton, David, and Etienne, Anne. (2007). *Theatre censorship: from Walpole to Wilson*. Oxford University Press.

Thomas, Mark. (2015). *100 acts of minor dissent*. September Publishing.

Thorpe, Vanessa. (2012). Cinemas open screens to opera and ballet. *Observer*, p. 22. 4 March 2012.

Traynor, Kerry. (2015). Birmingham, Alabama 8; Birmingham, UK 1: local television in the United Kingdom and an ethnographic case study of one service in the north of England. *International Journal of Digital Television*, 6(2), 163–83.

Trueman, Matt. (2013). The surprise success of NT Live. *Guardian*. 10 June 2013. www.theguardian.com/stage/2013/jun/09/nt-live-success

Tryon, Chuck. (2009). *Reinventing cinema: movies in the age of media convergence*. Rutgers University Press.

Tryon, Chuck. (2013). *On-demand culture: digital delivery and the future of movies*. Rutgers University Press.

Turner, Amy. (2012). Famous for 15 seconds. *Sunday Times*, pp. 12–19. 11 March 2012.

Turner, Alwyn. (2014). *A classless society: Britain in the 1990s*. Aurum.

UKIE. (2013). UKIE welcomes autumn statement announcements of support for business, urges government to push games production tax credits through. 5 December 2013. http://ukie.org.uk/content/ukie-welcomes-autumn-statement-announcements-support-business-urges-government-push-games-pr

UKIE. (2013). UKIE responds to announcement of European Commission tax breaks investigation. 16 April 2013. http://ukie.info/content/ukie-responds-announcement-european-commission-tax-breaks-investigation

Upton, Julian. (2016). Electric blues: the rise and fall of Britain's first pre-recorded videocassette distributors. *Journal of British Cinema and Television*, 13(1), 19–41.

Upton, Julian. (2017). Innocence unprotected? Permissiveness and the AA certificate 1970–82. *Journal of British Cinema and Television*, 14(1), 64–76.

Uricchio, William. (2009). The future of a medium once known as television. In Pelle Snickars and Patrick Vonderau (eds), *The YouTube reader* (pp. 24–39). National Library of Sweden.

Uricchio, William. (2011). The recurrent, the recombinatory and the ephemeral. In Paul Grainge (ed.), *Ephemeral media: transitory screen culture from television to YouTube* (pp. 23–36). British Film Institute.

Uricchio, William. (2014). Film, cinema, television … media? *New Review of Film and Television Studies*, 12(3), 266–79.

Uricchio, William. (2014). The greatest art form of the twentieth century. *Journal of Visual Culture*, 13(1), 104–6.

Vaizey, Ed. (2013). Digital radio action plan (speech). *Go Digital Conference*. 16 December 2013. www.gov.uk/government/speeches/go-digital-conference-16-december-2013-check-against-delivery

Vaizey, Ed. (2015). Letter to Siobhán Kenny (CEO, RadioCentre). 4 November 2015. www.gov.uk/government/uploads/system/uploads/attachment_data/file/473720/Radio_letter.pdf

van Doorn, Niels. (2010). Keeping it real: user-generated pornography, gender reification, and visual pleasure. *Convergence: The International Journal of Research into New Media Technologies*, 16(4), 411–30.

Video Standards Council. (2015). *Annual report and accounts 2014*

Walden, Ian, Edwards, Chris, and Savage, Nigel. (1990). *Information technology and the law*. Palgrave Macmillan.

Walker, James, and Bellamy, Robert. (2010). DVRs and the empowered audience. In John Allen Hendricks (ed.), *The twenty-first century media industry* (pp. 41–60). Lexington.

Walters, James. (2008). A taste for leeches: DVDs, cultural hierarchies and queer consumption. In James Bennett and Tom Brown (eds), *Film and television after DVD* (pp. 45–62). Routledge.

Westbrook, Caroline. (1995). Movies? How terribly 80s. *Empire*, p. 128. January 1995.

Wiggins, Benjamin. (2014). The culture industry, new media, and the shift from creation to curation; or, enlightenment as a kick in the nuts. *Television and New Media*, 15(5), 395–412.

Williams, David. (1997). The 'Cinematograph Act' of 1909: an introduction to the impetus behind the legislation and some early effects. *Film History*, 9(4), 341–50.

Williams, David. (2002). Never on Sunday: the early operation of the Cinematograph Act of 1909 in regard to Sunday opening. *Film History*, 14(2), 186–94.

Williams, Raymond. (1974). *Television: technology and cultural form*. Fontana.

Wilson, Timothy, and Zackariasson, Peter. (2012). Through the looking glass sharply. In Peter Zackariasson and Timothy Wilson (eds), *The video game industry: formation, present state, and future* (pp. 57–75). Routledge.

Woods, Lorna. (2009). Legal and extra-legal regulation. In David Goldberg, Gavin Sutter, and Ian Walden (eds), *Media law and practice* (pp. 335–72). Oxford University Press.

World Intellectual Property Organisation. (2013). *The legal status of video games: comparative analysis in national approaches*. www.wipo.int/export/sites/www/copyright/en/activities/pdf/comparative_analysis_on_video_games.pdf

Wortham, Jenna. (2010). Apple bans some apps for sex-tinged content. *New York Times*, p. B1. 23 February 2010.

Wragg, Paul. (2014). Leveson's vision for press reform: one year on. *Communications Law*, 19(1), 6–11.

Wu, Tim. (2011). *The master switch: the rise and fall of information empires*. Atlantic.

Yates, Nigel. (1983). *The Oxford Movement and Anglican ritualism*. Historical Association.

Yelton, Michael. (2005). *Anglican Papalism: a history: 1900–1960*. Canterbury Press.

Yeomans, Henry. (2012). *Spirited measures and Victorian hangovers: public attitudes to alcohol, the law and moral regulation*. (PhD), University of Plymouth.

Yoo, Christopher. (2014). Technological determinism and its discontents. *Harvard Law Review*, 127(3), 914–49.

Zick, Timothy. (2009). *Speech out of doors: preserving First Amendment liberties in public places*. Cambridge University Press.

Index

For Product Safety Concerns and Information please contact our EU representative GPSR@taylorandfrancis.com Taylor & Francis Verlag GmbH, Kaufingerstraße 24, 80331 München, Germany

Batch number: 10725973

Printed by Printforce, the Netherlands